FUNDS OF KNOWLEDGE

Theorizing Practices in Households,
Communities, and Classrooms

FUNDS OF KNOWLEDGE

Theorizing Practices in Households, Communities, and Classrooms

Edited by

Norma González
University of Utah

Luis C. Moll
University of Arizona

Cathy Amanti
Tucson Unified School District

 LAWRENCE ERLBAUM ASSOCIATES, PUBLISHERS
2005 Mahwah, New Jersey   London

Lawrence Erlbaum Associates, Inc., Publishers
10 Industrial Avenue
Mahwah, New Jersey 07430

Cover design by Sean Trane Sciarrone

Library of Congress Cataloging-in-Publication Data

Funds of knowledge : theorizing practices in households, communities, and classrooms /
edited by Norma González, Luis Moll, and Cathy Amanti.
    p. cm.
Includes bibliographical references and index.
ISBN 0-8058-4917-3 (cloth : alk. paper) — ISBN 0-8058-4918-1 (pbk. : alk. paper)
    1. Home and school—United States.   2. Teachers and community—United States.   3. Place-
based education—United States.   4. Children with social disabilities—Education—United
States.   5. Teaching—Social aspects—United States.   I. González, Norma.   II. Moll, Luis C.
III. Amanti, Cathy.

LC225.3.T54   2005
371.19′ 2—dc22   2004048707
                                                       CIP

Printed in the United States of America
10   9   8   7   6   5   4   3

Contents

PART II.   TEACHERS AS RESEARCHERS

PART III.   TRANSLOCATIONS: NEW CONTEXTS,
NEW DIRECTIONS

PART IV. CONCLUDING COMMENTARY

Preface

This book is written for educators who are willing to venture beyond the walls of the classroom. It is for those teachers and teachers-to-be who are willing to learn from their students and their communities. It is for those who are willing to be accountable not only to state-mandated tests, but to the nurturing of students' strengths and resources. At a time when national educational discourses swirl around accountability through testing, we present a counterdiscourse to scripted and structured educational packages. We feel instruction must be linked to students' lives, and the details of effective pedagogy should be linked to local histories and community contexts. We also call for greater teacher autonomy and stronger preservice professional preparation and in-service professional development that involves collaborative research to build an empirical understanding of the life experiences of students.

Our perspective is that learning does not take place just "between the ears," but is eminently a social process. Students' learning is bound within larger contextual, historical, political, and ideological frameworks that affect students' lives. This perspective is as relevant today, despite the focus on standards and high-stakes testing and accountability, as it was when the ideas presented in this book were first conceptualized. This work is a call to invest the time and effort to create enabling structures and greater levels of professionalism for teachers, as we develop deeper insights and understanding of the sociopolitical context of diversity.

The concept of *funds of knowledge*, which is at the heart of this book, is based on a simple premise: People are competent, they have knowledge, and their life experiences have given them that knowledge. Our claim is that first-hand research experiences with families allow one to document this competence and knowledge. It is this engagement that opened up many possibilities for positive pedagogical actions. The theoretical concepts presented in this book, a funds of knowledge approach, facilitates a systematic and powerful way to represent communities in terms of resources, the wherewithal they possess, and how to harness these resources for classroom teaching. Cummins (1996, p. 75) has argued, "Our prior experience provides the foundation for interpreting new information. No learner is a blank slate." The approach to students' households presented in this book is one key to unlock and capitalize on the knowledge students already possess.

This book presents an approach to local households where teachers, in their role as researchers and learners, visit families to document funds of knowledge. This approach should not be confused with parent participation programs, although increased parental involvement is often a fortuitous consequence of the work described herein. This is also not an attempt to teach parents "how to do school," although that could certainly be an outcome if the parents so desired. Neither does this work imply that curriculum can only be related to individual students' experiences; however, by critically examining what is taught and why it is taught it becomes an important aspect of our research. Instead, the approach presented in this volume attempts to accomplish something that may be even more challenging: to alter perceptions of working-class or poor communities and to view these households primarily in terms of their strengths and resources (or funds of knowledge) as their defining pedagogical characteristic.

We acknowledge that the households we studied may or may not, individually or collectively, have the challenges and problems that are commonly associated with poverty and urban schools. But very often these issues—such as drugs, gangs, and violence—have been transformed into the primary defining characteristic of these households or their communities, erasing the resiliency and fortitude of individuals and communities. What is often invisible is that the normative characteristic of these households is not dysfunction, but exactly the sorts of experiences and knowledge that we present in this book. These are people living, working, thinking, worrying, and caring. In the course of their lives, as individuals and as a group, they constitute households that have generated and accumulated a variety of funds of knowledge that are the intellectual residues of their activities. In a sense, we are attempting to re-present households in a way that is respectful to issues of voice, representation, and authenticity. How we go about conceptualizing, identifying, documenting, and using these funds of knowledge in classrooms is the story we tell in these pages.

At the heart of our approach is the work of teachers who conducted research in their students' households. The teachers in our study, in contrast to other approaches that emphasize home visits, venture into their students' households and communities, not as teachers attempting to convey educational information, as valuable as that may be, but as learners, as researchers with a theoretical perspective that seeks to understand the ways in which people make sense of their everyday lives. To accomplish this work, we relied on a mix of guided conversation and interviews, a sort of ethnographic inquiry. The principal task, we have come to learn, is not primarily to elicit information, but to foster a relationship of trust with the families so they can tell us about their lives and experiences. The interview, as we elaborate in later chapters, became an exchange of views, information, and stories, and the families got to know us as we got to know them. By focusing on understanding the particulars, the processes or practices of life (in Spanish, *los quehaceres de la vida*), and how people lived experiences, we gained a deep appreciation of how people use resources of all kinds, prominently their funds of knowledge, to engage life.

HOW THIS BOOK IS ORGANIZED

In this book we attempt to accomplish three objectives. The first is to give readers the basic theory and methods that we followed. The second is to present the teachers' voices as the central protagonists in this work. The third is to explore the pedagogical implications that can come about by knowing the community deeply and personally. Because the authors of the chapters have had different experiences and purposes in engaging in this type of work, the voices that you read are multiple and diverse. There is no impersonal authorial stance or unified voice that connects these chapters. Instead, each chapter reflects the author's own telling of his or her experience in connecting with communities. Some authors were teachers in our original project. Others have taken some basic premises and applied them to other contexts. Still others have redefined in creative ways how teachers and schools can learn from communities. Because we hope this book can be used for preservice teacher training and inservice professional development, we have written a series of "Reflection Questions" at the end of each chapter. These can guide the reader to deeper and more extensive discussions on the material that is presented.

The organization of this book reflects our objectives. The book is organized into four parts: (I) Theoretical Underpinnings, (II) Teachers as Researchers, (III) Translocations: New Contexts and New Directions, and (IV) Concluding Commentary. Each of the first three parts begins with an introduction to the themes of the chapters that can serve as a road map to the reader. Because this work has been ongoing for some time and has been published in other venues, some of the material that is presented may be familiar to the reader. We have selected key texts that encapsulate the diverse threads of this work. In Part I, Theoretical Underpinnings, we present reprints of three published articles that describe the theoretical basis for the work. Part II, Teachers as Researchers, describes the firsthand experiences of teacher-researchers who have participated in the project and who present their own insights and challenges in going beyond the classroom walls. In Part III, Translocations: New Contexts and New Directions, we present examples of how the basic methodology has been adapted and transformed to meet particular contextual needs. Part IV, the concluding chapter, attempts to connect deeply with theory and research, and reflects on the implications of the work.

ACKNOWLEDGMENTS

Because this work has a long history, we find that there are many people who should be thanked for bringing it to this point. First and foremost, we acknowledge and thank the students and students' families who have graciously allowed us into their homes. Of equal importance are the teachers who have participated in the various stages of the work, teachers from many schools who have been willing to go beyond their classroom walls. In addition, we gratefully acknowledge the principals who have supported and permitted this project in their schools. We would like to especially thank Gene Benton, Assistant Superintendent of Tucson Unified School District when we began our work, for his vision in caring about communities, households, and schools.

As in most work of this nature, it could not have progressed without the able support of dedicated and grossly underpaid graduate students. We thank these many colleagues for their participation. We also acknowledge the deep influence of Carlos Vélez-Ibáñez and James Greenberg on the formulation of our theoretical understanding. We are also grateful for funding from the W. K. Kellogg Foundation, the Center for Research on Diversity and Second Language Learning, and the Center for Research on Education, Diversity, and Excellence. We also express our appreciation to the Bureau of Applied Research in Anthropology and to the Department of Language, Reading, and Culture, both at the University of Arizona. Finally, we thank Naomi Silverman of Lawrence Erlbaum Associates for her unflagging support and professionalism.

REFERENCE

Cummins, J. (1996). *Negotiating identities: Education for empowerment in a diverse society*. Ontario, CA: California Association for Bilingual Eduation.

Chapter 1

Introduction: Theorizing Practices*

Norma González
University of Utah

Luis Moll
University of Arizona

Cathy Amanti
Tucson Unified School District

> *The problem with many empirical data, empirically presented, is that they can be flat and uninteresting, a documentary of detail which does not connect with urgent issues. On the other hand, the 'big ideas' are empty of people, feeling and experience. In my view well-grounded and illuminating analytic points flow only from bringing concepts into a relationship with the messiness of ordinary life, somehow recorded.*
>
> —Paul Willis (2000, p. xi)

In this introduction, we present a brief description of how we have brought our theoretical concepts into this sort of relationship with the "messiness of ordinary life." These are the everyday practices that we attempt to theorize, practices that are at times emergent, perhaps counterintuitive, and sometimes opaque. Yet these practices do not emerge from nowhere; they are formed and transformed within sociohistorical circumstances. Practices are also constructed by and through discourses, the ways of knowing that populate our streams of talk. The lives of ordinary people, their everyday activities, and what has led them to the place they find themselves are the bases

---

*Portions of this chapter appeared in González, N., & Moll, L. (2002), Cruzando el puente: Building bridges to funds of knowledge. *Journal of Educational Policy, 16*, 623–641; McIntyre, E., Rosebery, A., & González, N. (2001), *Classroom diversity: Connecting curriculum to students' lives*, Portsmouth, NH: Heinemann.

for our theorizing of practices. It is in the richness of telling these stories that we can find not only evocative human drama, but social analysis that emerges from its organic roots. Because this work has been a collaborative endeavor, we have relied on an interdisciplinary perspective. We have not always operated within a unified paradigm, although there are foundational premises that we have accepted as axiomatic, such as the power of social relationships in the construction of knowledge. The following section describes the emergent nature of jointly negotiating the process. Because we like to think of ourselves as engaged in a conversation, we present here the give-and-take of multiple perspectives, starting with the anthropological view.

THE ANTHROPOLOGIST'S VIEW (NORMA GONZÁLEZ)

We like to make much of the fact that in this project we are all learners: teachers as learners, researchers as learners, students as learners, communities of learners, and so forth. Actually, when I look back on the years that we carried out this work, the person who most needed to learn was me. I came into this project flush with anthropological theory, convinced that if only educators could appreciate the power of ethnography, the experience of schooling would be radically changed. It took a while for me to realize that what needed to change radically was the implicit ideology that had insidiously crept into my thinking: that to fix teachers was to fix schools. Although I continue to have the deepest respect for the teachers who have struggled through this process, I now wince as I recall my naïveté regarding the burdens under which teachers work. How can collaborative ethnography, where teachers are actively engaged in researching and applying local knowledge, be sustained when institutional constraints mitigate its continuation? An emancipatory social research agenda calls for empowering approaches that encourage and enable participants to change through self-reflection and a deeper understanding of their situations. Yet these empowering approaches must contend with a context that isolates practitioners, mutes autonomy, and pushes for standardization and homogenization.

Rereading some of my writing concerning those initial stages, I realize that I was quite taken with the postmodernist and poststructuralist discourses which, in the parlance of the times, interrogated hegemonic relationships and have done an admirable job of locating asymmetries of power and domination. What is not evident is how practitioners, within the limits of their very real structural constraints, can realistically carry out emancipatory and liberatory pedagogies when they themselves are victims of disempowerment and their circumstances preclude full professional development. Discourses of critical pedagogy have often become circumscribed within academic circles, peripheral to the very people they purport to affect because of a turgid literary style and an apparent lack of connection to everyday life in classrooms. It is the quintessential instance of being able to talk the talk, but not walk the walk.

How does the funds of knowledge concept differ from other approaches, and how is it useful? What did we do and how did we do it? What have we learned, and what can we claim? What could we have done better?

First of all, it is important to note that this project did not emerge fully formed, but evolved through incremental steps, some more useful than others. Tracing the anthropological trajectory of this project, I look at the early work of Carlos Vélez-Ibáñez in *Bonds of Mutual Trust* (1983), a study of rotating credit associations in central Mexico and the Southwest. Drawing on work by the Mexican anthropologist Larissa Lomnitz, Vélez-Ibáñez developed a fine-grained analysis of networks of exchange and *confianza*. Emphasizing *confianza* as the single most important mediator in social relationships, Vélez-Ibáñez (1983) claimed that *confianza en confianza*, trust in mutual trust, was an overriding cultural intersection for Mexican-origin populations (p. 136).

As director of the Bureau of Applied Research in Anthropology (BARA) at the University of Arizona in 1983, Vélez-Ibáñez continued this research interest in relationships of reciprocity. In 1984, he and fellow BARA anthropologist James Greenberg received funding from the National Science Foundation to carry out a study on nonmarket systems of exchange within the Tucson, Arizona, Mexican-origin community. This study ("The Tucson Project") involved extensive ethnographic interviews with households in two segments of the population, roughly falling into working-class and middle-class descriptions. This work clearly demonstrated the extent to which kin and non-kin networks affected families and households (see Vélez-Ibáñez, 1996, pp. 143–181). The ethnographic interviews revealed "core" households, households (usually the mother's) that were central to providing information, goods, mutual help, and support to a whole circle of other households. Because I was an ethnographer on the Tucson Project and a graduate student at the time, I realized firsthand the transformative effect of knowing the community in all of its breadth and depth. I had been born and raised in Tucson and felt that I was quite familiar with the cycles of life here, but the experience of talking firsthand to families, hearing their stories of struggle and hardship, of survival and persistence, magnified hundredfold the puny insights I held. I learned personally of the warmth and respect given to interviewers, and of the responsibility we held as part of *confianza*. In many ways, the Tucson Project set the groundwork for the methodological and theoretical bases of the Funds of Knowledge project.

THE EDUCATIONAL RESEARCHER'S VIEW
(LUIS MOLL)

Here is where I enter the story. I arrived in Tucson in 1986 after working at the University of California, San Diego. I was not only new to Tucson but considered an outsider both culturally (I am Puerto Rican) and in terms of my academic background, as I am an educational psychologist collaborating with anthropologists. With the help of several colleagues, especially Esteban Díaz, and in collaboration with teachers, I had conducted studies in San Diego that borrowed from ethnographic methods in researching both classroom dynamics and home life, primarily with Mexican children and families. Furthermore, inspired by Vygotsky's cultural–historical psychology, which emphasizes how cultural practices and resources mediate the development of thinking, I had been exploring how to combine insights gained from reading Vygotsky (and others) with the cultural emphasis of anthropological approaches. I will say more about this topic later in this chapter.

Two of our studies in San Diego were the immediate precursors of the Funds of Knowledge projects. In one study we used classroom observations and videotapes of lessons to analyze the social organization of bilingual schooling. We were struck by how English-language instruction did not capitalize on the children's Spanish-language abilities, especially their reading competencies. With the teachers' help, we experimented with the organization of reading lessons, creating a new reading arrangement in English that moved away from a sole emphasis on decoding and concentrated instead on developing the students' reading comprehension while providing support in both languages to help them understand what they read. We were able to show that students relegated to low-level reading lessons in English were capable of much more advanced work, once provided with the strategic support of Spanish in making sense of text (see Moll & Díaz, 1987).

A second study, conducted in middle schools and with the assistance of several teachers, focused on the teaching of writing in English to learners of that language. The study also featured home observations and interviews with families to document the nature and extent of family literacy. We formed a study group with the teachers which allowed us to meet regularly in a community setting to discuss what we were learning from the home observations and how it could be used in the classrooms. It was especially important that the teachers agreed to experiment with their instruction by including topics of relevance to broader community life and to keep a reflective journal of their attempts at change, which we would then discuss in the study group. Their instructional changes included more emphasis on the process of writing and in creating opportunities for the students to talk about what they wrote, which generated more writing by the students and many more opportunities to teach. We also found that the teachers' study group served as an important "pivot." This was a setting where we could turn to what we were learning from the home visits while addressing how to improve the teaching of writing (Moll & Díaz, 1987).

These two studies formed the bases of the design of the first funds of knowledge study in 1988, funded by the Office of Bilingual Education and Minority Language Affairs of the U.S. Department of Education. The idea was as follows: to replicate the three-part design implemented in San Diego—the home observations, the after-school study group, and the classroom work—but to base the household observations on the Tucson findings of Vélez-Ibáñez and Greenberg regarding funds of knowledge. We called the study the Community Literacy Project (CLP). The central thrust of the work was to document the funds of knowledge and literacy practices of the homes we studied and observe the teaching of literacy in selected classrooms while helping teachers use our household data to generate new forms of literacy instruction in their classrooms (see Moll & Greenberg, 1990).

This project convinced us of the great theoretical utility of the concept of funds of knowledge in developing a systematic approach to households. In particular, we realized that we could visit a wide variety of households, with a range of living arrangements, and collect information reliably that would inform us about how families generated, obtained, and distributed knowledge, among other aspects of household life. We established that these homes and communities should be perceived primarily, as their defining pedagogical characteristic, in terms of the strengths and resources that they possess.

We also confirmed in that first project the importance of creating collaborative working arrangements with teachers. As in the earlier San Diego study, the teachers' study group quickly became the coordinating center for the project's pedagogical activities. Within these groups, teachers were able to think about their classrooms and what they wanted to change, and consider how to use data on funds of knowledge to change their instruction. This first study provided us with the initial case studies of teachers successfully using the study's ideas and data as part of their teaching. It also became clear, however, that just as we were approaching households as learners, we needed to approach classrooms in a similar way to learn from the teachers' work, even as we helped them rethink their classroom practices. So far, the teachers had contributed greatly to the pedagogical thinking and analysis of our research team but had played no role in the data collection of the household funds of knowledge. We set out to remedy that imbalance by creating the prototype of the funds of knowledge approach.

HOW DO ANTHROPOLOGY AND EDUCATION
FIT TOGETHER? ANTHROPOLOGY AGAIN
(NORMA GONZÁLEZ)

We return to the anthropological perspective. Many of the assumptions and methods for a funds of knowledge approach are rooted in participatory ethnography, and in anthropological theory.

What Did We Do?

The pilot Funds of Knowledge study began in 1990 with 10 teachers and funding from the W. K. Kellogg Foundation. A sister project, with four teachers, was funded in that same academic year by the National Center for Research on Diversity and Second Language Learning at the University of California, Santa Cruz. Although the groups met separately, the methods and format were similar.

The underlying rationale for this work stems from an assumption that the educational process can be greatly enhanced when teachers learn about their students' everyday lives. In our particular version of how this was to be accomplished, ethnographic research methods involved participant observation, interviews, life-history narratives, and reflection on field notes. These helped uncover the multidimensionality of student experience. Teacher–ethnographers ventured into their students' households and communities seeking to understand the ways in which people make sense of their everyday lives. Although the concept of making home visits is not new, entering the households of working-class, Mexican-origin, African American, or American Indian students with an eye toward learning from these households is a departure from traditional school-home visits.

Who Are the Teachers?

We strongly felt that only teachers who voluntarily participated should be included. Any project that adds to teachers' duties and the demands on their time has to take into account the extra burden that it places on teachers' schedules and lives. There can be little benefit gained from mandating visits where a teacher does not want to be in the household, nor the household members want to receive them. However, when there is sincere interest in both learning about and learning from a household, relationships and *confianza* can flourish.

Teachers participating in the project in its various iterations were primarily elementary school teachers, although middle school teachers from a variety of backgrounds and ranges of teaching experience were recently included. Minority and nonminority teachers said they benefited from the process. Even teachers from the local community said that conducting household visits was "like coming home to my grandmother's house" and triggered childhood memories for them. One point that I found interesting was that the nonminority teachers who participated in the project seemed to share a background of exposure to other countries and cultures. Some had lived or traveled in Latin America, Africa, or Asia in their formative years. Others had parents in the armed forces, which had given them global experiences in the process. Teachers participating in the project were paid for their extra duty time.

A TEACHER'S VIEW (CATHY AMANTI)

As Norma points out, those of us who participated in the original Funds of Knowledge project were a diverse group. We represented a multitude of background experiences and became involved for a variety of reasons. We were all practicing teachers, however, and we were all volunteers.

When I became involved in the Funds of Knowledge project, I had recently earned my bilingual education teaching credentials. I was interested in this project because the first time I attended college in the early 1970s I intended to major in anthropology and was now planning to earn a graduate degree in that field. I heard about this project from Luis Moll, who had been one of my undergraduate professors. The school where I began teaching was targeted as one of the schools for involvement in the project.

What originally interested me in this project was the opportunity to combine my interests in education and anthropology. But what kept me involved was the impact it had on my thinking about teaching and the role teachers and parents play in schools. The school where I taught at the time was situated in a predominantly working-class, Latino neighborhood. During my teacher training, I was led to believe that low-income and minority students were more likely to experience failure in school because their home experiences had not provided them with the prerequisite skills for school success in the same way as the home experiences of middle- and upper-class students. The result has been that traditionally low-income and minority students have been offered lessons reduced in complexity to compensate for these perceived deficits.

My teaching experience did not validate the expectations I garnered from my teacher preparation studies. In my daily teaching practice I saw high levels of academic engagement and insight in my students who had typically been labeled "at risk" because of their demographic characteristics. I saw they were as capable of academic success as students from any other background. Additionally, most were fluent in two languages! Participating in the Funds of Knowledge project allowed me to delve into this seeming paradox.

This points to something else all of us teachers participating in the original Funds of Knowledge project had in common—the desire to improve our teaching practice and a willingness to step out of our comfort zones to achieve that end. The first thing we had to do was step into the world of ethnography and become trained in "participant observation." This was the catalyst for us to begin looking at our students and the communities surrounding our schools in a new light. Going on ethnographic home visits, then meeting in study groups to process those experiences, allowed us to take advantage of the reflexivity inherent in ethnographic research. We went from viewing our students as one-dimensional to being multidimensional, and at the same time we gained the tools we needed to create the bridge between our students' knowledge, background experiences, and ways of viewing the world and the academic domain.

I would like to point out, however, that unlike typical ethnographers, we were not detached observers of our school communities. Nor were we engaged in ethnographic research simply to document the home lives of our students or rework social theory. We already had a relationship established with the students whose homes we visited, and our purpose for gathering information on these visits was, again, to improve our teaching practice.

HOW DO WE FIND OUT ABOUT THE KNOWLEDGE IN THE COMMUNITY? (NORMA GONZÁLEZ)

In recent years, building on what students bring to school and their strengths has been shown to be an incredibly effective teaching strategy. The Center for Research on Education, Diversity, and Excellence (CREDE) at the University of California, Santa Cruz has developed five research-based standards for effective pedagogy (http://www.crede.ucsc.edu). One of these standards, *contextualization,* is concerned with making meaning and connecting school to students' lives. What better way to engage students than to draw them in with knowledge that is already familiar to them and to use that as a basis for pushing their learning? But here is the challenge and dilemma: How do we know about the knowledge they bring without falling into tired stereotypes about different cultures? How do we deal with the dynamic processes of the life experiences of students? How can we get away from static categorizations of assumptions about what goes on in households? How can we build relationships of *confianza* with students' households?

Our answer to these questions focuses on the talk born of ethnography: respectful talk between people who are mutually engaged in a constructive conversation.

What Are the Methods for Doing This?

As the Funds of Knowledge project evolved, the approach to ethnographic training shifted as we learned more about what works and what does not. Not surprisingly, what works is exactly our basic assumption: The more that participants can engage and identify with the topic matter, the more interest and motivation they will have. What does not work is a top-down classroom style approach in which participants can learn methodological technique, but that strips away the multidimensionality of a personal ethnographic encounter. In other words, we learn ethnography by doing ethnography.

It is difficult to reduce a complex process to formulaic terms because anything called ethnography is always in jeopardy of reductionistic misuse. However, there are certain important points that are key in adopting an anthropological lens. The first step was reading ethnographic literature. Teachers were provided with a reader that contained numerous examples of ethnographic work relating to educational settings. Secondly, we role-played and discussed a nonevaluative, nonjudgmental stance to the fieldwork the teachers will be conducting. We may not always agree with what we hear, but our role is to understand how others make sense of their lives. Sense-making processes may be contradictory or ambiguous, but in one way or another, understanding what makes sense to others is what we are about. The third step is to be a good observer and pay attention to detail.

The household visit begins long before the actual entrance into the home. As we drive down the street, we observe the neighborhood, the surrounding area, and the external markers of what identifies this as a neighborhood. We look for material clues to possible funds of knowledge in gardens (botanical knowledge?), patio walls (perhaps someone is a mason?), restored automobiles (mechanical knowledge?), or ornaments displayed (made by whom?).

During our initial training session (I hesitate to call it training because ethnography is not something one can be trained in, but must experience), we would show a video that contained two short segments of ordinary community scenes and ask participants to discuss what they noticed. This kind of preparation for participant observation allowed teacher-researchers the opportunity to hone their observational skills as well as focus on paying attention to the details of household life.

The first video contained a family yard sale with a great deal of activity going on at once. We stressed that this is usually what happens on a household visit. Life doesn't stand still in these homes just so we can observe it. The vignette usually elicited comments on what is being sold, such as wooden doll furniture, which might indicate carpentry skills. Others noticed the interactions where older siblings were caring for the younger babies, indicating cross-age care-taking. Many teachers noticed the use of language and commented on the code-switching between Spanish and English evident throughout. It was fascinating to notice how our own interests and our own funds of knowledge often colored and filtered what we observe. One teacher commented that he noticed a fountain in the backyard because he was installing one himself.

The second video segment that we used is particularly rich for tapping into potential curricular applications. It showed a nine-year-old boy in a backyard workshop, working with his father to build a barbecue grill. The scene is replete with measurement, estimation, geometry, and a range of other household mathematical practices. Because we do not often think of routine household activities as containing mathematics, this slice of life helped to conceptualize the academic potential of community knowledge.

Finally, and perhaps most importantly, we asked respectful questions and learned to listen to answers. The dialogue that comes about in the face-to-face interaction of the ethnographic interview is key to building bridges between community and school and between parent and teacher. Asking questions with the intent to learn more about others is a powerful method for establishing the validation of community-based knowledge.

What About Culture?

Because the term *culture* is loaded with expectations of group norms and often-static ideas of how people view the world and behave in it, we purposely avoided reference to ideas of culture. The term presumes coherence within groups, which may not exist. Instead, we focused on practice—what households actually do and how they think about what they do. In this way, we opened up a panorama of the interculturality of households, that is, how households draw from multiple cultural systems and use these systems as strategic resources. Because of the problematic nature of the term culture, the term has been used less in anthropology. The question then becomes how do we conceptualize difference? How do we replace the contribution made by culture while minimizing its limitations? We chose to focus on the practices, the strategies and adaptations that households have developed over time, and the multiple dimensions of the lived experiences of students. The question of culture is further explored in the next chapter.

The dialog of the ethnographic interviews provided a rich source of discourse, which encapsulates how people were thinking about these experiences. Together, discourse and practice form the basis for our approach to viewing households (see Abu-Lughod, 1991).

What Kinds of Questions Do We Ask?

It is important to remember that the interviews emerged as a type of conversation rather than a survey or research protocol. We asked permission of the households first, careful to explain that pseudonyms would always be used and confidentiality maintained. We also asked for permission to audio record the interview, if the family was willing, and permission forms were signed. We also explained why we were doing the interviews, with a focus on enhancing the educational experiences of students. We have found that the vast majority of parents are willing to participate, especially if it will help their children or other people's children. In fact, one comment that has circulated among us is that our problem has never been getting into the household. It has been getting out. That is to say that once parents are convinced that there is true and genuine interest in the everyday routines of their lives, we found that deep relationships of sharing took place. Still, it is important to explain to the family that the household is under no obligation to participate and may withdraw at any time.

On the basis of our previous experience in household interviews, we distilled critical topics into three basic areas. These areas correspond to three questionnaires that were generally covered in three visits. Using questionnaires as a tool was useful for teachers, as ethnographers, to signal a shift in approaching the households as learners. Entering the household with questions, rather than answers, provided the context for an inquiry-based visit. Questionnaires were used as a guide, suggesting possible areas to explore, and used previous information as a platform for formulating new questions. However, precisely because of this scaffolding, rather than providing protocols in this book for the home visits, we instead suggest broad topics that can be explored in a mutually educative manner.

The first interview was based on a family history and labor history. The questions were open-ended and we invited stories about families. We began by asking how and when the family happened to be here, which in our case, was Tucson, Arizona. This generally led to a conversation of family roots, tracing the movements of the family from locale to locale. We also asked about other households in the city and the region with whom they have regular contact. This helped us to conceptualize the networks within which the family operates. For example, we heard many stories of families who followed other family members to Tucson. They were then able to tap into knowledge about the area and job market that others had accumulated, establishing a form of social capital upon their arrival. The narratives that emerged from these household histories are incredibly powerful and often are testimonies to the resiliency and resources of people whose lives are often lived at the economic margins. We found that we would often ask only

one or two questions about family history before we were swept away with
sagas of migration, resiliency, and survival.

These histories often had a deep impact on the teacher-researchers because of the obstacles that had to be overcome, as well as the current challenges of household members. One teacher was deeply impressed with a
household she visited, an immigrant home in which 15 people lived, with
each adult member working in labor-intensive jobs in order to contribute
to the pool of resources. Teachers regularly encountered households that
could only survive because of the networks of exchange that surrounded
them. These networks are important sources for the diversity of funds of
knowledge to which children are exposed.

The knowledge of grandparents, aunts and uncles, and extended family
relations are also resources that go beyond the nuclear family. We have
found that the very experience of relating a family history, rich in its own
complexity, often evinced a historical consciousness in parents of their origins and where life has taken them. As parents related stories of their own
mothers and fathers, grandmothers and grandfathers, life histories came
tumbling out in a fashion that is not often elucidated. Mexican-origin
households told evocative stories of crossing into the United States on foot,
of working in territorial mines and railroads, and of kinship networks that
pulled them to their location in Tucson. African American households told
stories of relocations and settlements, of grand matriarchs of extended families, and of their own views of community. American Indian households related to teacher-researchers the importance of participating in local traditional ritual Easter ceremonies and the impact that those rituals can have
on a child's identity. Embedded within the experience of narrating one's
own particular life trajectory is the extraction of deeper meanings from our
own experiences. As family members narrated the stories of how they got to
be where they are, everyday experiences came to be imbued with insights
and coherence that led to alternate forms of learning.

The foundation of a family history often served as a platform for asking
about the labor history of the household. We have found that labor histories
are very rich sources for the funds of knowledge that a household possesses.
The jobs that people work often provide them with a varied and extensive
wealth of information. However, the types of jobs and labor histories that are
common within a particular location are linked to regional patterns of political economy. In the Southwest, we found funds of knowledge consolidated in
the ecologically pertinent arenas of mining and metallurgy, ranching and animal husbandry, ethnobotany, and transborder transactions. One interesting
finding within household labor histories was that many families had approached a jack-of-all-trades strategy as a viable and necessary option in
dealing with the fluctuations of the soft economy of Tucson, Arizona. For
non-white-collar workers, survival is often a matter of strategic shifts in em-

ployment trajectories when a particular marketable skill bottoms out. This strategy was articulated by one father who stated, "If you want to stay in Tucson and survive, you have to be able to do everything: construction, carpentry, roofing, mechanics, or whatever. Otherwise, you'll starve."

For many households who do not see relocation as an option, the economic climate of the region drives households into a wide breadth of marketable skills in a multiplicity of areas. Children are not only exposed to the funds of knowledge that these shifts engender, but also to the strategic shifts in employment goals. This ability to shift strategies in mid-stream is a skill that the successful and productive citizen of the future must embody. These children are keenly aware that survival is often a matter of making the most of scarce resources and adapting to a situation in innovative and resourceful ways.

We found family members engaged in diverse occupations that gave them skills in many areas. For example, carpenters and seamstresses both engage in mathematical practices, which are often intuitive, based on common sense, and not based on academics. Yet these practices yield efficient and precise results, because errors are costly and can affect their livelihood. One important point to remember is that a labor history does not necessarily mean a job in the formal labor market. For that reason, we asked about informal labor history. Many women, for example, sell items out of their homes, such as tortillas and tamales, or sell cosmetics, or have a regular stand at the local swap meet (flea market). These are not often counted as jobs, but they are ripe with potential for children's formation of knowledge. One student was able to negotiate a barter system with a fellow swap-market vendor, which enabled him to purchase some particular clothes he wanted.

The second interview was based on regular household activities, in an attempt to capture the routine "practices" of the household. Children are often involved in ongoing household activities that can incorporate car repair, gardening, home improvement, child-care, or working in a family business or hobby. One child participated in bicycle repairs and was able to acquire a high level of competency in this area. We asked about music practices, sports, shopping with coupons, and other aspects of a child's life, which helped us develop a composite and multidimensional image of the range of possible funds of knowledge. We asked about any daily, weekly and/or monthly routines in which the family participated, and who they interacted with in these activities. We also asked about the kinds of literacy and mathematical activities that might be embedded in these practices, making the leap from informal out-of-school knowledge to formal academic knowledge.

The third interview was the most complex, and teacher-researchers reported that it was often the most revealing and lengthy. This area of understanding processes of sense-making involved how parents view and construct their roles as parents and caretakers. This interview asked questions about parenthood, raising children, and the experience of being a parent. Parents were asked about their own school experiences, and asked how it contrasted with their children's school experiences. Immigrant parents were asked about school experiences in their home country, and to contrast it with the educational system in this country. There were also questions about language use for bilingual families, including when a particular language is spoken, and under what circumstances.

It is important to remember that questions were not asked in an intrusive way, and any question that seemed inappropriate was simply not asked. Teacher-researchers developed a set of skills in asking questions within a conversation in a way everyone found comfortable. None of the questions were prescriptive, and there was wide latitude in how the interview was conducted. For anyone wishing to conduct this type of home visit, we suggest that these topics form the basis for the interviews. However, because the strength of this approach is local context, the questions that can give us these insights will vary from locale to locale. We suggest a careful appraisal of the questions that can be asked respectfully within local circumstances.

A TEACHER'S VIEW OF THE QUESTIONNAIRES (CATHY AMANTI)

The interview questionnaires we used were instrumental in creating the positive focus for the visits we made to our students' homes. The types of information we gathered prompted us to change our perspective of our students' homes and communities from, at best, being irrelevant to the educational process and, at worst, being the cause of our students' lack of educational progress, to being rich resources for teaching and learning. This change in perspective was not limited to the students whose homes we visited. After going through the process of getting to know a few students on a deeper level by visiting them in their homes and seeing how little we really knew about them just from our classroom interactions, we began to realize that even those students whose homes we had not visited were bringing multiple resources to school. From our experience with the questionnaires we learned how to ask the right questions, even in the classroom, to get at what funds of knowledge these other students possessed.

HOW IS THE HOUSEHOLD SELECTED? (NORMA GONZÁLEZ)

There was wide latitude involved in the selection of households. Teacher-researchers had full flexibility to choose any student. Some adopted a lottery system, picking a name at random, and others identified particular households because they had previous contact with them, or had an interest in getting to know the family better. It was important that the family be willing to participate, that they be informed that they could withdraw at any time, and that they be aware that it involved a time commitment. Children often clamored to have their homes visited, and teachers were invariably welcomed as honored guests and with the utmost respect and courtesy. Conversations about family histories often brought out picture albums, yellowed newspaper clippings, and elaborate genealogies. Topics about work and hobbies often produced handcrafted items or tours of home improvement projects. Talk about schools generated diplomas and awards. Teachers were often invited back informally to participate in family gatherings or church and community functions. Telling their story became an important and valued experience for parents, when there was a truly engaged and interested listener and learner.

How Many Households Are Interviewed?

It goes without saying that it is impossible to interview the household of every student in a classroom. In fact, teachers typically conducted complete interviews with three students and their families. This may seem like a small number, but it actually represents a great deal of investment in time on the part of the teacher. Hectic schedules of both teachers and household members preclude frequent visits. Most visits were spaced out over a period of several months. Even when teachers were able to conduct only one in-depth series of interviews with a household, they still found it to be a powerful process. As we might expect, the more households were interviewed across a number of school years, the greater the insights into the community. However, we cannot underestimate the power of engaging in a long-term sustained relationship with only a few families.

What About Language?

As we have mentioned, the teachers we have worked with represent a diversity of background and experience. Although some of the teachers have been bilingual, others were not. Still, bilingualism has played an important role in our work. Bilingual teachers have, for the most part, carried out the interviews by themselves. However, we did recommend that teachers consider going in pairs to interviews, and this strategy worked well with non-bilingual teachers. These teachers were often accompanied by classroom paraprofessionals, who are almost always bilingual and who generally have a good sense of community context. In these cases, the bilingual paraprofessional was able to facilitate the connection to the household. However, this also means that paraprofessionals should be a part of the ethnographic training and participate in other professional development activities (see Rueda & Monzó, 2002). In one case, a monolingual teacher was accompanied by her bilingual principal, and they engaged in a rich, dual-language interview. Because the aim of the household interviews is to come to a deeper and more nuanced understanding of community practices, it is important that the formation of relationships be the guiding principle. The interview is not only meant to gather information, but to create new linkages between parents and teachers. The language of the interview becomes an important context for these relationships, and a great deal of thought should precede how communication will take place.

In addition, the study group discussion most often occurred in both English and Spanish, depending on the topic and the discussants. All of the questions used in the interviews are available in both languages because many of the interviews are conducted not only in one language or another, but in a combination of both. The writing of field notes also reflects bilingual language practices, prominent features of the households and communities we have studied. This bilingualism has been part of the texture of the interviews, so much so that in many ways we could not imagine conducting the research monolingually. Thus, this code-switching, this interplay of codes, often censored in schools, has become the language of research and yet another cultural resource as we attempt to represent and understand the communities within which we work.

What Happened After the Interview?

The field notes were important in reflecting on the interviews and visits. We asked the families' permission to tape-record the interview, since this helped to reconstruct the experience. The field notes documented the findings and details of the visit in a way that helped to further process the experience. The writing of field notes can be time-consuming, but the written expression helped to collectively share the insights gained from the visit in the study group. Following their forays into the field, teacher-researchers were asked to write field notes, as all field workers do, based on each interview, and these field notes became the basis for the study group discussions. Teachers overwhelmingly remarked on the time-consuming nature of this process. After a hectic school day, taking the time to conduct interviews which often stretched into two or three hours, and then to later invest four to five hours in writing field notes was an exacting price to pay for a connection to the household. They cited this one factor as precluding wholesale teacher participation in this project. Yet, in spite of the strain of the task, the teachers felt that the effort was worth it. It was in the reflexive process involved in transcribing that teachers were able to obtain elusive insights that could have easily been overlooked. As they replayed the audiotapes and referred to notes, connections and hunches began to emerge. The household began to take on a complex reality that had taken root in the interview and reached its fruition in reflexive writing. Writing gave form and substance to the connection forged between the household and the teacher.

THE STUDY GROUP SETTINGS (LUIS MOLL)

I want to underscore the importance of developing study-group settings with teachers. These settings, mentioned in several chapters in this volume, are deliberately created to facilitate interactions between teachers and researchers about the work at hand. It is difficult to underestimate the importance of such settings for a funds of knowledge approach. We have come to call them the "center of gravity" of the project. These are the places where we conduct all project business. It is where we discuss the background readings, introduce observations and note-taking, revise interview procedures, review findings from each visit, and discuss classroom practices and implications. It is also the place where we initially get to know each other and create relationships among participants through the discussions about the work.

The study group is also the place where we examine ethical considerations in the study. Any project involving multiple participants visiting various households has the potential to encounter ethical dilemmas. One such issue, for example, is whether teachers are being unnecessarily intrusive in visiting households. Although this is a concern of some teachers at the beginning of each study, this is a topic that to our knowledge has never been raised by the families themselves. This may be because we carefully negotiate entry into the households, usually by working with the teachers in contacting parents and explaining the work and our request to visit. Although we have not kept statistics, in the great majority of cases the families accede readily to the visits. Once we start the visits, we reiterate the purpose of the study as often as necessary, and assure the respondents of confidentiality, that they need not answer any question they do not like, and we offer to give them copies of the interview tapes or of the transcripts. In our experience, the families have never refused to answer any question. On the contrary, our experience has been that the families engage us in an extended dialog during each of the visits.

A question we get often during presentations about the work is whether we encounter many dysfunctional families, whatever the definition of this term. The answer is no. This may be because of the way we sample families, usually based on the suggestions of teachers, with an eye toward gaining access to the household. It could also be that if a family is having extreme difficulties, it would not become a candidate for a visit or consent to it if asked. But more than likely, it is that the perception of dysfunctionality in working-class neighborhoods is misleading and exaggerated. As we have pointed out often, the families we visit represent the status quo in their communities. In other words, they are working folks; these are not families that form part of any "underclass," a term that has unfortunately come to characterize low-income families in general (see Vélez-Ibáñez, 1983). We do not mean to suggest, however, that low-income communities do not have problems, especially as produced by structural factors; of course they do (see Vélez-Ibáñez, 1996, ch. 5). The perspective that we reject is that these problems characterize entire communities, removing from consideration the ample and positive resources families possess.

Another important aspect of study-group settings is their mobility. We usually meet after school and at the school, as a matter of convenience. However, we have also met at our homes, at restaurants, libraries, and other locations. We have also used university courses as study-group settings of sorts. The course routines ensure weekly meetings, which gives a study continuity. However, the course structure places the university-based teacher in the position of authority, given the requirements of assignments, assessments, and grades, a contradiction to the symmetry we call for in our collaborations.

In any case, regardless of location, the study-group settings serve similar "mediating" functions between the household visits and the classroom work. The term mediation has a special meaning in our studies, one that we borrow from the writings of Vygotsky (1978). A major point in his theory is how culture provides human beings with tools and other resources to mediate their thinking. In a nutshell, from birth one is socialized by others into particular cultural practices, including ways of using language(s) and ways of using artifacts that become the "tools for thinking" through which we interact with our social worlds. Thus, from a Vygotskian perspective, human thinking has a sociocultural character from the very beginning, because all human actions, from the mundane to the exotic, involve "mediation" through such objects, symbols, and practices. Put another way, these cultural tools and practices—some which are stable, and some which change across generations—are always implicated in how one thinks and develops.

There are three main ways that these Vygotskian ideas are found in our work. First, notice how these ideas relate to the analysis of household funds of knowledge (see Moll & Greenberg, 1990). As emphasized throughout this book, funds of knowledge are generated through the social and labor history of families and communicated to others through the activities that constitute household life, including through the formation of social networks that are central to any household's functioning within its particular environments. From this perspective, then, funds of knowledge represent one of the household's most useful cultural resources, an essential tool kit that households need to maintain (mediate) their well-being.

A second way is that funds of knowledge become cultural resources for teachers as they document their existence and bring them to bear on their work. But to carry out these tasks, teachers must themselves acquire, or appropriate, certain specialized tools to conduct research that come to mediate their thinking about these matters. It is this idea of "appropriating," of taking over, certain procedures, artifacts, discourses and reasoning, that applies so well to how the study groups function in our approach.

To elaborate on this, I want to highlight two aspects of these study groups that have to do with the production of theoretical (re)presentations. A major role of the study group has been to help facilitate the participants' comprehension of social life in the households they study. The process by which these understandings are created varies, but it starts with the preparations to conduct the household visits. As explained earlier, entering the households with questions is essential in developing such an inquiry-based approach. Equally important is for teachers to gain an understanding of funds of knowledge as a "fluid" concept, and that its content and meaning are negotiated through discussions among participants. Also, it is through the process of writing field notes and discussing them that one gives theoretical form and substance to the connections forged empirically between the households and the teachers.

Our approach to understanding families and their cultural resources also includes raising possibilities for changes in classroom practice. This is the third way that the Vygotskian formulations have played a role in our work, especially as combined with an anthropological perspective, in understanding classrooms as cultural settings. During the course of our studies we made the decision to take a more ethnographic stance toward the teachers' classroom practices. Our task shifted from stimulating changes in practice, especially as related to literacy instruction, to understanding how teachers made use of their experiences and resources within classroom contexts. The teacher-authored chapters included in this book reveal the multiple conditions and strategies followed in transporting experiences from their research into their practice. To be sure, this process of transportation is not to be thought of as a simple transfer of skills from one setting to the next. As the reader will appreciate, it involves a much more complicated process of recontextualizing not only the knowledge obtained through the research, but the perspectives and methods of inquiry that led to that knowledge.

Perhaps the connecting thread among the teachers who participated in our studies is a renewed emphasis on an inquiry model of teaching, one in which the students are actively involved in developing their knowledge. It is through an inquiry process, conceptualized in several ways, given the various participants within different work situations and curricular exigencies that one can create conditions for fruitful interactions between knowledge found inside and outside the classroom. The key for any inquiry method is to expand the resources available for teaching and learning within classroom settings (Moll, 1990, 1992, 1998, 2002).

STUDY GROUPS AS PEDAGOGICAL MODEL
(CATHY AMANTI)

It is no accident that an inquiry approach to teaching is a common thread in curriculum developed by teachers participating in the Funds of Knowledge project. As teachers engage in theorizing household knowledge and practices in the study group context, they are at the same time "socialized" into a particular type of pedagogy. As mentioned earlier, study groups are reciprocal, collaborative, and democratic; where teachers learn from researchers, researchers learn from teachers, and teachers and researchers learn from households; where what each person brings to the context is valued as one more piece to the puzzle of how to ensure academic success for all our students. In the study-group setting, university researchers serve as facilitators rather than instructors, acting as guides as teachers construct new knowledge about teaching and learning based on their experiences in their students' homes as well as their previous classroom experiences. The type of learning that takes place within the study group context by teachers has become the model for the curriculum that has been developed by funds of knowledge participants and the role the university researchers take in study groups is the one teachers have taken in their own classrooms.

The study groups are also supportive, nonjudgmental settings where teachers feel safe to share tentative conjectures and hypotheses about the importance and significance of what they are experiencing during their household visits. And they create the conditions where teachers can become risk-takers, willing to experiment and try out new strategies and practices in their classrooms. Those are exactly the conditions we want to recreate for our students in our own classrooms so that they become safe, nonjudgmental environments where students feel free to take risks and test their own hypotheses about what they are learning.

THEORIZING PRACTICES
(LUIS MOLL AND NORMA GONZÁLEZ)

It is important to note at this juncture that the theorizing of practices involves both households and classrooms. Very often theory and practice are presented as a matter of course in terms of putting "theory into practice." We suggest an alternative view to this binary. We suggest that as the practices of households are theorized, we as educators can come to deeper understandings of the complexities of students' lives. As ideas of practice are often based on the work of Bourdieu (1977), who theorized not coherence, but contradiction, and nuances rather than linear connections, we can see the theorizing of practices as an important step in comprehending the contexts of students' experiences. But the theorizing of practices is not only meant for households. As we met in the study groups, household practices were strategically related to classroom practices. Teachers were free to make connections to their classrooms in any of the content areas or in thematic units. Some teachers, because of school-based curricular requirements, were more restricted in the way they could incorporate household knowledge into the classroom. During the study group, an exploration of possibilities resulted in a wide array of opportunities to affect classroom practice. One teacher (Ayers, Fonseca, Andrade, & Civil, 2001) explored a construction unit with his students, based on their ideas of "building their own dream house." In this unit, students began by exploring two-dimensional floor plans of their dream houses and then progressed to drawings of blueprints of actual floor plans, using the correct architectural symbols for doors, windows, sinks, and so forth. They then went on to conceptualize and abstract geometrical concepts, calculating areas, perimeters and angles of sections of regular polygons. Finally, the students made scale models of their dream project, presenting it to an audience of students and teachers. (For an exploration of classroom practices that stem from a funds of knowledge approach, see McIntyre, Rosebery, & González, 2001.)

The process of theorizing practices addresses the critical task of representing the households and by implication the school's community, a task that all teachers engage in one way or another whether or not they participate in a research study. As mentioned, our strategy has been to get close to the phenomena of household life by making repeated visits in our role as learners, armed with a particular theory and method. The elaboration of field notes, journals, and academic articles are, by necessity, a strategic reduction of household life, a partial representation of reality, for that reality is too complex to understand without reducing it for specific purposes. Here is where the concept of funds of knowledge plays a major role as a "cultural artifact," in the Vygotskian sense, that helps mediate the teachers' comprehension of social life within the households. This key concept (and related ideas), then, serves as a conceptual organizer, a strategic way of reducing theoretically (but with plenty of respect) the complexity of people's everyday experiences, without losing sight of the rich and dynamic totality of their lives.

Notice how important this understanding of the concept is, especially for novices visiting households. It is a matter of entering the households with theoretical provisions and methodological guidance that will give order to the often unmanageable task of learning about other people's lives. It is also a matter of learning how to use these theoretical tools wisely, carefully, and in consultation with others. Thus, our research starts with the theoretical questions we bring into households, but our data result from the translation of the information gathered into theoretically informed narratives.

The field notes and other artifacts, therefore, such as audio- and videotapes, the tools of our trade, provide a social context for our interpretations and actions. These artifacts are central in helping us develop a "new attitude" toward the cultural resources found in local households. But also notice that, in a sense, we first create this new attitude toward the text, toward the slice of life that we have represented in writing, as facilitated by the documentation of funds of knowledge, and then we generalize that attitude to the families with whom we work, the sources of the data. This interaction between text and social life, between word and world, is a constant process in the approach.

Of course, most of us are predisposed to think well of the families anyway, but even those who are not convinced or who have not given the topic much thought are influenced by the process, or they at least develop a new vocabulary to refer to household practices. Terms such as *funds of knowledge, networks of exchange, reciprocal relations,* or the creation of *confianza* become part of the theoretical lexicon of teachers. Thus, it is important to emphasize that we do not create these new attitudes, or the vocabulary, about the families simply by visiting them, but through theoretically inspired text analyses and reflections, that is, by theorizing practices.

How Can I Carry Out a Similar Project in My School?

The success of our project depended on the confluence of a number of factors that may or may not exist in other contexts. For example, the presence of a large research university, as well as an alignment of interdisciplinary research interests, may not always be the case. Nevertheless we do believe that the basic methodologies and assumptions are portable and generalizable and that each school can gain knowledge of its local context through these methods. We would suggest a careful reading of this volume in order to appropriate the themes and topics that would be relevant to your school. In addition, we suggest that this be undertaken with a group of like-minded teachers, as a certain critical mass is important. We also strongly suggest readings on ethnographic methods, such as Carolyn Frank's *Ethnographic Eyes: A Teacher's Guide to Classroom Observation* or Annette Lareau and Jeffry Shultz' book *Journeys Through Ethnography: Realistic Accounts of Fieldwork*. It is also important to obtain support from school administrators and any other concerned stakeholders. Our process was greatly facilitated by support from external sources as well as the local university. If these resources are available, all possibilities for collaboration should be explored. Most importantly, however, is a commitment to connect to students' lives, as well as a commitment to grow professionally as a researcher and producer of knowledge.

Is This Scientifically Based Research?

Of course it is. The nature of the phenomena we studied, the purposes of our inquiry, our theoretical principles, our collaboration with teachers, and other contextual considerations "specified" our methods, not the other way around. To be brief, our particular qualitative methods suited our inquiry. The current reductionist rhetoric by federal policymakers regarding what constitutes scientifically based research is myopic, not to mention terrible policy, in that it contributes to a very narrow and distorted view of science. As Feuer, Towne, and Shavelson (2002) commented, the extremist view that only certain positivist modes of inquiry (e.g., randomized field trials) are acceptable in educational research denigrates "the legitimate role of qualitative methods in elucidating the complexities of teaching, learning, and schooling" (p. 8).

Indeed, as Pellegrino and Goldman (2002) have asserted, in also criticizing the attempt of the government to legislate scientific methods, "the complexity of issues, questions, and problems in education often demand a melding of approaches to achieve innovative problem formulation and successful problem solving" (p. 15). This book represents one such melding of approaches, especially in the adaptations to involve teachers authentically in research collaborations that lead to innovations in both theory and practice.

That said, we are not opposed, in principle, to quasi-experimental studies in education, or to randomized field trials for that matter. It is simply the case that these are inappropriate choices of design given the purposes of our work and our collaboration with teachers as reported in this volume.

We have also been asked whether we collected test data on the students to "prove" that the approach works. The answer is no. We did collect test data in several classrooms in an earlier version of the study that included matched comparison groups, but found much of this information uninterpretable given variations among classrooms, differences in instruction, and other confounding aspects of practice. In general, our main strategy in terms of documenting changes in practice has been twofold: to produce theoretically informed case studies of classroom attempts at incorporating funds of knowledge, and to rely on teacher-produced narrative accounts of their classroom work. The appeal, and we hope the readers will agree, is that these data, these case narratives, preserve the concrete conditions under which the work is conducted, the agency and improvisations of teachers in conducting the work, the actions of the students, and the qualitative transformations that took place within their classrooms. We believe that, in the pages that follow, we have made the crucial interplay among theory, methods, and findings clear for our readers. Ultimately, it is up to each reader to judge the worthiness of our efforts.

REFERENCES

Abu-Lughod, L. (1991). Writing against culture. In R. G. Fox (Ed.),*Recapturing anthropology: Working in the present* (pp. 137–162). Santa Fe, NM: School of American Research Press.

Ayers, M., Fonseca, J. D., Andrade, R., & Civil, M. (2001). Creating learning communities: The "Build your Dream House" unit. In E. McIntyre, A. Rosebery, & N. González (Eds.), *Classroom diversity: Connecting curriculum to students' lives* (pp. 92–99). Portsmouth, NH: Heinemann.

Bourdieu, P. (1977). *Outline of a theory of practice* (R. Nice, Trans.). Cambridge, UK: Cambridge University Press.

Feuer, M., Towne, L., & Shavelson, R. (2002). Scientific culture and educational research. *Educational Researcher, 31,* 4–14.

Lee, C. D., & Smagorinsky, P. (2000). *Vygotskian perspectives on literacy research: Constructing meaning through collaborative activity.* Cambridge, UK: Cambridge University Press.

McIntyre, E., Rosebery, A., & González, N. (2001). *Classroom diversity: Connecting curriculum to students' lives.* Portsmouth, NH: Heinemann.

Moll, L. C. (1990). *Vygotsky and education.* Cambridge, UK: Cambridge University Press.

Moll, L. C. (1992). Bilingual classroom and community analysis: Some recent trends. *Educational Researcher, 21,* 20–24.

Moll, L. C. (1998). Turning to the word: Bilingualism, literacy and the cultural mediation of thinking. *National Reading Conference Yearbook, 47,* 59–75.

Moll, L. C. (2002). Through the mediation of others: Vygotskian research on teaching. In V. Richardson (Ed.), *Handbook of research on teaching* (4th ed.). Washington, DC: American Educational Research Association.

Moll, L. C., & Díaz, S. (1987). *Bilingual communication skills in classroom contexts.* Final Report, Laboratory of Comparative Human Condition, University of California, San Diego.

Moll, L. C., & Greenberg, J. (1990). Creating zones of possibilities: Combining social contexts for instruction. In L. C. Moll (Ed.), *Vygotsky and education* (pp. 319–348). Cambridge, UK: Cambridge University Press.

Pellegrino, J., & Goldman, S. (2002). Be careful what you wish for—you may get it: Educational research in the spotlight. *Educational Researcher, 31,* 15–17.

Rueda, R., & Monzó, L. D. (2000). Apprenticeship for teaching: Professional development issues surrounding the collaborative relationship between teachers and paraeducators. *Teaching and Teacher Education, 18,* 503–521.

Vélez-Ibáñez, C. (1983). *Bonds of mutual trust: The cultural systems of rotating credit associations among urban Mexicans and Chicanos.* New Brunswick, NJ: Rutgers University Press.

Vélez-Ibáñez, C. (1996). *Border visions: Mexican cultures of the Southwest United States.* Tucson, AZ: University of Arizona Press.

Vygotsky, L. S. (1978). *Mind in society.* Cambridge, MA: Harvard University Press.

Willis, P. (2000). *The ethnographic imagination.* Cambridge, UK: Polity Press.

THEORETICAL UNDERPINNINGS

This part of the book lays out the theoretical groundwork for the funds of knowledge perspective. It begins with a discussion about culture, and how we can come to a deeper appreciation of the dynamic and emergent conditions of lived experiences by moving away from stereotypical notions of culture. In her chapter, Norma González attempts to connect conceptualizations of culture to the construct of funds of knowledge. The two terms are not synonymous. Although culture has been a powerful tool to counter claims about the variability of human populations, it has become, for many anthropologists, more of a burden than a productive tool. The funds of knowledge of a community are not a laundry list of immutable cultural traits, but rather are historically contingent, emergent within relations of power, and not necessarily equally distributed. This chapter is an attempt to trace the genesis of the term *culture* and relate its changing usages to educational concerns.

In the next three chapters, it is evident how we have drawn from sociocultural perspectives in designing a methodology that views the everyday practices of language and activities as constructing knowledge. These three articles are reprints and describe the work as it was developing and transforming throughout the 1990s. One caveat to the reader: Because these reprints represent ongoing work that was published in different venues, there is some overlap and redundancy in laying out the fundamental premises of the work. These articles are presented as they first appeared in print and are foregrounded in order to trace the trajectory of the evolving work.

The first reprinted article, "Formation and Transformation of Funds of Knowledge," by Carlos Vélez-Ibáñez and James Greenberg, is an anthropological perspective on households and their social capital. This chapter provides a theoretical framework for conceptualizing households as repositories of knowledge. By tracing the economic and political transformations that have given rise to the historical context of the southwestern United States, this chapter locates funds of knowledge within plural strategies of survival that households have deployed. Vélez-Ibáñez and Greenberg explain how Mexican-origin families have "crisscrossed the border in response to the intermittent booms and busts of the border economy," and how these cross-border relations have been significant in the formation of localized funds of knowledge. The importance of social networks is key to this formation, for it is through exchanges with kin and non-kin alike that these bodies of knowledge grow and transform. Often these systems of exchange are activated through the clustering of households around one core household, usually a parent or grandparent. This is an important concept, as we found that teacher-researchers could position the classroom within this system of household clusters. That is, the classroom becomes another node in an information exchange system that encompasses multiple bodies of knowledge. The classroom can thus activate the funds of knowledge within a social network as it becomes a part of that social network.

As Vélez-Ibáñez and Greenberg explain, funds of knowledge are not only received from others, they are also modified, discarded, or produced, depending on specific circumstances. By extension, teacher-researchers can modify or adapt these resources as the basis for the creation of new knowledge specific to classroom circumstances. This implies a dynamic aspect to the transformation of funds of knowledge, as they are ever-forming as pedagogical resources.

Because the labor market significantly affects household strategies, labor histories are critical in the production of funds of knowledge. However, we are always cautious to include the informal economy within this sphere. Women's marketing of food items, informal sale of goods and services, as well as women's exchange systems, can be obscured by a narrow focus on a waged economy.

Although this particular article does not deal with teachers and researchers, it did provide the conceptual glue which has held our approach together: Understanding the social, historical, political, and economic context of households is of critical importance in understanding teaching and learning.

In chapter 3, authored by Luis Moll, Deborah Neff, Cathy Amanti, and Norma González, the conversation between anthropology and education is embodied in the interaction between a teacher-researcher making her first forays into the field and a more experienced ethnographer trying to connect with local knowledge. We discern the apprehension of the teacher-researcher in engaging with a then-unfamiliar role, and the surprise of the ethnographer at the ease with which the teacher-researcher fits into the role. The ready acceptance of the teacher into the household setting is appreciated because it deals with the apprehension anthropologists often face while working in the field.

In the dialog that ensues, we see Amanti, the teacher-researcher, make insightful and deep connections to the family's history and practices. Because we had often touched upon the networks that connect households, sometimes across borders, she quickly identifies her students' cross-border experience as an often-unrecognized fund of knowledge. Carlos, her student, is embedded in a web of kinship in Magdalena, Sonora, Mexico, a web that has facilitated economic and material resources to the family. Because of his binational experience, Amanti affirms, "These children have had the background experiences to explore in-depth issues that tie in with a sixth grade curriculum, such as the study of other countries, different forms of government, economic systems, and so on."

But the connection does not end there. Because Amanti and Neff had witnessed Carlos selling Mexican candy to a neighbor during the household visit, Amanti decided to use this seemingly unremarkable interaction as the basis for a curriculum unit on candy. On the surface, the topic of candy might not seem to fit in with culturally relevant or critical pedagogy. Yet it had emerged from the lived experiences of the child, and the teacher was quick to recognize the pedagogical significance of elaborating the topic within the scientific method. She was able to incorporate elements of science, math, social studies, and language arts curricula within this unassuming topic.

More importantly, a mother, Mrs. Rodríguez, came into the classroom and taught the students from her own store of funds of knowledge. In a powerfully symbolic transformation, the mother of a student, an immigrant woman with limited formal education, becomes the imparter of knowledge. Her background experiences might easily have gone unrecognized but are instead validated as worthy of pedagogical notice. As Amanti notes, "My respect and awe of Mrs. Rodríguez grew by leaps and bounds that morning."

Finally, we find the students engaged in their own production of knowledge. The teacher has become a mediator, providing strategic assistance that would facilitate the students' inquiry and work. In this dialog we can see the ripple effect of teachers engaging in qualitative household research. As teacher-researchers develop more complex theories of households, they are able to connect with broader sociopolitical contexts.

In the final chapter in this part, the voices of teacher-researchers take center stage. The continuing professional development of teachers has been and continues to be an area of considerable theoretical and practical debate. Our approach to professional development has been in engaging teachers as researchers in their own school communities. Rather than formulaic generalizations about the communities where schools are located, teachers are presented with an array of theoretical tools that can help them discover for themselves the funds of knowledge within their reach. The social processes within which students are embedded take on a new dimension. This is particularly important as schools, teachers, students, and parents attempt to construct communities of learners.

In this chapter, we offer an insider's look at how teachers can realistically engage in researching their students' communities. As we reiterate, there is no cookie-cutter recipe that will work equally well at all school sites. Although we believe that our methods and practices are transportable, we do not rely on rigid replication of a model. Instead we offer some general principles that undergird the reflexive process of engaging parents in face-to-face interaction. Stories of resilience, of hope against all odds, and of survival erupt in all shapes when the narratives that dwell within households are uncovered. For teachers, this can be both inspiring and exhausting.

We have tried to present the teachers' own voices and narratives of this experience. An emphasis on the joint construction of knowledge helped us see our work as multiauthored and polyvocal. This collaborative type of professional development provided a space for interactive research within an inquiry-based environment. We were all learners. Yet, we found, that engagement in a teacher study group did not end at the door to the school grounds. Parents and community members engaged in a reflexive process of telling their own stories, which itself engendered a form of historical consciousness of how they came to be where they are now.

Finally in this article, we suggest the basic principles that we have found to be critical in the process, as well as identify problematic areas. Professional development is not accomplished with only one strategy or method. Our focus has been on helping ourselves elaborate a theory of households, of households' function within a wider sphere, and thus of the sociopolitical context of local schools.

Chapter 2

Beyond Culture: The Hybridity of Funds of Knowledge*

Norma González
University of Utah

> *The encounter with persons, one by one, rather than categories and generalities, is still the best way to cross lines of strangeness.*
> —Mary Catherine Bateson (2000, p. 81)

The concept of culture is one of those seemingly commonsense words that implies a taken-for-granted meaning. After all, we all know what we mean when we talk about Japanese culture, corporate culture, or, on the other hand, to be a cultured individual in art and music. As educators, we are urged to be aware of cultural issues and try to incorporate culturally sensitive pedagogy. Yet, once we start to peel back the layers of this common usage, we find a complex history, a variety of definitions, and wide disparity in theories of culture.

ABBREVIATED HISTORY OF THE CONCEPT OF CULTURE

Because the idea of culture is so embedded in our everyday conversations, it is somewhat startling to realize that it is a relatively recent newcomer in the history of ideas. Raymond Williams (1958), the British social theorist, traced the idea of culture as it developed in Britain from the late eighteenth cen-

---

*Portions of this chapter appeared in a different form in: González, N. (2004). Disciplining the discipline: Anthropology and the pursuit of quality education. *Educational Researcher, 33*(5), 17–25.

tury. Before this time, the word had mostly signified the growth of an organism, as in agri*culture* or horti*culture*. It then evolved from meaning

> "the tending of natural growth," and then, by analogy, a process of human training. But this latter use, which had usually been a culture *of* something, was changed, in the nineteenth century, to *culture* as such, a thing in itself. It came to mean, first "a general state of habit of the mind," having close relations with the idea of human perfection. Second, it came to mean "the general state of intellectual development, in a society as a whole." Third, it came to mean "the general body of the arts." Fourth, later in the century, it came to mean "a whole way of life, material, intellectual and spiritual." It came also, as we know, to be a word which often provoked either hostility or embarrassment. (Williams, 1958, p. xvi)

Williams also claimed that the idea of culture emerged as a contestation to the upheaval caused by the Industrial Revolution. "The idea of culture represented the last line of defense against the idea that society consists of nothing more than mechanistic, market-based transactions, with 'cash payment as the sole nexus' " (Stolzenberg, 2001, p. 443). Thus, culture, in the British tradition, came to be thought of in nonmaterial terms, as the aspirations of the human mind and of artistic endeavor. However, it is in Germany that we find the deepest roots of the culture concept. In late 19th century Germany, we encounter the term "culture-history" which grew out of the earlier emphasis on the "history of the spirit" (Wax, 1993, p. 103). This is significant because the person most responsible for developing the culture concept within U.S. anthropology, Franz Boas, was trained as a natural scientist in Germany, and he later transmitted his ideas about culture as being the "genius of a people."

CULTURE AS THE ANTIDOTE TO SCIENTIFIC RACISM

Prior to about 1900, "culture" both in the German and in the Anglo-American tradition was heavily influenced by the evolutionary tenets in vogue at the time. Culture was associated with "the progressive accumulation of the characteristic manifestations of human creativity: art, science, knowledge, refinement—those things that freed man from control by nature, by environment, by reflex, by instinct, by habit, or by custom" (Stocking, 1968, p. 201). Evolutionism in social terms conceived of the progress of human societies in terms of evolutionary stages, from the simple (or, in evolutionary terms, more primitive) to the more complex. These stages encompassed all areas of social life: marriage and kinship forms, art and artistic development, forms of government, religious life, the development of myth, and so forth. This form of evolutionism was congruent with the then-accepted ranking of racial groups in terms of intelligence and biogenetic inheritance. It was a commonly held belief where "leaders and intellectuals did not doubt the propriety of racial ranking—with Indians below whites, and blacks below everybody else" (Gould, 1981, p. 31). Indeed, there was a relegation of "the dark-skinned savage to a status very near the ape" (Stocking, 1973, p. lxx, cited in Gould, 1981, p. 73).

The "scientific" basis for ascribing these hierarchies came from a number of measures, especially craniometry and evolutionary distance from other primates. The measurement of skull size was held to correlate to brain capacity (and hence intellectual capacity), and other anthropometric measurements gauged the "apishness" of traits. Thus, it was unremarkable that in 1890 the anthropologist Brinton, in what was not anthropology's finest hour, could claim:

> The adult who retains the more numerous fetal, infantile, or simian traits, is unquestionably inferior to him whose development has progressed beyond them. . . . Measured by these criteria, the European or white race stands at the head of the list, the African or Negro at its foot. . . . All parts of the body have been minutely scanned, measured and weighed, in order to erect a science of the comparative anatomy of the races. (Brinton, 1890, p. 48, as cited in Gould, 1981, p. 116; for an overview of this history, see Gould, 1981)

It is against this backdrop that Franz Boas began to argue against the unilineal progression of evolutionary stages and, more importantly, against the racial implications of this argument. His answer to this reigning paradigm was the elaboration of the concept of culture.

Prior to Boas, the culture concept had been defined primarily by E. B. Tylor in his book, *Primitive Culture* (1873/1958). His definition was accepted as the most comprehensive view: "Culture or Civilization, taken in its wide ethnographic sense, is that complex whole which included knowledge, belief, art, morals, law, custom, and any other capabilities and habits acquired by man as a member of society" (p. 1). Tylor, however, was also an evolutionist, and he regarded stages of development as the outgrowth of culture. While Boas did not redefine culture, he did put the evolutionary framework to the test of actual rigorous and scientifically tenable ethnographic fieldwork. Through his extensive time in residence with various North American Indian groups, he was able to critique the claims of evolutionary stages and argued for a historical comparative method that recognized the possibility of multiple historically conditioned cultures that often strategically borrowed from each other. This process of cultural diffusion was a challenge to key evolutionary assumptions. If societies borrowed cultural traits, according to Boas, it was not necessary to independently invent each institution anew. Some societies could have invented traits, but others could have borrowed these. In this way, by arguing that human behavior could be conditioned by the historical circumstances in which it arises, he transformed the biogenetic argument of human development. If something extrinsic to the human organism, something called "culture," could account for human behavior, then a powerful argument could be made for the relativism of human societies. No longer could race and hierarchical racial classifications be scientifically defensible. Thus, "by changing the relation of 'culture' to man's evolutionary development, to the burden of tradition, and to the processes of human reason, [Boas] transformed the notion into a tool quite different from what it had been before" (Stocking, 1968, p. 233).

The implications of this paradigm shift were enormous. Although many social scientists continued to see race as a way to account for human differences, "Boas, almost single-handedly, developed in America the concept of culture, which, like a powerful solvent, would in time expunge race from the literature of social science" (Degler, 1991, p. 71). Yet, this does not mean that social science was marching evenly, onward and upward, toward a vision of racial and social justice. In fact, there are some who argue that the attempt to expunge race from social science, by assigning it to biology, actually resulted in a continuation of scientific racism (Visweswaran, 1998). Because culture came to stand for race, without a sociohistorical construction of race, "culture is asked to do the work of race" (p. 76). In fact, the concept of culture can make race invisible, and race becomes "a metonym for culture; and it does so only at the price of biologizing what is culture or ideology" (Appiah, 1986, p. 36, as cited in Visweswaran, 1998, p. 76).

PROLIFERATION OF THE USAGE OF CULTURE

As Boas and his students transformed the use of culture, it became in many ways the central organizing concept of anthropology. As such, it was differentiated and elaborated in myriad ways. By 1952, in a well-known review of definitions of culture, the anthropologists Alfred Kroeber and Clyde Kluckhohn discovered more than one hundred and fifty definitions of "culture."

Even though there was no consensus among cultural anthropologists in terms of a definition of or a theorizing of culture, there eventually came to be an accepted view that "everyone knew what it was." Says George Spindler, one of the founders of the field of Anthropology and Education:

> In the 1940s, when I began my fieldwork, everybody knew what culture was—culture was what everybody had in a predictable, bounded sense; everyone was recognizable by their laundry list of cultural traits. (Spindler, 1996)

Indeed, anthropology came to be dominated, from about 1940 to about 1980, by a view of culture that emphasized a holistic and integrated view of culture, a neat "package deal . . . [in which] cultures were believed to have neat boundaries, inside of which were all sorts of traditions and structures, such as marriage practices, gender roles, religion, death rituals, child-rearing practices, language, power, and authority structures, food, and so forth" (Henze & Hauser, 1999).

In addition, there was an assumption that culture provided particular rules for behavior that everyone in a culture abided by. Our culture determined our behavior, and culture was thought of in a holistic and pervasive sense. Although this thread of cultural determinism was woven through most concepts of culture, there did emerge a proliferation of approaches to culture. In 1974, Roger Keesing published an article that outlined the general strands of theories of culture at the time. The two main divisions, between what might be termed *mentalist* (culture is inside the head) and *materialist* (culture is a response to dealing with the material conditions of existence) theories of culture, formed a bifurcation in the anthropological understanding of culture. On the one hand, the materialists saw culture as an adaptive system that connected human communities to their ecological and subsistence settings. In this sense, culture was a mechanism that had allowed human groups to survive in a number of ecosystems. Thus, "technology, subsistence economy, and elements of social organization directly tied to production are the most adaptively central realms of culture [and] . . . economies and their social correlates [were viewed] as primary, and ideational systems—religion, ritual, world view [were viewed as] secondary, derived, epiphenomenal" (Keesing, 1974, p. 76).

On the other end of the divide, some anthropologists privileged "ideational" theories of culture, that is, cultures as systems of ideas. Here Keesing divides this camp into three major groups: cultures as cognitive systems, cultures as structural systems, and cultures as symbolic systems. Within the first camp, cultures were seen as systems of knowledge. Ward Goodenough, one of the prime proponents of this view, summarized this perspective:

> A society's culture consists of whatever it is one has to know or believe in order to operate in a manner acceptable to its members. Culture is not a material phenomenon, it does not consist of things, people, behavior or emotions. It is rather an organization of these things. It is the form of things that people have in mind, their models for perceiving, relating and otherwise interpreting them. (Goodenough, 1957, p. 167, as cited in Keesing, 1974)

A further variation was cultures as structural systems, which posited that universal processes of the human mind develop diverse but formally similar patterns. The logic of relations and transformations provides an order that can transcend boundaries of language and custom. Thus, proponents of this approach (most notably Claude Levi-Strauss) were more interested in human Culture (with a capital C) than in individual cultures and saw the human mind as containing structural elements that would give rise to similar formations of myth, symbolism, and social structure.

The paradigm that would prove most alluring to ideational anthropologists was the interpretive turn instantiated in large part by Clifford Geertz. For Geertz, as described by Keesing (1974, p. 79), meanings are not "in people's heads," but are shared between social actors. In this sense, they are public, not private. For Geertz, to study culture is to study shared codes of meaning, a semiotic interpretation of ongoing practices and "webs of significance." His major metaphor was to treat culture as "an assemblage of texts," and the idea of textual representation and interpretation of cultures took root (Geertz, 1973).

Dividing these two approaches to culture—anthropology as an empirical science or as a humanist interpretive field—was a deeper issue.

CULTURE WITHIN ANTHROPOLOGY
AND EDUCATION

Central to our concern here, though, is how the concept of culture came to be transferred into the educational arena. Although one might suppose that the concept of culture as applied to diverse populations would be a positive affirmation of diversity, this was not always the case. In fact, several trends viewed the culture of poor and minoritized students as the cause of educational failure. Because culture was now viewed as a holistic configuration of traits and values that shaped members into viewing the world in a particular way, these rules for behavior among diverse populations were seen as the root of educational failure. By explaining educational achievement disparities and differential social mobility through recourse to forces within the culture (in the domestic realm and hence outside of the public purview), the dominant writing of social theory legitimized the marginalization of many students. The idea that poor students shared a "culture of poverty" that was considered to be antithetical to school achievement led to the development of "cultural deficit" models in schooling. Poor and minoritized students were viewed with a lens of deficiencies, substandard in their socialization practices, language practices, and orientation toward scholastic achievement (see Valencia, 1997, for an overview of the evolution of deficit paradigms).

Even today, although we would hope that these deficit conceptualizations would belong to the dustbin of history, we can still find evidence in some teacher training programs and in the popular mind that students' culture within their households is viewed as deficient in cognitive and social resources for learning. We remember the comments that caused an affirmative action furor when a University of Texas law professor, Lino Graglia, claimed that minority students are not academically competitive with whites in selective institutions, saying "It is the result of primarily cultural effects. They have a culture that seems not to encourage achievement. Failure is not looked upon with disgrace" (Mattos, 1997). Clearly the culturological deficit conceptions of how the "other" lives and thinks are alive and well.

Within the field of Anthropology and Education, the emphasis on culture took another turn. As academic attention was directed to educational disparities of minoritized children, there emerged a discourse that centered on educators coming to "know the culture" of their students. Predicated on the assumption that classroom cultural and linguistic patterns should be in congruence with cultural and linguistic community patterns, researchers and practitioners sought to bridge what came to be regarded as the discontinuity or mismatch gap. This approach was an outgrowth of the cultural difference approach that sought to counter and debunk cultural deficit concepts. The tenets of this extension of culture held that school culture was linguistically and/or materially a different cultural world for underrepresented children and that educators should seek to engage in community-based linguistic and cultural patterns. Although these were powerful concepts that held sway for almost 30 years, this paradigm nonetheless focused primarily on microinteractional processes—that is, on classroom and language practices—and generally assumed that all members of a particular group share a normative, bounded, and integrated view of their own culture. This approach masked the underlying issues of economic and power relations between dominant and minoritized populations and sought answers through "fixing" teachers' interactional patterns.

Two works emerged in the late 1970s that interrogated some of these assumptions. The first was a critique formulated by John Ogbu (1978) who proposed that some students (recent immigrant students for instance) who are culturally very different tend to do well in school, while minoritized populations do not fare as well. He argued for a "cultural frame of reference" toward schooling that implicated historical conditions, echoing in some way Boas's earlier admonition to look carefully at particular histories. Ogbu elaborated his theme to account for the reasons that "caste-like" involuntary minorities often see school in negative terms, while historical circumstances cast a different light on schooling for immigrant students, who are voluntary (having chosen to immigrate) minorities. This formulation shifted the gaze from the micro to the macro, and questioned larger structural issues. Levinson and Holland (1996), in reflecting on the impact of Ogbu's reconfiguration, noted how the cultural difference approach ignored relations of power:

> Neglecting to emphasize how communication styles, cognitive codes, and so on were the cultural practices of *variably* empowered groups, historically pro-

duced within relations of power, the cultural difference approach tended to essentialize the cultural repertoires of minoritized groups. As Ogbu (1981) has pointed out, the absence of such a critical analysis permitted confident reformists to attempt amelioration of school-based conflicts in cultural styles through remedial programs and "culturally responsive" pedagogies. The deeper structural context of cultural production and school failure remained obscure and largely unaddressed. (p. 8)

A second problematization of the idea of culture emerged with the work of Paul Willis in his book *Learning to Labour* (1977). In this work, Willis took on the concept of *agency*, that is, how individuals actively appropriate certain elements of cultural practices, while discarding others. In a detailed ethnographic study of working-class "lads" in England, he formulated the notion of "cultural production." Within this framework, students were seen as resisting certain structures and as active agents in constructing their own identities and ideologies. They were not passive recipients of reproductionist modes of culture. As Willis wrote:

> Social agents are not passive bearers of ideology, but active appropriators who reproduce existing structures only through struggle, contestation and a partial penetration of those structures. (p. 175)

Implicit in both of these perspectives was the assumption that students were not passive receptacles of an immutable culture. In Willis' approach, students were able to appropriate or discard cultural elements in the cultural production of their own identities. Ogbu's work focused on historical, political, and economic forces that produced particular cultural frames of reference for schooling. Although Ogbu has been criticized, correctly in my view, for repeating the error of essentializing and typologizing groups, in both these approaches we see that the concept of culture, rather than forcing individuals into prefabricated molds, was seen as an adaptive mechanism, a way for students to exercise some agency in their encounters with schooling. Culture had expanded into realms that posited individuals not as "cultural dopes" doomed to endlessly reproduce a static and unyielding culture, but as manipulating and tinkering with cultural elements, although not always to their educational benefit.

ANTHROPOLOGICAL CRITIQUES OF CULTURE

To further fragment the culture concept, anthropologists began critically reviewing the whole idea of culture, which resulted in a major paradigm shift in anthropology. Culture had lost much of its utility as a way to describe the diversity within societies. It came to be viewed as freighted with excess baggage of its historical use and abuse and in some ways was considered more of a burden than a useful tool. Some anthropologists suggested doing away with the term altogether. Lila Abu-Lughod, in her essay "Writing Against Culture," explained that individuals often improvise daily decisions and do not always adhere to cultural norms and prescriptives:

> The particulars suggest that others live as we perceive ourselves living, not as robots programmed with "cultural" rules, but as people going through life agonizing over decisions, making mistakes, trying to make themselves look good, enduring tragedies and personal losses, enjoying others, and finding moments of happiness. (1991, p. 58)

For the past 15 years or so, anthropologists began to write "against" culture (Abu-Lughod, 1991), "beyond" culture (Gupta & Ferguson, 1992), "critiquing" culture (Marcus & Fischer, 1986), "revisiting" culture (Keesing, 1994), putting "culture in motion" (Rosaldo, 1989), examining the interstitial space for "locating" culture (Bhabha, 1995), as well as the "breakdown" (Fox, 1995) and "demise" (Yengoyan, 1986) of the culture concept, and "forgetting" culture (Brightman, 1995). As is evident, anthropologists have not moved in uniform step toward any single vision of what does or does not constitute culture. It continues to be contested terrain, with convergences, divergences, as well as exit points.

One alternative to the static and frozen ideas about human groups, processual approaches, began to take shape. Processual approaches, as Renato Rosaldo (1989) noted, stress the case history method and show how ideas, events, and institutions interact and change through time. Such studies "more nearly resemble the medical diagnosis of a particular patient rather than law-like generalizations about a certain disease . . . and resist frameworks that claim a monopoly on truth" (p. 92). More and more, culture was viewed as dynamic, interactional, and emergent.

THE HYBRIDITY OF CULTURE

Increasingly, the boundedness of cultures gave way to an idea of the interculturality and hybridity of cultural practices. Often these concepts were predicated on examining borderlands, which are often riddled with emergent practices and mixed conventions that do not conform to normativity. Borderlands came to be a fertile metaphor for observing flux and fluidity, literally and metaphorically. Gupta and Ferguson (1992), for instance, examined the "assumed isomorphism of space, place and culture," noting that:

> The fiction of cultures as discrete object-like phenomena occupying discrete spaces becomes implausible for those who inhabit the borderlands. Related to border inhabitants are those who live a life of border crossings—migrant

workers, nomads, and members of the transnational business and professional elite. What is "the culture" of farm workers who spend half a year in
Mexico and half a year in the United States? (p. 7)

Another theorist, Homi Bhabha, in his provocative work *The Location of
Culture* (1995), argued for examining "border lives" as exemplars of moments "of transit where space and time cross to produce complex figures of
difference and identity, past and present, inside and outside, inclusion and
exclusion" (p. 1). It is these "in-between" spaces, he argued, that

> provide the terrain for elaborating strategies of selfhood—singular or com-
> munal—that initiate new signs of identity, and innovative sites of collabora-
> tion, and contestation, in the act of defining the idea of society itself. (p. 1)

Hybridity is closely tied in with economic globalization, that is, the penetra-
tion of goods and services into every corner of the globe. Increasingly students draw from an intercultural and hybrid knowledge base, appropriating multiple cultural systems, as youth culture permeates greater and
greater spheres.

POSTMODERNISM AND POSTSTRUCTURALISM

Within a postmodern perspective, the idea of general models and grand
theories gave way to considering contradiction and ambiguity and local and
contingent ways of positioning knowledge. The idea of knowledge as being
intimately connected with power was theorized by Michel Foucault, and an
increasing emphasis on textuality and "discourse" came to dominate discussions about the cultural. The notion of "discursive field," also emerging
from the writings of Foucault, became theoretically ubiquitous. In addition,
a suspicion of science and of the positivistic assumption that an objective
understanding of the social world is possible created a climate in which
texts and representations were examined for the way in which they constructed knowledge claims. Discussions of culture gave way to the exploration of discourses that have the capacity to construct, rather than merely reflect, our realities. In this perspective, a scientific study of culture is not only
impossible, but unworkable.

IMPLICATIONS FOR EDUCATORS

So, where does this leave us as educators, trying to make use of a powerful
concept that in many ways cannot be replaced? Do we throw out the baby
with the bathwater? How do we account for diversity if the central concept

that led us to that place is both vilified and marginalized? In a recent series of essays on culture, anthropologists took up a conversation that has not yet been resolved. In a preface to the article "When: A Conversation With Culture" (Borofsky, Barth, Shweder, Rodseth, & Stolzenberg, 2001), the editors of *American Anthropologist* made this observation:

> For decades now culture has been a topic anthropologists argue about: WHAT it does or does not mean. IF it should or should not constitute a central concept of the discipline. This essay steps outside these arguments to rephrase the issue and our approach to it. It explores WHEN it makes sense to use the cultural concept. (p. 432)

In the words of one author in this series of essays:

> The concept of culture serves the basic need of naming such ineffable and inexplicable features of human existence as "meaning" and "spirit" and living together with others. Stop thinking of it as a name for a thing, and come to view it instead as a placeholder for a set of inquiries—inquiries which may be destined never to be resolved. (Stolzenberg, 2001, p. 444)

Perhaps, therefore, we can think of culture as a set of inquiries. Indeed, in our work this is very much the position we have taken in considering the hybridity of funds of knowledge.

The struggle of anthropologists of education to deal with the practical and ever-present effects of practicing theories and theorizing practices belies the unmet challenge to anthropology: As anthropology continues to privilege the academic and theoretical dimensions of the discipline, very often the pragmatic, practice-based implications of those theories are not well thought out, or, more commonly, they are ignored. In the debate over the abandonment of the heuristic value of culture, there is never any mention of the fact that for teachers, culture has been a central unifying concept that has been engaged in both reactive and proactive ways. To deconstruct culture because of the theoretical abuse and misuse of the term completely obscures the battle that brought culture to the forefront in the first place: How do we account for human diversity without recourse to a discourse of biogenetic difference? What tools can be put in the hands of educators that can replace a concept that went so far in breaking down barriers of racial and cultural divisiveness? Can we, in our anthropological theoretical conceit, claim that only theory and not the implications of that theory are the focus of our concern? We must always be ready to lay out the "So what?" question to our theoretical formulations, or risk the very abuse and misuse of anthropological theory that is now bemoaned. If we do not lay out the implications ourselves, think deeply and thoughtfully about the ways in which our use of theory will affect real students in real classrooms in real urban areas, we are neglecting our ultimate responsibility.

As anthropologists, we must clearly be aware of the call for civic scholarship, for a scholarship that is not validated by doing fieldwork thousands of miles away, but looks to the communities that surround our universities and the schools that are the basic building blocks of those communities. As this retrospective look on culture has suggested, anthropology can bring unique theoretical and methodological insights into the studies of schools and schooling. One such key anthropological insight was developed early on that suggests that one must look beyond the school itself to understand the local meanings and impact of schooling.

CULTURE AS THE LIVED EXPERIENCES OF STUDENTS: FUNDS OF KNOWLEDGE

What we describe in this book is an alternative perspective on students' lives and background. This is not to suggest that we are, in turn, replacing concepts of culture with another concept, or implying that this is all that is needed to address the pressing issues of schools. However, it is one way in which the context for respectful relationships between schools and communities is fostered. In this perspective, we have interrogated many of the assumptions of a shared culture, and have chosen instead to focus on "practice," that is, what it is that people do, and what they say about what they do. This processual approach coalesces with our use of qualitative and ethnographic methods to counter deficit models. The bridging of the chasm between household and school, the instantiation of reciprocal relationships between parents and teachers, the pedagogical validation of household knowledge with which students come to school, and the development of teachers as researchers, go beyond the view of culture as a "problem." Rather than simply documenting a mismatch between the school and the community, we have actively engaged households in a dialog that can address the often unequal relations between school and community. In addition, teachers have developed skills as researchers, activating their own knowledge bases by engaging in professional development that can directly affect their classroom practice.

The concept of culture emphasized in schools has focused on how shared norms shape individual behavior and on discovering standardized rules for behavior. However, when we move away from uniform categorizations of a shared group culture, issues of contestation, ambiguity, and contradiction are often the focus of ethnographic analysis. Initially, as we moved in and out of our encounters with culture, we adopted processual approaches to culture that take into account multiple perspectives that could reorient educators to consider the everyday lived experiences of their students. Processual approaches focus on the processes of everyday life, in the form of daily activities, as a frame of reference. These daily activities are a manifestation of particular historically accumulated funds of knowledge that households possess. Instead of individual representations of an essentialized group, household practices are viewed as dynamic, emergent, and interactional. Sally Falk Moore, an early proponent of the term *processual,* explained that

> process conveys an analytic emphasis on continuous production and construction without differentiating in that respect between repetition and innovation. A process approach does not proceed from the idea of a received order that is then changed. Process is simply a time-oriented perspective on both continuity and, change. . . . An event is not necessarily best understood as the exemplification of an extant symbolic or social order. Events may equally be evidence of the ongoing dismantling of structures or of attempts to create new ones. Events may show a multiplicity of social contestations and the voicing of competing cultural claims. (Moore, 1987, p. 729)

The issue of voicing competing claims is particularly important because critical educators have begun to examine seriously the issue of student experience as a central component in developing a theory of schooling. The pedagogical applications of entering households with an eye toward using the knowledge base of children draws on this concern. Giroux noted that "the ways in which student experience is produced, organized, and legitimated in schools has become an increasingly important theoretical consideration for understanding how schools function to produce and authorize particular forms of meaning" (1992, p. 180). Thus the validation of the experiences of students and the lived practices of households is an important aspect of critical pedagogy. For these theorists, pedagogy is not defined as simply something that goes on in schools. Rather, it is posited as central to any practice that "takes up questions of how individuals learn, how knowledge is produced, and how subject positions are constructed" (p. 81). The issue of student voice is paramount to these critical theorists, and pedagogy in this context can draw on local histories and forms of knowledge.

DISCOURSE AND POWER

In addition to classroom practice, a second domain that was powerfully affected by household ethnographic encounters centers on the parental narratives that were evoked during the dialog between parents and teachers. In the attempt to discover household knowledge on its own terms rather than as a reflection of group knowledge, teachers and parents engaged in open-ended interviews that detailed the life histories of the households. As parents responded with personal narratives concerning their own unique and singular life courses, a heightened historical consciousness began to emerge. The articulation of the trajectory that brought parents to be where they are now engendered an awareness of the historical character of their experiences. In this way, the Freireian notion of dialog as an emancipatory educational process can be developed in the households (Freire, 1981). As other researchers have stated, ethnography can be seen as a tool for social action (Savage, 1988) that can enable persons to transform the limitations of their circumstances. In the powerful dialog that this ethnographic interview can spark, parents can and did find a passageway to the schools. As the teachers validate the households' experiences as those from which rich resources or funds of knowledge can be extracted, parents themselves come to authenticate their skills as worthy of pedagogical notice.

The discursive properties of the household interviews provide a viable vehicle for reflection and consciousness. One parent, after relating her own educational experiences, opted to return to continue her curtailed education, and others, having developed a relationship of *confianza* with the teachers, reaffirmed their own abilities in a redefinition of how educational systems could work. Although parental involvement is the mantra of every educational reform program, it is often categorically and narrowly defined as parents (usually the mothers) entering the classroom to facilitate the teacher. This is the barometer of parental interest and support. Yet, if educational institutions are serious about creating partnerships with the community, the relationship cannot be an asymmetrical alliance, with one component defining and limiting the role of its counterpart.

CONCLUSIONS

As discourses come to recognize the situated nature of knowledge and the partiality of all knowledge claims, the metaphor of borders and border-crossers has been foregrounded. However, the ultimate border—the border between knowledge and power—can be crossed only when educational institutions no longer reify culture, when lived experiences become validated as a source of knowledge, and when the process of how knowledge is constructed and translated between groups located within nonsymmetrical relations of power is questioned. As minoritized students continue to be subjected to standardized and prescriptivist tests, the issue of whose knowledge and whose voice are embedded in these measures can be answered only as we cross this furthest border between knowledge and power. We cannot claim that because teachers make connections to households that students will not be enmeshed in high-stakes testing, nor will some funds of knowledge be considered more valued than others. Yet, the very act of transcending the boundaries of the classroom in itself ruptures the flow of circulating discourses of deficiency and difference (McIntyre, Rosebery, & González, 2001).

In summary, theory that has been developed within the interpretive paradigm of anthropology has often been criticized as irrelevant to practical and applied approaches to social issues. The methodology that has been described here assumes a postmodern perspective on issues of local knowledge, multivocality, and hegemonic relations. Yet, within this discourse, there has emerged a viable yet reflexive method for addressing the multiply mediated worlds of "the other." Rather than assuming a mosaic or tapestry approach to multicultural education, we acknowledge competing circulating discourses and emphasize that "practice" supplies us with a panorama of activities that may or may not coincide with normative cultural behavior. The interculturality of households, drawing on multiple cultural systems and using these systems as strategic resources, emerges from this perspective. In addition, the notion of engendering dialogs of historical consciousness has a profound effect on interlocutors. As a corollary to this kind of validation, a further parameter of transformation was implemented in importing household knowledge into classroom practice. One significant point should be stressed, however. The purpose of drawing on student experience with household knowledge is not to merely reproduce household knowledge in the classroom. Working-class students are not being taught construction, plumbing, or gardening. Instead, by drawing on household knowledge, student experience is legitimated as valid, and classroom practice can build on the familiar knowledge bases that students can manipulate to enhance learning in mathematics, social studies, language arts, and other content areas.

But the ultimate value of going beyond culture is that it opens up spaces for the construction of new fields wherein students are not locked into an assumed unilineal heritage. It allows for variability within populations rather than only between populations. More importantly, the funds of knowledge of a community occupy that space between structure and agency, between the received historical circumstances of a group, and the infinite variations that social agents are able to negotiate within a structure.

In the following chapters, we provide a picture of the evolution of the funds of knowledge concept, and examples of how teachers can use communities' funds of knowledge in proactive and life-affirming ways, not just as a source of differences that are compared with mainstream practices.

As we focus on the social networks that interconnect households with their social environments, we do not attempt to restrict the parameters of interaction of these often overlapping spheres of influence. As the chapters in this volume indicate, students move in and out of their social networks and draw resources and funds of knowledge from the intersection of these activities. For example, in an attempt to focus on "kid-based funds of knowledge," Jan Nespor (1997) describes how multiple funds of knowledge and social networks can coalesce in one activity setting:

> Earl's computer use was at the intersection of a family network (he was learning with his mother who was taking computer classes), a friendship network (with Duane), and various commercial networks (the games and software he bought). Everyday life is made from such articulations. In this case, the three networks blended together to create a heterogeneous fund of knowledge that connected Earl and his friends to distant and unknown groups of kids (who would also be fashioning identities in interaction with games and computers) and shaped their relationships to one another in their immediate environment. (p. 171)

Using the concept of funds of knowledge as a heuristic device provides teachers with a pragmatic avenue to engage with their students' lives. It allows the possibility of seeing beyond the classroom and glimpsing the circulating discourses and shifting fields of power that shape students' lives. Most importantly, we are able to begin to conceptualize the hybridity that emerges from the intersection of diverse funds of knowledge. To wrap back around to the quote from Mary Catherine Bateson at the beginning of this chapter, it is only through face-to-face interaction and one-to-one encounters with persons, through a mutually respectful dialog, that we can cross the constructions of difference.

REFLECTION QUESTIONS

1. What is meant by a "processual approach"?
2. How does a funds of knowledge approach differ from the idea of culture?
3. How can the idea of culture be problematic?

REFERENCES

Abu-Lughod, L. (1991). Writing against culture. In R. G. Fox (Ed.), *Recapturing anthropology: Working in the present* (pp. 137–162). Santa Fe, NM: School of American Research Press.
Appiah, A. (1986). The uncompleted argument: DuBois and the illusion of race. *Critical Inquiry, 12,* 21–37.
Bateson, M. C. (2000). *Full circles, overlapping lives: Culture and generation in transition.* New York: Random House.
Bhabha, H. K. (1995). *The location of culture.* London: Routledge.

Borofsky, R., Barth, F., Shweder, R., Rodseth, L., & Stolzenberg, N. M. (2001). When: A conversation about culture. *American Anthropologist, 103,* 432–446.

Brightman, R. (1995). Forget culture: Replacement, transcendence, reflexification. *Cultural Anthropology, 10,* 509–546.

Degler, C. (1991). *In search of human nature: The decline and revival of Darwinism in American social thought.* New York: Oxford University Press.

Fox, R. (1995). The breakdown of culture. *Current Anthropology, 36,* i–ii.

Freire, P. (1981). *Education for critical consciousness.* New York: Continuum.

Geertz, C. (1973). *The interpretation of culture.* New York: Basic Books.

Giroux, H. (1992). *Border crossings: Cultural workers and the politics of education.* New York: Routledge.

Goodenough, W. (1957). Cultural anthropology and linguistics. In P. Garvin (Ed.), *Report of the Seventh Annual Round Table meeting on Linguistics and Language Study,* 9. Washington, DC: Georgetown University Monograph Series on Language and Linguistics.

Gould, S. J. (1981). *The mismeasure of man.* New York: Norton.

Gupta, A., & Ferguson, J. (1992). Beyond "culture": Space, identity and the politics of difference. *Cultural Anthropology, 7,* 6–23.

Henze, R., & Hauser, M. (1999). *Personalizing culture through anthropological and educational perspectives.* Educational Practitioner Report 4. Retrieved from Center for Research on Education, Diversity and Excellence (CREDE) Web site: http://www.crede.ucsc.edu/products/print/eprs/epr4.html

Keesing, R. M. (1974). Theories of culture. *Annual Review of Anthropology, 3,* 73–97.

Kroeber, A., & Kluckhohn, C. (1952). Culture: A critical review of concepts and definitions. *Papers of the Peabody Museum, Harvard University, 47.*

Levinson, B., & Holland, D. (1996). The cultural production of the educated person: An introduction. In B. A. Levinson, D. E. Foley, & D. C. Holland (Eds.), *The cultural production of the educated person: Critical ethnographies of schooling and local practice.* Albany, NY: State University of New York Press.

Marcus, G. E., & Fischer, M. J. (1986). *Anthropology as cultural critique: An experimental moment in the human sciences.* Chicago: University of Chicago Press.

Mattos, J. (1997, September 16). Fighting words spark affirmative-action action. *Time.* Retrieved 3/4/04 time.com/time/nation/article/0,8599,9406,00.html

McIntyre, E., Rosebery, A., & González, N. (2001). *Classroom diversity: Connecting curriculum to students' lives.* Portsmouth, NH: Heinemann Press.

Moore, S. F. (1987). Explaining the present: Theoretical dilemmas in processual ethnography. *American Ethnologist, 14,* 727–736.

Nespor, J. (1997). *Tangled up in school: Politics, space, bodies, and signs in the educational process.* Mahwah, NJ: Lawrence Erlbaum Associates.

Ogbu, J. (1978). *Minority education and caste: The American system in cross-cultural perspective.* New York: Academic Press.

Rosaldo, R. (1989). *Culture and truth: The remaking of social analysis.* Boston, MA: Beacon.

Savage, M. (1988). Can ethnographic narrative be a neighborly act? *Anthropology and Education Quarterly, 19,* 3–19.

Spindler, G. (1996). Comments from Exploring Culture Institute, San Francisco, CA. In Henze and Hauser, *Personalizing culture through anthropological and educational perspectives.* [Educational Practitioner Report #4 Center for Research on Education, Diversity and Excellence (CREDE).] Retrieved from http://www.crede.ucsc.edu/products/print/eprs/epr4.html

Stocking, G. W. (1968). *Race, culture and evolution: Essays in the history of anthropology.* New York: Free Press.

Stocking, G. W. (1973). From chronology to ethnology. James Cowles Prichard and British anthropology 1800–1850. In facsimile of 1813 ed. of J. C. Prichard, *Researches into the physical history of man* (pp. ix–cvii). Chicago: University of Chicago Press.

Stolzenberg, N. M. (2001). What we talk about when we talk about culture. In Borofsky et al., When: A Conversation about Culture. *American Anthropologist, 103*, 432–446.

Tylor, E. B. (1958). *Primitive culture*. New York: Harper. (Original work published 1873)

Valencia, R. (Ed.). (1997). *The evolution of deficit thinking: Educational thought and practice*. Washington, DC: Falmer Press.

Visweswaran, K. (1998). Race and the culture of anthropology. *American Anthropologist, 100*, 70–83.

Wax, M. L. (1993). How culture misdirects multiculturalism. *Anthropology and Education Quarterly, 24*, 99–115.

Williams, R. (1958). *Culture and society 1780–1950*. New York: Columbia University Press.

Willis, P. (1977). *Learning to labor: How working class kids get working class jobs*. London: Saxon House.

Yengoyan, A. (1986). Theory in anthropology: On the demise of the concept of culture. *Comparative Studies in Society and History, 24*, 368–374.

Chapter 3

Formation and Transformation of Funds of Knowledge*

Carlos Vélez-Ibáñez
James Greenberg
University of Arizona

Our purpose in this work is to provide a broad anthropological context for possible educational reforms of the public schools that serve U.S.-Mexican populations[1] in the southwestern United States. Our position is that public schools often ignore the strategic and cultural resources, which we have termed *funds of knowledge*, that households contain. We argue that these funds not only provide the basis for understanding the cultural systems from which U.S.-Mexican children emerge, but that they also are important and useful assets in the classroom. Many assumptions about these cultural systems informing policy and practice in public schools are not supported by the actual culture of these populations, since, as Greenberg has said,

---

*This article first appeared in the journal *Anthropology and Education Quarterly* (1992, Vol. 23, pp. 313–335) and is reprinted with permission from the American Anthropological Association.

[1] We use the term *Mexican* to describe both those born in Mexico and those of Mexican parentage born in the United States. Although *Chicano* or *Mexican American* are also used for those born in the United States of Mexican heritage, Mexican is the generally preferred term used by the U.S.-born population. Although there is an extended discussion that links the rise of ethnic consciousness to the collapse of rural and commercial control by Mexicans in the United States in the 1880s (see Camarillo, 1979; Griswold de Castillo, 1984) and their encapsulation in urban ghettos, our position is that this leaves out the importance of cross-border relations both due to the constant reintroduction of kin and culture from Mexico and due to the obvious retention of the Spanish language over time. Mexican households continue to define themselves as Mexicans culturally and, more important, socially (see Garcia, 1982, pp. 295–314; Vélez-Ibáñez, 1983).

"the difficulty in educating our children begins in the separation in industrial societies of the work place from the home" (1990, p. 317). This separation makes an understanding of the cultural system necessary to build constructive relationships between teachers, students, and parents, relationships which are needed to improve the educational quality, and equity in schools that serve U.S.-Mexican populations.

We argue that grasping the social relationships in which children are ensconced and the broad features of learning generated in the home are key if we are to understand the construction of cultural identity and the emergence of cultural personality among U.S.-Mexican children. We explain why educational structures and practices often militate against such cultural identity and why we should consider alternative policies. By examining the historical processes by which U.S.-Mexican cultural identity has been constructed, we hope to provide a critical perspective on the deficiency model or a minority model of instruction used for culturally different students.[2]

As case material shows, each generation struggled against different historical forces, yet their defenses, for the most part, were invariant—human creativity coupled with an enormous ability to mobilize and expand social relations. The case study illustrates the effect of struggles on households and their ability to maintain their security and support the emergence of personal and cultural identity.

HISTORICAL DIMENSIONS OF FUNDS OF KNOWLEDGE FOR U.S. MEXICANS

The key to understanding the forces that shape U.S.-Mexicans lies in the historical struggle of their households for control of their labor and resources, and for economic security. We argue that the economic and political transformations that accompanied the rise of capitalism in the southwestern United States have profoundly shaped such households. We also argue that since the late 19th century, the combination of the historical forces of industrialization and their accompanying immigration policies has contributed binationally to the rise of U.S.-Mexican ethnicity. As well,

---

[2]The deficiency model of minority groups, either directly or indirectly, underlies most instructional strategies concerning culturally different populations. For example, Spanish-speaking "minority" students placed in so-called ability groups are exposed to learning based on the assumption that they are not "ready" for comprehension and must be treated to an array of decoding exercises in which text-bound skills are underscored and a generally reductionist, "tiny-bite" approach to skills acquisition is emphasized. Despite the fact that many Spanish-speaking students have great comprehensive abilities in Spanish, the deficiency model excludes already-developed comprehension as a strength and substitutes a learning model that is noncontextual, piecemeal, and hierarchical.

these forces have led both to the formation of binational families and to the distribution of Mexican households in residential clusters. These forces have also led to repeated transformations of the cultural and behavioral practices, or funds of knowledge (Vélez-Ibáñez, 1987, 1988a, 1989, 1992b; Vélez-Ibáñez & Greenberg, 1990), that form the core of regional U.S.-Mexican cultural identity.

The best way to explain what we mean by funds of knowledge is to relate them to Wolf's (1966) discussion of household economy. Wolf distinguishes several funds that households must juggle: caloric funds, funds of rent, replacement funds, ceremonial funds, social funds. Entailed in these are wider sets of activities requiring specific strategic bodies of essential information that households need to maintain their well-being. If we define such funds as those bodies of knowledge of strategic importance to households, then we may ask such pertinent questions as How were such assemblages historically formed? How variable are they? How are they transformed as they move from one context to another? How are they learned and transmitted? How are they socially distributed?

SETTING

Since the late 19th century there has been a continual struggle for control of U.S.-Mexican households in the border region. Large-scale and industrially organized technologies (Vélez-Ibáñez, 1992a) have been drawn to the 2,000-mile-long political border and have created a region that includes 52 million persons in the 10 border states,[3] half of whom live within a 400-mile-wide belt dissected by the border (Martínez, 1988). Since 1950 the population of the six Mexican border states has increased threefold, while the population of the four U.S. states has increased from 20 million to 42 million since 1980. Such growth stems from uncontrolled industrialization on both sides of the border, created by a series of symbiotic economic and technological relations in manufacturing, processing, industrial agriculture, labor markets, and twin plants development (Diez-Canedo, 1981; Fernández-Kelly, 1987; García y Griego, 1983; González-Archegia, 1987; Martínez, 1983; Porras, n.d.; Tiano, 1985). Such relations in the borderlands continue to shape the formation of Mexican households, as well as their cultural and social responses.

United States border policy exacerbates such structural conditions and influences how Mexican households on both sides cope with changing economic and political fortunes. Whether yesterday's Mexican national be-

---

[3]The 10 states that make up the U.S.-Mexican border region are, on the Mexican side, Baja California Norte, Baja California Sur, Sonora, Chihuahua, Nuevo Leon, and Tamaulipas; and on the U.S. side, California, Arizona, New Mexico, and Texas.

comes today's U.S. citizen is very much dependent on the region's economic health. Even ethnicity among U.S.-Mexicans in the Southwest, and its attending political implications (Vélez-Ibáñez, 1992a), is of very recent origin and largely a product of post-Depression border policies.

DYNAMIC OF FUNDS: HISTORICAL FORMATION

The historical conditions that produced the dynamic qualities of the border region have their roots in the incessant introduction of large-scale technological and capital-intensive investments (Vélez-Ibáñez, 1992). Such development created binational labor markets that proletarianized rural populations and pushed persons back and forth across the border. As new technologies and productive activities, such as mining, construction, railroads, and industrial forms of agriculture, were introduced into the borderland arena, populations responded in kind. For most of the 19th century and the early 20th century, labor markets were open to both U.S. and Mexican-born workers.

Before 1929, the north and south movement of persons between border communities was relatively uninterrupted. *Cross-border families*, with portions of large extended kin networks residing on both sides, were common (Alvarez, 1987; Heyman, unpublished manuscript). It still is not uncommon for parents who reside in a Mexican borderland town or city to send children to elementary and secondary schools in the United States. Such cross-border kinship systems, as Heyman points out, were really "a series of bilaterally related households and networks scattered between similar types of neighborhoods on both sides of the border" (Heyman, unpublished manuscript, p. 7).

Yet, after 1929, the massive repatriation and deportation policies and practices of the 1930s began to interfere with the formation and maintenance of the cross-border families. As Heyman pointed out, the new legal context of visa regulation that was put into effect during the heyday of the repatriation period "caused the differentiation of documented and undocumented entrants, and divided Mexican from Mexican-American kin in a manner not seen in the period before 1929" (Heyman, unpublished manuscript, p. 1).

After 1929, legal citizenship rather than culture became the hallmark of ethnic identity. For many Mexicans born in the United States, immigration restrictions on Mexican kin created a they–us differentiation that interrupted the easy flow of kin between extended cross-border familial networks. As American schools, under the guise of "Americanization" programs, relegated the Spanish language to a secondary position and denigrated its use, self-denial processes set in. This experience led some U.S.-Mexicans to change their names, anglicize their surnames, and internalize self-hatred and self-deprecation (Rodríguez, 1982).

Differentiation has repeatedly been accentuated by systematic processes of deportation, repatriation, and voluntary departure, such as "Operation Wetback" in 1954,[4] or the recent immigration sweep, "Operation Jobs," in 1982. The intent of the Immigration Reform and Control Act (IRCA) passed in 1986 was to stem undocumented immigration. IRCA, however, has had no striking impact on the labor sectors of which Mexican undocumented workers are a part (Chávez, 1988; Chávez et al., 1992; Cornelius, 1988). What it has done is to legalize Mexican migrants, guarantee their permanent settlement, and increase the flow of individual workers and families back and forth to the United States with newly acquired legality (Cornelius, 1988, p. 4).

The more profound consequence of IRCA is that it has created further division between eligible and noneligible Mexicans. Even within the same extended family, the legalization of one family member sharply contrasts with the illegality of others. Because reform bills such as IRCA immigration are usually followed by immigration sweeps, each roundup further emphasizes the "foreignness" of the population in Mexico and further differentiates them from U.S. Mexicans.[5] Such demographic and political splitting between Mexican-born and U.S.-born Mexicans establishes the cultural basis for the creation of an ethnic U.S. Mexican, and the denial of cultural continuity between these populations.

CROSS-BORDER RELATIONS

Yet, despite the political and cultural divisions that have arisen, cross-border families and *clustered households*[6] continue to balance the effect of the disruption of identity and self-reference. As a result, Mexican house-

---

[4]"Operation Wetback" was an INS-sponsored program of expulsion of undocumented Mexican labor during fiscal year 1954 and allegedly resulted in the departure of 1.3 million "illegals," according to INS authorities (U.S. Department of Justice, 1954, p. 31).

[5]The cultural implication for some U.S.-Mexicans is to differentiate themselves as "American Mexicans" from the *mojados* (wetbacks). Analogous processes become set in motion for Mexicans in Mexico with differentiations made between themselves as real Mexicanos and the despised *pochos* from the United States.

[6]One important type of variant further removed from the border in this regard is that familial "clustering" of households, or extension of families beyond the nucleated household increases rather than lessens with each succeeding generation. We have termed these *cross-border clustered households* because 77.1% of our sample have relatives in Mexico, and of the total sample, a significant proportion (61%) organize their extended kin relations in the United States in a clustered household arrangement of dense bilateral kin and maintain kin ties with their Mexican relatives. Recent studies (Keefe, 1979, p. 360; Keefe et al., 1978, 1979; Griswold del Castillo, 1984, pp. 129–132) have shown that, despite class, Mexican extended families in the United States become more extensive and stronger with generational advancement, acculturation, and socioeconomic mobility. These findings as well are supported by findings in a na-

holds are typically nested within extensive kinship networks that actively engage them in the lives of relatives on both sides of the border. Because many Mexicans work in highly unstable labor markets, in their struggle to make a living they are not only forced to crisscross national boundaries, but they must also depend on one another to gain access to resources found on each side.

As Mexican families have crisscrossed the border in response to the intermittent booms and busts in the border economy, they have produced an associated phenomenon, one we term *generational hop-scotching* (Vélez-Ibáñez, 1992a). In such families, one or more members of a given household are born in Mexico, and others are born in the United States. As well, one generation may be born in the United States, a second in Mexico, and a third in the United States. Although such hop-scotching has both negative and positive consequences for members of a given household, the phenomenon provides a legal advantage in gaining access to personal or institutional resources on either side of the U.S.-Mexico border.

FORMATION PROCESSES

The dynamic processes of the border economy directly affect the way local populations respond to the loss of control over the means of production. One manifestation of this loss is an increasing separation between the functions of knowledge in the workplace and the home. We may better understand the impact of this separation by examining their previous integration. For example, most Mexican families in the Southwest either have ancestors who were farmers and ranchers or were engaged in commercial or craft and manufacturing activities in a rural setting, or they have relatives who are engaged in these activities now.

Historically, these households not only produced or bartered for much of what they consumed, but their members also had to master an impressive range of knowledge and skills. To cope and adapt to changing circumstances and contexts, household members had to be generalists and possess a wide range of complex knowledge. In the countryside, many segments of the population understood the characteristics of local ecosystems—soils, plants, pests, hydrology, and weather (Sheridan, 1988). Given the frailty and complexity of arid land environments, water management, flood control, and climate variations were important parts of the knowledge base for survival. As cattle producers, topics such as animal husbandry, range management, and veterinary medicine were part of the "natural systems" of

---

tional study that has found that the clustered residential households we describe for Tucson, Arizona were more common among U.S.-born Mexicans than they were among Mexican immigrants or Anglos (see Vélez-Ibáñez, 1992a).

household information. The maintenance of equipment made knowledge of blacksmithing and mechanics essential. As well, to avoid reliance on specialists, some knowledge and skills in construction and repair were mandatory (i.e., bodies of knowledge about building plans, masonry, carpentry, and electrical wiring, and also formulas for mixing cement, mortar, and adobe). Where there was a lack of physicians or where medical costs were prohibitive, rural and folk medical knowledge of remedies, medicinal herbs, and first aid procedures were often extensive. In time of economic and labor crises, such skills become crucial in adjusting income and searching for work. For instance, after the Great Arizona Mine Strike of 1983, many striking U.S.-Mexican miners still skilled in ranching became cowboys to make ends meet (O'Leary, interview with author, 1991).

Taken together, these largely rural skills, experiences, and technical knowledge of habitat and survival make up the adaptive strategies that we have called funds of knowledge for much of the Arizona-Sonora Mexican population.

CLUSTERING IN THE LIFE CYCLE AND THE FORMATION OF FUNDS OF KNOWLEDGE: A CASE STUDY IN SOCIAL EXCHANGE FORMATION AND CULTURAL EMERGENCE

The following case study[7] shows that, no matter the historical context in which they emerge, the specific characteristics of household clusters all seem to converge on very similarly organized and structured networks of relationships based on dense exchange. In other words, each household has characteristic emphasis, a type of cultural "shape" that differentiates one household from another and that is derived from historical circumstances.

In addition, each household cluster has accumulated and discarded funds of knowledge that form the basis of material survival, so each contains much of the previous generation's repertoire of information and skills used for subsistence. The case study has, at its core, funds of knowledge rooted in either historical or contemporary rural experience of each household or cluster. The borderland region is also an important historical and contemporary cultural reference point for such funds. Because such funds are rooted in useful daily skills and information of a very broad nature, and because they include mechanical, historical, creative, computational, and design mastery, they are expressed in a broad range of contexts.

Such funds are not only found within households, but they also are part of the repertoire of information contained within the clusters of house-

---

[7]The case study uses pseudonyms to protect the identity of the informants and to maintain confidentiality; some events have been changed.

holds where younger generational cohorts learn their substance and have the opportunity to experiment with them in a variety of settings. These funds are the currency of exchange not only between generations but also between households, and so form part of the "cultural glue" that maintains exchange relations between kin. This case study shows that such funds of knowledge are dynamic in content and change according to changes in empirical reality.

Serranos Family Background: From Mines to City, From Repatriate to Patriot

The focus of most of 58-year-old Hortencia Serrano's personal and social attention is the cluster of relations that consists of her husband, Tomás, a former aircraft maintenance worker; her four children, three of whom are married and live nearby, and their children; her mother and father, who live 50 yards behind them, in Hortencia's old home; and her mother's sister and family, who live next door to her mother. Her job as a bank teller has been her primary occupation since graduating from high school in 1954. Even when she followed Tomás to the various army bases to which he was transferred, Hortencia supplemented their income by working part-time while raising their children. Unlike Tomás, Hortencia has always had her own stable platform, in spite of her early childhood, during which her mother and father and his brothers moved from mining town to mining town in Arizona, searching for work both during the Depression and later, when the mines began to be exhausted. It was only after her father was injured in a mine accident that they moved to Tucson, where he and his brothers began a handyman's service. Thus, much of Hortencia's early household experience centered on her father's relations and their households; she also helped keep the books for the handyman's service.

Tomás's household experience was almost opposite to that of Hortencia. It began in Phoenix, the city where he was born, when his parents, who had migrated from Mexico to seek work, were "repatriated." While attending school intermittently in Sonora, Tomás sold vegetables with his father on the streets of a northern Mexican border town; their income barely supported the family of six. After his father's death in 1945, Tomás, aged ten, moved to Tucson by himself. He lived in the storage closet of a grocery store, which the store's owner allowed him to use in exchange for his labor. Soon afterwards, Tomás was taken into custody by the police for truancy. He was placed in a foster home where he remained until he was of legal age. With a seventh-grade education, he joined the army. For the next 10 years he attended several service-connected schools and was trained as a maintenance mechanic for army planes and helicopters. After his discharge from the service in 1962, he and Hortencia returned to Tucson to be near her family of orientation, and Tomás joined the Arizona Army National Guard, where he has worked as a maintenance person for 25 years.

GENERATIONAL FUNDS AND THEIR TRANSMISSION

For both Hortencia and Tomás, however, since the mid-1980s the focus of all their activities has been their grandchildren, their children, their church, and their country. The children of their eldest son and eldest daughter are frequent visitors. Hortencia and Tomás care for their four grandchildren at least three times a month, as well as for the entire weekend at least twice a month. Hortencia especially enjoys being with her grandchildren and her mother while preparing the Sunday dinners that are held either in the great grandparents' home or in Hortencia's. The great grandchildren and grandchildren help with the housecleaning, marketing, cooking, and table preparation.

Hortencia devoted much effort to teaching each of her children, and now her grandchildren, the computational skills in which she excels after so many years as a bank teller. Almost nightly, Hortencia posed simple problems to her children, progressing to increasingly more difficult ones. She had them compete with her and with one another until someone made an error and was eliminated. Hortencia has begun the same process whenever her older grandchildren visit.

Tomás takes the grandchildren to recreational and entertainment activities. He also allows them into the well-stocked woodworking shop, directly behind his home, to observe and occasionally to experiment in the repair or construction of household items. For Tomás there is no better exercise than hard manual labor, or the labor in which one's hands shape an object from scratch. Tomás takes pride in having expanded their tract home from two to four bedrooms and having added both a dining room and two full baths. With assistance from his sons and daughter, they converted a small plasterboard home into a large and spacious brick-faced house that serves as a model for many other families in this predominantly Mexican neighborhood.

Tomás's two sons and his daughter are employed in highly technical, skilled blue-collar occupations. All three attribute their abilities to the entire family's participating in Hortencia's computational games and in Tomás's home repairs and construction.

THE ROLE OF RELIGION AND IDEOLOGY

Hortencia and Tomás credit the kids "turning out right" to the importance of religion within the household and the reverence for the ritual activities within the church. Tomás is a member of the Knights of Columbus, and

Hortencia is a member of its auxiliary. Both of them have participated intensively in the movement through the association's hierarchy. Tomás attires himself in full regalia for important ecclesiastical events in which he serves as part of the honor guard for church dignitaries. This ideological commitment to Catholicism is equaled by their investment in conservative points of view. They are archconservatives regarding national defense, the importance of a strong military, and the support for political figures like Ronald Reagan and Evan Mecham, the impeached governor of the state of Arizona. Tomás has created an altar-like wall in one of his storage rooms on which are displayed myriad plastic emblems of army units, air force squadrons, and models and pictures of astronauts, aircraft, and tracked military vehicles. He has a large collection of military caps and emblems displayed in glass cases with his own military awards.

THE UNCERTAINTY OF THE LIFE CYCLE IN CONTEXT

Yet, the Serranos' patriotic and religious faiths have been shaken by three unforeseen developments: the possible blindness of their oldest and favorite son, the divorce of their second son, and the probable destruction of Tomás's immune system. Their first son, "Tomasito," seemed to have fulfilled their fondest wishes. A handsome and intelligent young man who presented them with their first grandson soon after his marriage, Tomasito received advanced technical training in communications from the local telephone company and was quickly promoted for his diligence and focused work. Unfortunately, his attention to detail caused a serious injury to his eyes. He ventured too close to a wire-wrapping device used in the maintenance of telephone wires and was nearly blinded. After two operations, Tomasito has lost most of his sight in one eye, and the sight in his other eye has begun to deteriorate.

Their second son, Robert, married with two small children, was recently divorced after his wife left him for one of their neighbors. For Tomás and Hortencia, divorce has always been something that other people who lack religious resolve have done. They place divorce in the same negative category with abortion. Both are culturally shocked, although members of Hortencia's family of orientation have been divorced. Yet the greatest shock for both is the inability to see their grandchildren with the same frequency as before, as well as the great chasm between them and their former daughter-in-law, who remarried shortly after the divorce.

The most deadly development is that Tomás has been diagnosed as suffering from a breakdown of his immune system. After having suffered incessant headaches, nausea, fainting spells, and loss of balance, he was diagnosed as having high blood pressure. His symptoms continued, in spite of the medication, until toxicity tests revealed a high concentration of toxic chemicals in his body fat. Tomás had never told his physicians that for almost 20 years he had sprayed strong industrial cleaning solvents, without gloves or a face mask, on aircraft engines and airframes as an aircraft maintenance man in the Army National Guard. When he was asked why he did not wear protective clothing, his response was that bulky gear interfered with his efficiency and productivity and that he did not want to be seen as a "lazy Mexican."

Neither Tomás nor Hortencia has been lazy or lacking in either motivation for hard work or sacrifice. They have committed themselves to the notion of nation and support for individuals and issues that espouse conservative points of view. The military occupation, which represented that commitment, is the factor that certainly will kill Tomás in the not-too-distant future. Neither their prayers nor their devotion can stop his process of physical degeneration.

THE IMPACT OF CAPITALIST DISLOCATIONS AND TECHNOLOGICAL CHANGES ON ADAPTATIONS OF HOUSEHOLDS

As households became dependent on wages, the locus of work activities moved away from the home, and the funds of knowledge required of workers became increasingly specialized. Moreover, funds of knowledge that households needed for their survival and reproduction were increasingly found not within the households, but distributed in their social networks or located in a variety of formal institutions to which they had to turn to solve their everyday problems. Such institutions included government offices, labor unions, and, of course, schools.

CLASS CHANGES

One paradox of funds of knowledge in urban contexts is that, although they help households, depending on their content and breadth, to be independent of the marketplace, individuals gain funds through work and through participation in labor markets. Yet, even as such funds help household obtain a degree of independence of the marketplace, there are major obstacles to their permanency or transmission from one generation to another. Succeeding generations often do not gain a complete and functional understanding of the funds that their ancestors had unless they remain within the same class segment or are able to translate such knowledge into a new, rewarding labor arena. Urban residents, nevertheless, often attempt symbolically to retain such funds by constructing equivalent conditions and contexts for their maintenance and transmission. Such attempts take the form of economic and ideological investments in small ranching and farming projects, which are often not profitable, but which aim to recapitulate early childhood experience. Because wages in highly segmented labor markets are low and unstable, working-class households have had to jump from one sector of the labor market to another, holding several jobs and pooling their wages to make ends meet. However, because the independence is problematic, the broad funds of knowledge alone, which they have acquired in this process, cannot guarantee their well-being or survival. Thus, the ability of households to cope in rough economic seas rests equally on the exchange relationships among them.

Depending on kin or friends is also fraught with problems. Besides the uncertainty experienced in the search for work, the frailty of having to depend on others for assistance with child care, household maintenance, and transportation leads people to make very determined efforts to enter primary labor markets. Such formal-sector jobs are prized not just because they pay better, but because they provide formal benefits that help underwrite the households' reproduction and lessen their dependence on others. This quest for stability is of single importance for U.S.-Mexican households. If they cannot find employment within primary labor markets, then they are willing to make extreme investments in education in the hope that their children will gain such an entrée. The irony is that educational institutions also serve as important mechanisms of denial for access to such labor markets.

Social Distribution of Funds of Knowledge

Significantly, nevertheless, funds of knowledge do become part of the implicit operational and cultural system of daily life. Friends and kin often provide a safety net and substantial aid in time of crisis. Such exchanges occur in such a routine and constant fashion that people are hardly aware of them. These exchanges take a variety of forms: labor services, access to information or resources (including help in finding jobs or housing or dealing with government agencies or other institutions), and various forms of material assistance besides money (such as putting up visitors).

Small favors are a constant feature of exchange relations. However, because they are reciprocal, they balance out in the long term and are less important economically than the exchange of information and special funds of knowledge. Indeed, help in finding jobs, housing, and better deals on goods and services, and in dealings with institutions and government agencies, is of far greater significance to survival than are the material types of aid that these households usually provide one another.

Because households depend on their social networks to cope with the borderland's complex political and changing economic environment, they are willing to invest considerable energy and resources in maintaining good relations with their members. One way they do this is through family rituals: birthdays, baptisms, confirmations, "coming out" rituals (*quinceañeras*), wedding showers, weddings, Christmas dinners, outings, and visitations. Not only do these events bring members of one's network together ritually to reaffirm their solidarity, but staging them also often requires members to cooperate by investing their labor or pooling their resources. Moreover, such rituals broadcast an important set of signals about both the sponsor's economic well-being and the state of social relations with other members—through both lavishness and attendance.

As well, the willingness to help stage family rituals is a measure of who one can count on for other things. These rituals form a calendrical cycle where Christmas, New Year's, and Easter are major rituals in which almost everyone participates. Life-cycle rituals, such as baptisms, confirmations, quinceañeras, weddings, and funerals, mark a secondary level of minor rituals that fit between the major rituals. Interspersed throughout these are myriad other smaller celebrations, such as birthdays, anniversaries, housewarmings, and ritualized visitations. This entire calendrical cycle is carefully monitored by the households involved and gives meaning to the social relations articulated through such events. Great effort, resources, and energies go into not only organizing such events, but also evaluating their social success.

Such formal rituals are but one mechanism through which social networks are maintained. Household visits, which are as important, are themselves informal rituals. Like their more formal counterparts, the frequency of visiting and the treatment that the visitor receives are important signals about the state of social relations. This frequent contact helps both to maintain social ties and to provide a context for the exchange of information through which funds of knowledge are constantly renewed and updated.

As well, each household cluster has accumulated and discarded funds of knowledge, forming the basis of material survival, that contain within them much of the previous generation's repertoire of information and skills. As each case study presented here illustrates, these funds have important historical and contemporary reference points. By paying attention to such funds, we may gain considerable insight into how funds of knowledge are mobilized and deployed daily in a broad range of relationships, and how Mexican children acquire their cultural identity.

The Emergence of the Mexican Child in Social Density

There is one other dynamic aspect that should be considered. The probability that the funds of knowledge that such clusters contain will be transmitted to the following generation rests not only on an appropriate economic and social context for their application, but also on the early expectations for learning that children gain in such contexts. Our evidence suggests that these clusters provide U.S.-Mexican children with a social platform in which they internalize these "thick" social relations and learn to have analogously "thick" social expectations.

However, because most studies of early childhood socialization have been attitudinal and not observational, the empirical record of process for Mexican children is scant. A recent study by Vélez (1983) of mother–infant interaction, however, provides some insights into the possible genesis of Mexican expectations and potentialities. Her work provides the probable link between early childhood experience and the formation of these expectations in clustered household settings and establishes the theoretical basis for understanding the phenomenon.

The original postulate in the work asserted that there would be significant variations in the mothering styles of Mexican-American mothers and those of Anglo mothers that could be attributed to cultural expectations, and that such expectations included the probability that Mexican mothers provide more proximal stimulation to infants, are more responsive to their infants' signals, and express such differences about infant rearing in their beliefs and values (Vélez, 1983, p. 11).

In her findings, there was little difference in the frequency or quality of the actual interaction between mothers and infants. Of greater significance for the emergence of the Mexican infant's social personality was the social context of interactions and the role that others played in the infant's early social experience (p. 80). Vélez found that although she introduced a variety of social and economic controls to match her sample, the Mexican mothers' social density was much greater, contact with infant and mother by other relatives was significantly more frequent, and greater stimulation of the infant by others was also statistically significant. The Mexican infant had a social context packed with tactile and sound stimulation. The child was surrounded by a variety of relatives, and, at the behavioral level, was seldom really alone. This last finding was also supported by the observation that although Mexican children had their own rooms available, 92% of the Mexican children slept in their parents' room, whereas 80% of the Anglo children slept in their own rooms.

Although this was a working-class sample, we have the impression from our present study that the same phenomenon extends to middle-class Mexican-American households. It would appear that the early "thick" social context that surrounds Mexican children leads to the emergence of social expectations that are different from those of non-Mexican populations that do not have equivalent social characteristics. Such differences, we suggest, may include the internalization of many other significant object relations with more persons, an expectation of more relations with the same persons, and expectations of being attentive to, and investing emotionally in, a variety of relations. Such psychodynamic and psychosocial processes entailed in cultural expectations of *confianza* (mutual trust)[8] are the cradle from whence anticipations for exchange relations emerge. Such early experiences give substance to cultural expectations for exchange, expectations that are reinforced by ritual and other forms of exchange throughout the life cycle.

Such "thick contexts" are the social platforms in which the funds of knowledge of the cluster of households are transmitted. So, by examining how such knowledge is transmitted, we gain some insight into the cultural conflicts that may arise when Mexican children confront educational models of the dominant society that seek to reshape Mexican children culturally and socially according to its values.

FUND TRANSMISSION AND THE BASIS
FOR CULTURAL CONFLICT

Further analysis of how information is transmitted to children in U.S.-Mexican households suggests that such knowledge is passed on through culturally constituted methods, that these methods have emotive implications for the self-esteem of children, and that they are possible sources of cultural conflict in the schools.

Because Mexican children are ensconced within "thick" multiple relations, they visit and become familiar with other households, households that contain other funds of knowledge and with whom they carry on a variety of social relationships. Such clustered households provide the opportunity for children to become exposed to an array of different versions of such funds. However, what is important is not only that the children are exposed to multiple domains in which funds of knowledge are used, but that they are also afforded the opportunity to experiment with them in each domain. Our studies (Vélez-Ibáñez & Greenberg, 1984; Moll et al., 1988) show that the transmission process is largely an experimental one. Although adults may manifest specific portions of a fund, the organization of learning is in the hands of the children themselves. Children are expected to ask questions during the performance of household tasks. Thus, the question-and-answer process is directed by the child rather than by the adult. Once children receive an answer, they may emulate adults by creating play situations for practicing the learned behavior.

---

[8] *Confianza* is a cultural construct indicating the willingness to engage in generalized reciprocity. For a full discussion, see Vélez-Ibáñez and Greenberg (1984, pp. 10–16).

Another important aspect in the transmission of funds of knowledge is the wide latitude allowed for error and the encouragement that children are given to experiment further. For instance, a child's observing and "assisting" an adult repair an automobile leads to attempts by the child to experiment on other mechanical devices, as well as on "junk" engines that may be available. The usual adult direction is to "finish it yourself and try your best, no matter how long it takes." Even when the child is stuck at one point, the adult usually does not volunteer either the question or the answer. Such sequences teach children to persevere, to experiment, to manipulate, and to delay gratification.

Because there are multiple occasions for experimentation, there are also multiple opportunities to fail and to overcome that failure in different domains. Because there are a variety of contexts in which children may observe and learn to do tasks adequately, children have more than one domain in which they may be successful. A major characteristic of the transmission of funds of knowledge is that multiple household domains provide children with a zone of comfort that is familiar yet experimental, where error is not dealt with punitively, and where self-esteem is not endangered. Because such transmission occurs in multiple domains, children can usually find nonstressful domains or neutral zones of comfort, where little criticism is expressed and where they will not be faulted. When an adult is impatient and judgmental, children often go to other adults in other domains who are more patient. Children thus learn very early to use a comparative approach to evaluate adults, avoiding discouraging or punitive persons because there are others available who are not so.

Because the feedback process is in the hands of the child, such zones of comfort also allow self-evaluation and self-judgment. The only exceptions are when children would be in danger or cannot physically do the tasks. Similarly, if their errors would prove costly, then children are not encouraged to experiment. Nonetheless, the outstanding characteristic of such experimentation is that children eventually develop enough familiarity with various domains to predict and manipulate them. Children learn quickly that there are constraints, but these are so obviously in their favor that such an understanding becomes the underlying basis for zones of comfort. In emic terms, such zones of comfort, and the relationships that support their expression, become the basis of *confianza* and place children within the appropriate cultural frame for adulthood.

The use of traditional pedagogical approaches to learning in public schools threatens the cultural frame of such zones of comfort. Our observations show that when little girls "play school," they emulate teacher-originated and directed sequences. The children taking the role of teacher allow for markedly little active student-controlled interaction, and imitate as well the expectations of rote or uncreative responses to instruction (Tapia,

1989). In addition, the school model of instruction is emphasized by parents during homework periods, with strong punitive measures either threatened or carried out if tasks are not completed. This use of the schooling model created one of the few sources of adult–child conflict in the households we observed. Such basic cultural conflict becomes further exacerbated when understood within a larger cultural framework of human emergence. For the U.S.-Mexican adult, who has emerged within both culturally constituted zones of comfort and formal educational settings, self-doubt, negation, and cultural resistance will emerge together. However, there are processes beyond any adult's control that mitigate even the zones of comfort within the household. These are the institutionalized processes of literacy fracturing within each household.

THE FRACTURING OF LITERACY COMPREHENSION
AND COGNITIVE DEVELOPMENT

U.S.-Mexicans, contrary to popular images, are a literate population, especially in Spanish. Although public schools should find this advantageous for political, economic, and legal reasons, little use is made of their native language literacy. For example, in our household sample we found that 68% read Spanish "well or very well," and an equal percentage wrote Spanish "well or very well." On the other hand, 59% read English "not at all" or only "a little," while 62% wrote English "not at all" or only "a little."

Rather than assuming that literacy and comprehension are found wanting in these households, it is the shift from Spanish to English that interrupts, or "fractures," an extended development of Spanish comprehension and literacy in reading and writing. For parents, most economic and legal functions demand English dominance. Because there is little use for Spanish in legal and economic realms, comprehension and literacy often begin to suffer from disuse. Thus, there is a marked shift from a tradition of Spanish literacy to one where Spanish is largely an oral tradition, commonly limited to household situations.[9]

---

[9]John Ogbu stated that for any child "there is discontinuity in the social–emotional socialization received in the home and school" (1982, p. 292), and went on to detail the discontinuity in the home of home language use, contextual learning, as well as the stylistics involved. Citing Cook-Gumperz and Gumperz (1981), who contended that there are shifts from the largely oral tradition of the home to the literate tradition of the school, Ogbu considered these as part of the larger problem of discontinuity. Within the context of literacy fracturing, however, we suggest yet a further type of discontinuity: literacy fracturing, that is, the elimination of the process, possibility, and practice of literacy activities in Spanish within the U.S.-Mexican household and a shift to the oral tradition. In the nonethnic English-language dominant home, no such structural condition is liable to occur other than illiteracy.

Such fracturing has several unintended and intended consequences. First, if parents speak only Spanish they are unable to participate in the initial literacy activities of their children. Because public schools demand an English literacy "script" be followed, the comprehensive abilities of the parents are either unrecognized or are unintentionally denied as being efficacious. Second, for parents, such abilities are often unused and unreinforced, except when writing letters to relatives in Mexico or reading popular magazines. The lack of opportunity to use literacy skills then "fractures" parental ability to communicate within their own generation and prevents the transmission of literacy in Spanish to the following one. Third, if their own children learn Spanish only as an oral traditional language, transmission of knowledge is constrained by the daily household vocabulary that makes little use of the technical terms and extensive vocabularies common in written materials. In this sense, then, the "literate" world is also denied the children of Spanish-literate dominant parents.

This process of fracturing has enormous implications for the acquisition of literacy abilities, cognitive understandings, and complex organizational thought. In a very specific sense, when such fracturing processes deprive children access to written materials in Spanish, their use of language is reduced to Spanish vocabulary and expressions that, for the most part, are devoid of the literary tradition. The version of Spanish they learn perforce will be constrained to a daily use that largely excludes broader arenas of application. Largely, children will be exposed to language directly associated with household functions and relations rather than to language associated with the broader economic, political, social, and cultural activities that provide substantive reinforcement to conceptual and cognitive development.

Because the version of English learned at school is directly defined by institutional requirements focusing on skills, coding, and specific problem-solving application, it, too, is largely disconnected from a reinforcing literate tradition. For, other than manipulative, functional, and immediate application, English is unconnected to a previous generation. In fact, children function largely as translators for parents whose own traditions, both oral and literate, are in Spanish. This fracturing process between generations, then, may be partly responsible for the type of negative academic performances too often associated with U.S.-Mexican children. The cumulative impact of these processes is to create pockets of populations in which the problem is not one of illiteracy, but one of literacy in, English and Spanish.

From an evolutionary point of view, it may be suggested that this process is a devolutionary one in which succeeding generations are placed at greater and greater risk of being less able than the previous generation to use literacy skills to manipulate their environment efficiently and productively.

CONCLUSIONS

The funds of knowledge that Mexican populations have historically acquired in the U.S.–Mexico borderland reflect the ongoing character of the organization of production and its technological basis. Consequently, the agrarian pursuits that the population followed in the rural countryside included a broad range of skills that could also be marketed in urban and industrial settings. Yet, their very success in adapting to the unstable labor markets contained the seeds of cultural demise. In moving from the countryside to the city, the social and cultural context in which their identities were forged was fundamentally altered, and the transmission of funds of knowledge, in some instances, was lost.

Yet, social exchange between households, clusters of households, and kinship networks not only continues to provide individuals access to historic funds of knowledge, but also provides them the cultural matrix for incorporating new understandings and relationships in a "Mexican" way. These funds and their functions in social relationships, thus, will continue to be characteristically "shaped" by the Mexican experience of structural changes in the economic and political environment. So, although the case studies reflect a common appreciation for religious values in each household, the differences between them are also striking. In the Serrano case, the attention paid to country and patriotism creates an emphasis that may be "ethnically" different from that of other families. This is a reflection of the continued intensity of the army experience for the Serranos, which provides a wider basis of identity reference to a national prism in which citizenship and culture are regarded as analogous. In spite of these differences, the basis of social density and the multiplicity of relations, regardless of rural–urban dimensions, occupation, or language preference, remain at the core of the way both households have unfolded within the life cycle. Identity formation and emergence as Mexicans in the United States thus arises from the matrix of social relations in the clusters of households, and not from "cultural" iota as such. Such identity becomes implicitly "cultural," in that, as other works (Vélez-Ibáñez, 1988b) have shown, these matrices become the social platforms from whence children emerge.

POLICY IMPLICATIONS

There are several policy implications that flow from an understanding of the full range of household strategies and their probable outcomes as mentioned in this study.

Educational Policy Reform

The implications of our findings for educational policy reform seem clear. What is needed is a critical reexamination of the cultural basis of evaluation and assessment of U.S.-Mexican children, a close analysis of the cultural basis of instruction and pedagogy, and field testing of the nature of the social relations between U.S.-Mexican children, their parents, and the educational institutions that serve them.

Concerning evaluation and assessment, we should pay some attention to more dynamic forms of assessment that seek to measure children's learning potential. The process would use mediated learning practices within the assessment context, with the assessor actively participating in the teaching of skills to the examinee. Such an approach is based on the modification of the examinee, not on stable, easily measurable characteristics. Using this approach, Feurestein (1979) showed significant gains for educable mentally retarded students through instruction based on learning potential.

Second, the very basis of instruction should be reexamined. In contrast with the traditional, highly individualized competitive instruction systems, "cooperative" learning systems might be more appropriate for children for whom such social interaction is both a highly developed skill and an expectation. Such systems are based on the idea that students accomplish their academic tasks in heterogeneous groups, where, although the tasks are usually assigned by the teacher, each student's effort contributes to the total group effort. Cooperative learning may be an important innovation in relation to education and culture for three reasons. First, it may be more compatible with the cultural norms and values of U.S.-Mexican children, and it seems highly compatible with their learning experiences. Second, it may contribute to their interethnic relations in the classroom. Third, and most important, such approaches lead to much higher academic gains for minority students (Kagan, 1986).

Next, both the social basis of instruction between children and teachers and the social basis of relations between teacher and parents must be carefully considered. If, as we have pointed out, the expectations of children and parents in relations with others are based on social density, then the school-based model of instruction is in direct contradiction and opposition to these expectations. If anything, the school-based model of instruction is organized around single-stranded teacher-to-student interaction, in which parental involvement is restricted to occasional contact or is defined within highly formalized contexts such as parent–teacher organizations. There is little in the triad of children, teacher, and parents that crosscuts either generational, class, educational, ethnic, or status differences except the single strand of informational and assessment authority directed by the teacher.

Last, the implications for teacher training and the elimination of institutionalized "literacy fracturing" seem paramount. We should pay greater attention to providing teachers with opportunities to learn how to incorporate the funds of knowledge from their students' households into learning modules that approximate the total reality of the population. As well, literacy instruction must maximize its use of the available literacy and within the home as a means to tap the vast funds of knowledge that parents have, but are seldom given the opportunity to share and express.

REFLECTION QUESTIONS

1. How do Vélez-Ibáñez and Greenberg conceptualize and define the idea of funds of knowledge?
2. How do the case studies they present help us to understand the formation and transformation of funds of knowledge?
3. How can literacy come to be fractured?
4. Why is the historical context important in framing funds of knowledge?

ACKNOWLEDGMENT

We acknowledge the support of the W. K. Kellogg Foundation for providing financial resources to carry out the research activities without which this work could not have been written.

REFERENCES

Alvarez, R. (1987). *Familia: Migration and adaptation in Baja and Alta, California*. Berkeley, CA: University of California Press.

Camarillo, A. (1979). *Chicanos in a changing society: From Mexican pueblos to American barrios in Santa Barbara and Southern California, 1848–1930*. Cambridge, MA: Harvard University Press.

Chávez, L. R. (1988). Settlers and sojourners: The case of Mexicans in the United States. *Human Organization, 47*, 95–108.

Chávez, L. R., Flores, E. T., & López-Garza, M. (1992). Here today, gone tomorrow? Undocumented settlers and immigration reform. *Human Organization, 49*, 193–205.

Cook-Gumperz, J., & Gumperz, J. J. (1981). From oral to written culture: The transition to literacy. In M. F. Whitehead (Ed.), *Variation in writing: Functional and linguistic-cultural differences* (pp. 89–109). Norwood, NJ: Ablex.

Cornelius, W. A. (1988). *The role of Mexican labor in the North American economy of the 1990s*. Paper prepared for the Fourth Annual Emerging Issues Program for State Legislative Leaders: The North American Economy in the 1990s. University of California, San Diego.

Diez-Canedo, J. (1981). *Undocumented migration to the United States: A new perspective.* Albuquerque, NM: Center for Latin American Studies, University of New Mexico.

Fenández-Kelly, P. (1987). Technology and employment along the U.S. Mexican border. In C. L. Thorup (Ed.), *The United States and Mexico: Face to face with new technology* (pp. 149–166). New Brunswick, NJ: Transaction Books.

Feurestein, R. (1979). *The dynamic assessment of retarded performers: The learning potential assessment device, theory, instruments, and techniques.* Baltimore, MD: University Park Press.

García, J. A. (1982). Ethnicity and Chicanos: Measurement of ethnic identification, identity, and consciousness. *Hispanic Journal of Behavioral Sciences, 43,* 295–314.

García y Griego, M. (1983). *Mexico and the United States: Migration, history, and the idea of sovereignty.* El Paso, TX: Center for Interamerican and Border Studies, University of Texas.

González-Archegia, B. (1987). *California-Mexico linkages.* Paper presented at the First Annual California-Mexico Business Conference, Los Angeles.

Greenberg, J. B. (1990). Funds of knowledge: Historical constitution, social distribution, and transmission. In W. T. Pink, D. S. Ogle, & B. F. Jones (Eds.), *Restructuring to promote learning in America's schools: Selected readings* (Vol. 2, pp. 317–326). Elmhurst, IL: North Central Regional Educational Laboratory.

Griswold del Castillo, R. (1984). *La familia: Chicano families in the urban Southwest, 1848 to the present.* Notre Dame, IN: University of Notre Dame.

Heyman, J. (n.d.). *The power of the United States border over Mexican lives: The case of cross-bordership.* Unpublished manuscript.

Kagan, S. (1986). Cooperative learning and socio-cultural factors in schooling. In S. Kagan (Ed.), *Young language: Social and cultural factors in schooling language minority students* (pp. 36–47). Los Angeles: California State University.

Keefe, S. E. (1979). Urbanization, acculturation, and extended family ties: Mexican Americans in cities. *American Ethnologist, 6,* 349–365.

Keefe, S. E., Padilla, M., & Carlos, M. L. (1978). *Emotional support systems in two cultures: A comparison of Mexican Americans and Anglo Americans.* [Occasional Paper No. 7.] Los Angeles: Spanish Speaking Mental Health Research Center, UCLA.

Keefe, S. E., Padilla, M., & Carlos, M. L. (1979). The Mexican American extended family as an emotional support system. *Human Organization, 38,* 144–152.

Martínez, O. (1983). The foreign orientation of the Mexican border economy. *Border Perspectives, 2.* El Paso, TX: Center for Interamerican and Border Studies, University of Texas.

Martínez, O. (1988). *Troublesome border.* Tucson, AZ: University of Arizona Press.

Moll, L. C., Vélez-Ibáñez, C. G., & Greenberg, J. B. (1988). *Community knowledge and classroom practice: Combining resources for literacy instruction.* Unpublished manuscript, Innovative Approaches Research Project Grant, Development Associates.

Ogbu, J. U. (1982). Cultural discontinuities and schooling. *Anthropology and Education Quarterly, 13,* 290–307.

Porras, A. S. (n.d.). *Crisis, maquiladoras y estructura sociopolítica en Chihuahua, Sonora y Baja California.* Unpublished manuscript.

Rodríguez, R. (1982). *Hunger of memory. The education of Richard Rodríguez: An auto-biography.* New York: D. R. Godine.

Sheridan, T. E. (1988). *Where the dove calls: The political ecology of a peasant community in Northwestern Mexico.* Tucson, AZ: University of Arizona Press.

Tapia, J. (1989). *The recreation of school at home through play.* Unpublished manuscript, Bureau of Applied Research.

Tiano, S. B. (1985). *Export processing, women's work, and the employment problem in developing countries: The case of the Maquiladora program in Northern Mexico, 22.* El Paso, TX: Center for Interamerican and Border Studies, University of Texas.

U.S. Department of Justice. (1954). *Annual report of the immigration and naturalization service.* Washington, DC: Author.

Vélez, M. T. (1983). *The social context of mothering: A comparison of Mexican American and Anglo mother infant interaction patterns.* PhD dissertation, Wright Institute of Psychology.

Vélez-Ibáñez, C. G. (1983). *Bonds of mutual trust: The cultural systems of rotating credit associations among urban Mexicans and Chicanos.* New Brunswick, NJ: Rutgers University Press.

Vélez-Ibáñez, C. G. (1987). Mecanismos de intercambio incorporados entre los Mexicanos en la zona fronteriza de Estados Unidos. In O. Martínez et al. (Eds.), *Memoria XII: Simposio de historia y antropología de Sonora* (pp. 413–482). Hermosillo, Sonora: Universidad de Sonora.

Vélez-Ibáñez, C. G. (1988a, November). *Forms and functions among Mexicans in the Southwest: Implications for classroom use.* Paper presented at the Invited Session, Forms and Functions of Funds of Knowledge Within Mexican Households in the Southwest, American Anthropological Association Annual Meeting, Phoenix, AZ.

Vélez-Ibáñez, C. G. (1988b). Networks of exchange among Mexicans in the U.S. and Mexico: Local level mediating responses to national and international transformation. *Urban Anthropology and Studies of Cultural Systems and World Economic Development, 17,* 27–51.

Vélez-Ibáñez, C. G. (1989, November). *Transmission and patterning of funds of knowledge: Shaping and emergence of confianza in U.S. Mexican children.* Paper presented at Society for Applied Anthropology, Annual Meeting, Santa Fe, NM.

Vélez-Ibáñez, C. G. (1992a). Plural strategies of survival and cultural formation in U.S. Mexican households in a region of dynamic transformation: The U.S.-Mexico borderlands. In S. Foreman (Ed.), *Diagnosing America: Anthropology and public engagement.* Ann Arbor, MI: University of Michigan Press.

Vélez-Ibáñez, C. G. (1992b). Problem solving and collaboration: A model for applied anthropology from the field. In D. R. Gross (Ed.), *Discovering anthropology* (pp. 402–403). Mountain View, CT: Mayfield Publishing.

Vélez-Ibáñez, C. G., & Greenberg, J. B. (1984). *Multidimensional functions of non-market forms of exchange among Mexicans/Chicanos in Tucson, Arizona.* Unpublished manuscript, National Science Foundation.

Vélez-Ibáñez, C. G., & Greenberg, J. B. (1990, November). *Formation and transformation of funds of knowledge among U.S. Mexican households in the context of the borderlands.* Paper presented at the America Anthropological Association Annual Meeting, Washington, DC.

Wolf, E. R. (1966). *Peasants.* Englewood Cliffs, NJ: Prentice Hall.

Chapter 4

Funds of Knowledge for Teaching: Using a Qualitative Approach to Connect Homes and Classrooms*

Luis Moll
Cathy Amanti
Deborah Neff
Norma González
University of Arizona

We form part of a collaborative project between education and anthropology that is studying household and classroom practices within working-class, Mexican communities in Tucson, Arizona. The primary purpose of this work is to develop innovations in teaching that draw on the knowledge and skills found in local households. Our claim is that by capitalizing on household and other community resources, we can organize classroom instruction that far exceeds in quality the rote-like instruction these children commonly encounter in schools (see e.g., Moll & Greenberg, 1990; Moll & Díaz, 1987).

To accomplish this goal, we have developed a research approach that is based on understanding households (and classrooms) qualitatively. We use a combination of ethnographic observations, open-ended interviewing strategies, life histories, and case studies that, when combined analytically, can portray accurately the complex functions of households within their sociohistorical contexts. Qualitative research offers a range of methodological alternatives that can fathom the array of cultural and intellectual resources available to students and teachers within these households. This approach is particularly important in dealing with students whose households are usually viewed as being "poor," not only economically but in terms of the quality of experiences for the child.

*This article first appeared in the journal *Theory Into Practice* (1992, Vol. 31, pp. 132–141) and is reprinted with permission.

Our research design attempts to coordinate three interrelated activities: the ethnographic analysis of household dynamics, the examination of classroom practices, and the development of after-school study groups with teachers. These study groups, collaborative ventures between teachers and researchers, are settings within which we discuss our developing understanding of households and classrooms. These study groups also function as "mediating structures" for developing novel classroom practices that involve strategic connections between these two entities (see Moll et al., 1990).

In this chapter we discuss recent developments in establishing these "strategic connections" that take the form of joint household research between classroom teachers and university-based researchers and the subsequent development of ethnographically informed classroom practices. We first present a summary of our household studies and the findings that form the bases of our pedagogical work. We then present an example of recent research between a classroom teacher and an anthropologist, highlighting details of their visit to a household, and the teacher's development of an instructional activity based on their observations. We conclude with some comments on the work presented.

SOME BASIC FINDINGS

As noted, central to our project is the qualitative study of households. This approach involves, for one, understanding the history of the border region between Mexico and the United States and other aspects of the socio-political and economic context of the households (see e.g., Vélez-Ibáñez, 1993; see also Heyman, 1990; Martínez, 1988). It also involves analyzing the social history of the households, their origins and development, and most prominently for our purposes, the labor history of the families, which reveals the accumulated bodies of knowledge of the households (see Vélez-Ibáñez & Greenberg, 1989).

With our sample,[1] this knowledge is broad and diverse, as depicted in abbreviated form in Table 4.1. Notice that household knowledge may include information about farming and animal management, information associated with households' rural origins, or knowledge about construction and building, related to urban occupations, as well as knowledge about many other matters, such as trade, business, and finance on both sides of the border (see e.g., Moll & Greenberg, 1990). We use the term *funds of knowledge* to refer to these historically accumulated and culturally developed bodies of knowledge and skills essential for household or individual functioning and well-being (Greenberg, 1989; Tapia, 1991; Vélez-Ibáñez, 1988).

---

[1]Our sample includes households of students in the project-teachers' classrooms, as well as students from other classrooms in the same general community. In total, including previous projects, we have observed in approximately 100 homes.

TABLE 4.1
A Sample of Household Funds of Knowledge

Agriculture and Mining	Material and Scientific Knowledge
Ranching and farming	Construction
Horse riding skills	Carpentry
Animal management	Roofing
Soil and irrigation systems	Masonry
Crop planting	Painting
Hunting, tracking, dressing	Design and architecture
Mining	Repair
Timbering	Airplane
Minerals	Automobile
Blasting	Tractor
Equipment operation and maintenance	House maintenance

Economics	Medicine
Business	Contemporary medicine
Market values	Drugs
Appraising	First aid procedures
Renting and selling	Anatomy
Loans	Midwifery
Labor laws	Folk medicine
Building codes	Herbal knowledge
Consumer knowledge	Folk cures
Accounting	Folk veterinary cures
Sales	

Household Management	Religion
Budgets	Catechism
Childcare	Baptisms
Cooking	Bible studies
Appliance repairs	Moral knowledge and ethics

Our approach also involves studying how household members use their funds of knowledge in dealing with changing, and often difficult, social and economic circumstances. We are particularly interested in how families develop social networks that interconnect them with their social environments (most importantly with other households), and how these social relationships facilitate the development and exchange of resources—including knowledge, skills, and labor—that enhance the households' ability to survive or thrive (see e.g., Moll & Greenberg, 1990; Vélez-Ibáñez & Greenberg, 1989; see also Keefe & Padilla, 1987).

Two aspects of these household arrangements merit emphasis here, especially because they contrast so sharply with typical classroom practices. One is that these networks are flexible, adaptive, and active, and may involve multiple persons from outside the homes: In our terms, they are "thick" and "multistranded," meaning that one may have multiple relationships with the same person or with various persons. The person from whom the child learns carpentry, for example, may also be the uncle with whom the child's family regularly celebrates birthdays or organizes barbecues, as well as the person with whom the child's father goes fishing on weekends.

Thus, the teacher in these home-based contexts of learning will know the child as a whole person, not merely as a student, taking into account or having knowledge about the multiple spheres of activity within which the child is enmeshed. In comparison, the typical teacher–student relationship seems thin and single-stranded, as the teacher knows the students only from their performance within rather limited classroom contexts.

Additionally, in contrast to the households and their social networks, the classrooms seem encapsulated, if not isolated, from the social worlds and resources of the community. When funds of knowledge are not readily available within households, relationships with individuals outside the households are activated to meet either household or individual needs. In classrooms, however, teachers rarely draw on the resources of the funds of knowledge of the child's world outside the context of the classroom.

A second key characteristic of these exchanges is their reciprocity. As Vélez-Ibáñez (1988) has observed, reciprocity represents an "attempt to establish a social relationship on an enduring basis. Whether symmetrical or asymmetrical, the exchange expresses and symbolizes human social interdependence" (p. 142). That is, reciprocal practices establish serious obligations based on the assumption of *confianza* (mutual trust), which is reestablished or confirmed with each exchange and leads to the development of long-term relationships. Each exchange with relatives, friends, and neighbors entails not only many practical activities (everything from home and automobile repair to animal care and music) but constantly provides contexts in which learning can occur—contexts, for example, where children have ample opportunities to participate in activities with people they trust (Moll & Greenberg, 1990).

A related observation is that children in the households are not passive bystanders, as they seem in the classrooms, but active participants in a broad range of activities mediated by these social relationships (see La Fontaine, 1986). In some cases, their participation is central to the household's functioning, as when the children contribute to the economic production of the home, or use their knowledge of English to mediate the household's communications with outside institutions, such as the school or government offices. In other cases they are active in household chores, such as repairing appliances or caring for younger siblings.

Our analysis suggests that within these contexts, much of the teaching and learning is motivated by the children's interests and questions; in contrast to classrooms, knowledge is obtained by the children, not imposed by the adults. This totality of experiences, the cultural structuring of the households, whether related to work or play, whether they take place individually, with peers, or under the supervision of adults, helps constitute the funds of knowledge children bring to school (Moll & Greenberg, 1990).

FUNDS OF KNOWLEDGE FOR TEACHING

Our analysis of funds of knowledge represents a positive (and, we argue, realistic) view of households as containing ample cultural and cognitive resources with great potential utility for classroom instruction (see Moll & Greenberg, 1990; Moll et al., 1990). This view of households, we should mention, contrasts sharply with prevailing and accepted perceptions of working-class families as somehow disorganized socially and deficient intellectually; perceptions that are well accepted and rarely challenged in the field of education and elsewhere (however, see McDermott, 1987; Moll & Díaz, 1987; Taylor & Dorsey-Gaines, 1988; see also Vélez-Ibáñez, 1993).

But how can teachers make use of these funds of knowledge in their teaching? We have been experimenting with the aforementioned arrangements that involve developing after-school settings where we meet with teachers to analyze their classrooms, discuss household observations, and develop innovations in the teaching of literacy. These after-school settings represent social contexts for informing, assisting, and supporting the teachers' work; settings, in our terms, for teachers and researchers to exchange funds of knowledge (for details, see Moll et al., 1990).[2]

In analyzing our efforts, however, we realized that we had relied on the researchers to present their findings to the teachers and to figure out the relevance of that information for teaching. Although we were careful about our desires not to impose but to collaborate with teachers, this collaboration did not extend to the conduct of the research. In our work with teachers, at least as far as household data were concerned, we relied on a "transmission" model: We presented the information, teachers received it, without actively involving themselves in the development or production of this knowledge. But how could it be otherwise? Was it feasible to ask teachers to become field researchers? What would they get out of it? Could they develop similar insights to those developed by the anthropologists in our research team? What about methods? Could they, for example, with little experience, understand the subtleties of ethnographic observations?

---

[2]For similar ideas regarding the development of teacher "labs" or activity settings, see, for example, Berliner (1985), Laboratory of Comparative Human Cognition (1982), and Tharp and Gallimore (1988). The creation of study groups is also a common practice among whole-language teachers and researchers (see Goodman, 1989).

In what follows we present a case example from our most recent work that addresses these questions. The goal of the study was to explore teacher-researcher collaborations in conducting household research and in using this information to develop classroom practices. As part of the work, 10 teachers participated in a series of training workshops on qualitative methods of study, including ethnographic observations, interviews, the writing of field notes, data management, and analysis.[3] Each teacher (with two exceptions) then selected for study three households of children in their classrooms. In total, the teachers visited 25 households (the sample included Mexican and Yaqui families) and conducted approximately 100 observations and interviews during a semester of study (for details, see Vélez-Ibáñez, Moll, González, & Neff, 1991).

Rather than provide further technical details about this project, however, we present an edited transcript from a recent presentation[4] by a teacher (Cathy Amanti) and an anthropologist (Deborah Neff) who collaborated in the study. They describe their experiences conducting the research and provide a revealing glimpse of the process of using qualitative methods to study households and their funds of knowledge.

STUDYING HOUSEHOLD KNOWLEDGE

In their presentation, Amanti and Neff first described some of their concerns in conducting the work, including how their assumptions and previous experiences may have influenced their observations. They also described their planning. Notice how they decided to divide the methodological responsibilities for conducting the interviews and observations.

Deborah Neff: We are going to share with you some of our experience in working as a team doing household interviews. We have chosen the

---

[3]Field notes are generally descriptive to provide context and background information, whereas interviews, usually based on a questionnaire, focus on topics of specific relevance to the project, such as the participation of children in a household activity. In the project described herein, all notes were prepared and coded using word-processing programs, and laptop computers were made available to the teachers. Anthropologists and graduate students assisted the teachers in interviewing and provided feedback on the consistency, completeness, and depth of the field notes. Given the constraints on teachers' time, we recommend that they obtain release time from teaching to conduct observations and interviews, and record and edit field notes. Release time, we should point out, is routinely granted for other purposes, such as participating in inservice workshops, so it very well could be used for documenting the knowledge base of the students' homes.

[4]The presentation (August 5, 1991) was before approximately 200 principals and other administrators (including the new superintendent) of the local school district.

López family, a pseudonym, as the focus of this brief talk. The Lópezes are the parents of one of Cathy's students, whom we will call Carlos.

In going into the homes, we carry with us cultural and emotional baggage that tends to color our understanding of interviews and observations. We have fears and assumptions, and perhaps misunderstandings. I for one did not know exactly what to expect when I first went into the López home with Cathy. I had heard talk of dysfunctional homes, lack of discipline, lack of support systems and so forth, but remained skeptical of these negative characterizations. Having done fieldwork before, I was accustomed to this kind of uncertainty.

Cathy Amanti: I, however, was nervous because I was going out in the field for the first time with someone who's had experience doing this type of research. Deborah had experience doing ethnography. I did not, and I was concerned about balancing doing interviews and observations with establishing and maintaining rapport. I was glad, though, that she was there, and I wanted her feedback to make sure I was getting what I should from the visit.

In 2 years of teaching, I had visited only a handful of homes. So, I had been into some of these homes before but only for school-related reasons, for example, delivering a report card, but I'd only visited for a brief period of time. These research visits were to be different—I had to observe, ask questions, take notes, and establish rapport—it was a lot to assimilate, with many activities to coordinate at the same time. One problem I had, for example, was deciding how closely to stick to the questionnaires.

DN: We discussed that and Cathy decided to stick closely to the questionnaire for the time being until she got more comfortable with the procedure. She would conduct the interviews in Spanish, the language of the parents, and we decided that both of us would take notes. I would concentrate more on observations, body language, and overall context, noting suggestions to improve our interview skills and topics to follow up on in future visits. Cathy would conduct the interview and respond to the parents' questions. We decided the first interview, in particular, would be to establish rapport.

We spent a lot of time first discussing the child, for example, Carlos's performance in Cathy's class. Cathy also informed Mrs. López of school activities she might want to be involved in, such as a culminating activity to a literature unit. It took us about 10 minutes to explain the project. The Lópezes had no difficulty understanding the potential benefits to the child, although they were not quite clear about what we wanted from them. That became clear as the interviews progressed. They were glad to participate, although Mrs. López preferred not to be tape-recorded.

CA: I was glad that she was able to tell us that so readily. Each time we went, we talked about the child, and tried to make astute observations. Some of these observations included, for example, noticing and asking about family photos and trophies. Encyclopedias on corner bookshelves provided a natural entrée into topics of family history and social networks of exchange, literacy, and the parents' pride in their child's achievements.

DN: At first, going into the López home, I felt a little nervous, too, because it was my experience to spend an enormous amount of time living with and interacting with the families before gaining the kind of entrée we were hoping to gain in this first interview. I didn't realize then that Cathy, as Carlos's teacher, had a natural entrée into the home, and had an implicit connection with Carlos's parents. I can't emphasize this enough. She was their son's teacher, and so we were treated with a tremendous amount of respect and warmth. I was amazed at how easily and quickly Cathy gained rapport with Mrs. López, and how much the Lópezes opened up to us.

The anthropologist noticed that the teacher held a special status with the family that could help establish the trust necessary for the exchange of information. After making sure that the family understood the purpose of the visit, the teacher started the interview and was surprised by how forthcoming the mother was with information. Cathy, the teacher, also realized that she was starting to blend her role as a teacher with her new role as researcher; as she gathered new information about the family, their history and activities, she started making connections to instructional activities she wanted to develop—a common experience among the teachers and a key moment in our work.

CA: Once we began the interview, it seemed that Ms. López was really enjoying talking about her family, her children, and her life. They had told us this in training, that people would open up once they get talking. For instance, when she got on the subject of the difference between Mexican and U.S. schools, she just kept talking, and we let her go with it, and got more out of it than if we had stayed strictly with the questionnaire. But we had to balance that with our agenda; and for the first interview the main thing was to get the family history so we would have a baseline for discussing literacy, parenting, attitudes toward school, and funds of knowledge.

The issue of balancing use of the questionnaire and letting it go to probe on emergent issues was never totally resolved for me. That's why it was helpful to have an anthropologist with me. For example, during one later interview, I was prepared to accept a short answer from a parent and go on to the next question, but at Deborah's urging, I probed further and ended up with good information on religious devotion as a fund of knowledge, something that I would have missed.

DN: Eventually, we returned to the questionnaire, moving on to discuss the family's labor history.

CA: As we progressed asking questions about family background and labor history, I began to relax, although I was concerned with whether I was getting enough material that would be useful later in developing a learning module. Actually I never totally disengaged from my role as a teacher, and when such things as cross-border trade came up, I thought this would be a great topic to use in my classroom and I tried to figure out how I could capture this resource for teaching.

SEEING BEYOND STEREOTYPES

An important aspect of the teachers' participation in the household research became the more sophisticated understanding they developed about the children and their experiences. There is much teachers do not know about their students or families that could be immediately helpful in the classroom, as the following comments illustrate.

DN: One of the things that we learned about the Lópezes that we didn't know before was the depth of the multicultural experiences their son, Carlos, had in cross-border activities. It wasn't just a superficial experience for him.

CA: Half of the children in my classroom are international travelers, and yet this experience is not recognized or valued because they are Mexican children going to Mexico. Anglo children may spend a summer in France and we make a big deal about it, by asking them to speak to the class about their summer activities! Carlos spends summers in Magdalena, Mexico, yet he's probably rarely been asked to share his experiences with anyone.

His visits to Mexico have been more than 1- or 2-day visits. He spends most summers there. He and his brothers are first-generation born in the United States but their social networks extend into Magdalena. His family's cross-border activities extend back generations. His parents were born in Magdalena. His father began coming to the United States during his summer vacations, when he worked as a migrant worker in

California. He eventually decided to stay here permanently and moved with some friends to Tucson.

Carlos's father's parents are involved in the import–export of major appliances between Sonora and Arizona and there are regular visits of relatives back and forth. His dad says they really live in both places. I'll read some of the notes from my interview with Carlos that describe his life in Sonora:

In Magdalena he and his family stay with different relatives. When he is there he plays with his cousins. They are allowed to wander freely around most of the town. They like to play hide-and-seek and sometimes they are taken places by older relatives. They like to visit a pharmacy that one of his aunts owns, and one of his older cousins is married to someone who works on three ranches.

Sometimes he goes to visit the ranches. Once he got to ride a horse. One thing he likes to do when he visits a ranch is play with a bow and arrow. He says his cousin's husband will give him and his cousins a thousand pesos if they find the arrows. Carlos also reports playing cards when he visits Magdalena and that he has gone fishing near Santa Ana with older cousins and an uncle.

DN: It is precisely through information of these kinds of social activities that we identify funds of knowledge that can be used in the classroom to help improve his academic development.

CA: Furthermore, because of these experiences, Carlos and many of my other students show a great deal of interest in economic issues, because they have seen the difference in the two countries. In immigration law, but also in laws in general; they would ask me why there are so many laws here that they don't have in Mexico. These children have had the background experiences to explore in-depth issues that tie in with a sixth grade curriculum, such as the study of other countries, different forms of government, economic systems, and so on.

Carlos himself is involved in what we could call international commerce. He's a real entrepreneur. Not only does he sell candy from Mexico, according to his mother he'll sell anything he can get anyone to buy, for example, bike parts. His mother says Carlos got the idea to sell candy from other children. We didn't uncover this only through questioning but from being there when one child came over to buy some candy from Carlos. He was really proud when he gave us each a piece to take home. Here was Carlos right in front of our eyes enacting a family fund of knowledge. This experience later turned out to be the seed for the learning module I developed for the project, which I will share with you in a few minutes.

The two presenters then discuss how the specific qualitative methods of study influenced not only the nature of the information collected from the family, yielding data about their experiences and funds of knowledge, but provided them with a more sophisticated understanding of the student, his family, and their social world. This more elaborate understanding helped the teacher transform this information into a useful instructional activity.

DN: It is so important to learn how culture is expressed in students' lives, how students live their worlds. We can't make assumptions about these things. Only a part of that child is present in the classroom. We had little idea what Carlos's life was really like outside of the classroom, and what he knew about the world.

CA: I couldn't have done this work without the anthropological perspective and methodological perspective I learned in the project. Ethnography is different from other forms of educational research. It's open-ended: You go in with an open mind, not prejudging, being totally receptive to everything you hear and see. I didn't want to know only if the parents read stories to their children or how many books they had. I wasn't tallying the hours of TV the children watched either. I feel that I learned much more than that with a greater breadth of knowledge because I was not narrow in my focus.

DN: Carlos is embedded in a home and world, continuous with his family's history and in a culture that is at times discontinuous from that found in school. How does one take advantage of these resources in the home? This experience of going into the home, taking off your lens for a moment, trying to step outside your assumptions to see Carlos on his own terms, in his own turf, is one way to do this.

We learned a lot during these three interviews that fractured stereotypes that we had heard others say about these households. Carlos's parents not only care, but have a very strong philosophy of child rearing that is supportive of education, including learning English. They have goals of a university education for their children, instill strong values of respect for others, and possess a tremendous amount of pride and a strong sense of identity—in addition to the more practical knowledge in which their children share on a regular basis. These values are not unique to this family. All of the households we visited possess similar values and funds of knowledge that can be tapped for use in the classrooms.

But the workshops and fieldwork experience are just the beginning. There's the extensive reflection and writing-up stage, the record of the experiences, from which we read segments a few minutes ago. This reflection process is not to be underemphasized, for it is not just what people say that matters, but the subtext, and our observations and interpretation; for example, the way Mrs. López's eyes lit up when she showed us the trophy her son had won in the science fair, Mr. López's pride in his philosophy of child rearing, and so forth. And then there is the translation of this material into viable lessons for the classroom.

The presenters pointed out that it is the teacher, not the anthropologist, who is ultimately the bridge between the students' world, theirs and their family's funds of knowledge, and the classroom experience. However, teachers need not work alone. They can form part of study groups, social networks that will provide the needed assistance and support in analyzing information and in elaborating instructional practices.

EXPERIMENTING WITH PRACTICE

The presentation concluded with a description by Cathy, the teacher, of the development of a theme study, or learning module, as we called them, based on information gathered from the households. Notice the emphasis on the inquiry process, on the students becoming active learners, and on strategically using their social contacts outside the classroom to access new knowledge for the development of their studies. Her summary follows.

CA: After we had completed our field work and written field notes for all our interviews, it truly was left up to us, the teachers, to decide how we were going to use the knowledge we had gained about our students and their families. We spent 2 days with consultants and everyone else who had been working on the project and brainstormed and bounced ideas off each other. I worked with two other teachers from my school, and together we developed a learning module with a rather unusual theme—candy. You've already heard that Deborah and I witnessed Carlos selling Mexican candy to a neighbor. The fifth grade teacher I worked with also uncovered this theme. He interviewed a parent who is an expert at making all kinds of candy. In a truly collaborative effort, we outlined a week's worth of activities we could use in our classes.

To focus students' thinking on the theme, I had students free-associate with the topic. I recorded their ideas on a large piece of white paper on the board. Next, I had them come up with a definition for the word *candy*. This was not as easy as you might think. They'd mentioned gum and sunflower seeds while brainstorming, which I wasn't sure should be included in this category. But I didn't tell them this because I wanted them to use their analytical skills to come up with their own definition. Actually, they got stuck deciding whether salty things like *pica-limón* and *saladitos* (Mexican snacks that include salt and spices) were candy. Next they categorized all the candies they'd mentioned.

After that we used the "know-want-learn" (KWL) method to organize our unit. For those not familiar with this method, we used a three-column chart. In the first column we recorded everything the students know about the topic. In the next column, we recorded what they want to know. The third column, is used at the end of the unit to record what the students learned during the study. After working with the project consultant, I added another W, or "want," at the end of the chart—a fourth column, something new for me—to record new questions students had, to help them see that learning is ongoing, that it does not consist of discrete chunks of knowledge. We then surveyed and graphed favorite candies of the class.

With the assistance of the teacher, the students pursued their interests by focusing their inquiry on a narrower topic and by specifying a research question. As is common in research, the class relied on all their resources, including the expertise of one of the parents, to elaborate their work. Notice, however, that this was not a typical parent visit to correct or sort papers; the purpose of the parent's visit was to contribute intellectually to the students' academic activity. This parent, in effect, became a cognitive resource for the students and teacher in this classroom (see also Moll & Greenberg, 1990).

CA: Next, we became a research team. Students chose one of the questions they'd generated to answer. They chose, "What ingredients are used in the production of candy?" I framed the pursuit of the answer using the version of the scientific method we use in schools. After writing their question on the board, the students developed a procedure to answer their question; then they hypothesized what ingredients they'd find on the candy labels they brought in the next day.

The next day, after students had made a class list of ingredients in the candy samples they'd brought in, they graphed the frequency of occurrence of the ingredients they'd found. Then I had them divide the ingredients into two lists—one of ingredients they'd found in the Mexican candy samples and one of ingredients they'd found in U.S. candy samples. We all learned something that day. We were all surprised to see that fewer ingredients are used in Mexican candies and that they don't use artificial flavors or coloring—just vegetable dyes and real fruit.

The next day one of the parents of my students, Mrs. Rodríguez, came in to teach us how to make *pipitoria*, a Mexican candy treat. This turned out to be the highlight of our unit. Before she came in that morning, the students divided up to make advertising posters and labels for the candy because we were going to sell what we made at the school talent show. When Mrs. Rodríguez arrived, she became the teacher. While the candy was cooking, she talked to the class for over an hour and taught all of us not only how to make different kinds of candy, but also such things as the difference in U.S. and Mexican food consumption and production, nutritional value of candy, and more. My respect and awe of Mrs. Rodríguez grew by leaps and bounds that morning. Finally, the students packaged and priced their candy.

The unit concludes, somewhat prematurely, as the teacher notes, with the students summarizing and reflecting on their work, and by identifying further topics for future research. The teacher, in turn, has become a "mediator"—providing strategic assistance that would facilitate the students' inquiry and work.

CA: The last day of the unit, students wrote summaries of what they'd learned and we recorded it on our chart. Then they began to formulate new questions. Examples of their new questions are "What is candy like in Africa?" and "What candy do they eat in China?" As you can see, if we'd had time to continue our unit, our studies would have taken us all over the world. We did, however, cover many areas of the curriculum in one short week—math, science, health, consumer education, cross-cultural practices, advertising, and food production.

From the questions the students came up with alone, we could have continued investigating using innumerable research and critical thinking skills for a considerable part of the year. If we had continued this type of activity all year, by the end we would have been an experienced research team, and my role would have been to act as facilitator helping the students answer their own questions.

CONCLUSION

We have presented a single aspect of a broader, multidimensional research project: teachers as co-researchers using qualitative methods to study household knowledge and drawing on this knowledge to develop a participatory pedagogy. The insights gleaned from approaching the homes ethnographically, and adapting the method to the educational goals of the project, were a result of a genuine teacher-researcher (in this case, teacher–anthropologist) collaboration. We have learned that it is feasible and useful to have teachers visit households for research purposes. These are neither casual visits nor school-business visits, but visits in which the teachers assume the role of the learner, and in doing so help establish a fundamentally new, more symmetrical relationship with the parents of the students.

This relationship can become the basis for the exchange of knowledge about family or school matters, reducing the insularity of classrooms, and contributing to the academic content and lessons. It can also become, as illustrated above, the catalyst for forming research teams among the students to study topics of interest to them, or important to the teacher, or for achieving curricular goals.

Our concept of funds of knowledge is innovative in its special relevance to teaching, we believe, and contrasts with the more general term *culture*, or with the concept of a culture-sensitive curriculum, and with the latter's reliance on folkloric displays such as storytelling, arts, crafts, and dance performance. Although the term *funds of knowledge* is not meant to replace the anthropological concept of culture, it is more precise for our purposes because of its emphasis on strategic knowledge and related activities essential in households' functioning, development, and well-being. It is specific funds of knowledge pertaining to the social, economic, and productive activities of people in a local region, not "culture" in its broader, anthropological sense, that we seek to incorporate strategically into classrooms.

Indispensable in this scenario are the research tools—the theory, qualitative methods of study, and ways of analyzing and interpreting data. These are what allow the teachers (and others) to assume, authentically, the role of researchers in household or classroom settings. They are also what help redefine the homes of the students as rich in funds of knowledge that represent important resources for educational change.

We are currently starting the next phase of study, involving teachers in five different schools serving both Mexican and Native American students.[5] The research design remains the same: developing our understanding of households and classrooms and collaborating with teachers in conducting the research and in developing academically rigorous instructional innovations. Now, however, we have teachers with research experience helping us organize the study groups, developing further the methodology for doing the home investigations, conceptualizing and implementing promising instructional activities, and evaluating the project. In this new study we plan to include principals, as co-researchers, and parents in the study groups as an attempt to rethink our respective roles and develop our collective funds of knowledge about teaching and learning.

---

[5]One of our goals for 1992–1993 is to develop the project in other regions of the country through collaborative ventures. For example, we are currently piloting an initial teacher–anthropologist component to collect baseline and background data on target schools and communities including demography, economy, migration, educational achievement level, and community resources, before developing questionnaires and conducting home interviews in different regions of the country. We are also developing assessment procedures to document project success, especially the academic benefits to the students, in order to improve our accountability to the schools and communities in which we work.

One of the hallmarks of qualitative research is that strategies often evolve within the process of doing. As teachers, administrators, and parents become more aware of the linkages that can be created using this methodology and become comfortable with the redefinition of roles that it entails, new strategies of implementation will emerge that are driven by the needs of the target community. As the research unfolds, the constitutive nature of the inquiry process becomes apparent, as teacher, researcher, parent, child, and administrator jointly create and negotiate the form and function of the exploration.

REFLECTION QUESTIONS

1. How does the conversation between the anthropologist and the teacher connect with the idea of theory into practice?
2. What do the authors mean by reciprocity?
3. In what ways are teachers also researchers?

REFERENCES

Berliner, D. C. (1985). Laboratory settings and the study of teacher education. *Journal of Teacher Education, 36,* 2–8.

Goodman, Y. (1989). Roots of the whole-language movement. *The Elementary School Journal, 92,* 113–127.

Greenberg, J. B. (1989, April). *Funds of knowledge: Historical constitution, social distribution, and transmission.* Paper presented at the annual meeting of the Society for Applied Anthropology, Santa Fe, NM.

Heyman, J. (1990). The emergence of the waged life course on the United States–Mexico border. *American Ethnologist, 17,* 348–359.

Keefe, S., & Padilla, A. (1987). *Chicano ethnicity.* Albuquerque, NM: University of New Mexico Press.

La Fontaine, J. (1986). An anthropological perspective on children in social worlds. In M. Richards & P. Light (Eds.), *Children of social worlds: Development in a social context* (pp. 10–30). Cambridge, UK: Polity Press.

Laboratory of Comparative Human Cognition. (1982). A model system for the study of learning difficulties. *The Quarterly Newsletter of the Laboratory of Comparative Human Cognition, 4,* 39–66.

Martínez, O. J. (1988). *Troublesome border.* Tucson, AZ: The University of Arizona Press.

McDermott, R. P. (1987). The explanation of minority school failure. Again. *Anthropology and Education Quarterly, 18,* 361–364.

Moll, L. C., & Díaz, S. (1987). Change as the goal of educational research. *Anthropology and Education Quarterly, 18,* 300–311.

Moll, L. C., & Greenberg, J. (1990). Creating zones of possibilities: Combining social contexts for instruction. In L. C. Moll (Ed.), *Vygotsky and education* (pp. 319–348). Cambridge, UK: Cambridge University Press.

Moll, L. C., Vélez-Ibáñez, C., Greenberg, J., Whitmore, K., Saavedra, E., Dworin, J., & Andrade, R. (1990). *Community knowledge and classroom practice: Combining resources for literacy instruction* (OBEMLA Contract No. 300-87-0131). Tucson, AZ: University of Arizona College of Education and Bureau of Applied Research in Anthropology.

Tapia, J. (1991). *Cultural reproduction: Funds of knowledge as survival strategies in the Mexican American community.* Unpublished doctoral dissertation, University of Arizona.

Taylor, D., & Dorsey-Gaines, C. (1988). *Growing up literate: Learning from inner city families.* Portsmouth, NH: Heinemann.

Tharp, R., & Gallimore, R. (1988). *Rousing minds to life: Teaching, learning, and schooling in social context.* Cambridge, UK: Cambridge University Press.

Vélez-Ibáñez, C. G. (1988). Networks of exchange among Mexicans in the U.S. and Mexico: Local level mediating responses to national and international transformations. *Urban Anthropology, 17,* 27–51.

Vélez-Ibáñez, C. G. (1993). U.S. Mexicans in the borderlands: Being poor without the underclass. In J. Moore & R. Pinderhughes (Eds.), *The barrios: Latinos and the underclass debate* (pp. 195–220). New York: Russell Sage Foundation.

Vélez-Ibáñez, C. G., & Greenberg, J. (1989). *Formation and transformation of funds of knowledge among U.S. Mexican households in the context of the borderlands.* Paper presented at the annual meeting of the American Anthropological Association, Washington, DC.

Vélez-Ibáñez, C., Moll, L. C., González, N., & Neff, D. (1991). *Promoting learning and educational delivery and quality among "at-risk" Mexican and Native American elementary school children in Tucson, Arizona: A pilot project.* Final Report to W. K. Kellogg Foundation. Tucson, AZ: University of Arizona Bureau of Applied Research in Anthropology.

Chapter 5

Funds of Knowledge for Teaching in Latino Households*

Norma González
Luis Moll
Martha Floyd Tenery
Anna Rivera
Pat Rendón
Raquel Gonzales
Cathy Amanti
University of Arizona

"Home visits are not new. I was doing home visits 20 years ago in the Model Cities program," asserted the principal of one elementary school. Her point is well-taken. The notion of home visits is neither novel nor unusual. Teachers may opt to visit the home of a student to discuss a particular problem, such as a student's disruptive behavior in the classroom, or to pinpoint difficulties with a particular subject matter. The teacher may simply introduce him- or herself to parents and elicit their cooperation. Some school programs require home visits for the teachers to mentor parents on the teaching of reading or math to their children, to provide suggestions on how to help the students with their homework, or to distribute books and supplies.

In this chapter, we describe a very different type of household visit by teachers. These are research visits, for the express purpose of identifying and documenting knowledge that exists in students' homes. In contrast to other visits, these visits are part of a "systematic, intentional inquiry by teachers," as Lytle and Cochran-Smith (1990, p. 84) define teacher research. We are convinced that these research visits, in conjunction with collaborative ethnographic reflection, can engender pivotal and transformative shifts in teacher attitudes and behaviors and in relations between households and schools and between parents and teachers (see González & Amanti, 1992; Moll, Amanti, Neff, & González, 1992).

---

*This article first appeared in the journal *Urban Education* (1995, Vol. 29, pp. 444–471) and is reprinted with permission from Sage Publications

Instead of presenting the (university-based) researchers' interpretations of ongoing work, as is common in these reports, we have chosen to emphasize the participating teachers' insights on the project: what they consider relevant and important to communicate to others, especially to other teachers, as a result of their own inquiry. Lytle and Cochran-Smith (1990) have noted that:

> Conspicuous by their absence from the literature of research on teaching are the voices of teachers themselves—the questions and problems teachers pose, the frameworks they use to interpret and improve their practice, and the ways teachers themselves define and understand their work lives. (p. 83)

In order to make explicit the transformative nature of the household visits, we have therefore selected a multivocal discourse that attempts to demystify the traditional authority of university-based researchers. As this research evolved, the authentic collaboration between teachers and researchers fashioned an alteration in the conventionally asymmetrical exchange between university and schools. In brief, we attempt to provide insights that corroborate the assertion that elementary school teachers are as capable of theoretical reflection as university professors (Savage, 1988).

In what follows, we first present an overview of the research project, highlighting what we refer to as funds of knowledge, a key theoretical concept in our work. This section is intended to provide the general context of the research and the goals of the investigation. A critical assumption in our work is that educational institutions have stripped away the view of working-class minority students as emerging from households rich in social and intellectual resources. Rather than focusing on the knowledge these students bring to school and using it as a foundation for learning, the emphasis has been on what these students lack in terms of the forms of language and knowledge sanctioned by the schools. This emphasis on "disadvantages" has provided justification for lowered expectations in schools and inaccurate portrayals of the children and their families.

We then introduce the teachers in the project and describe their participation in the study, including selected aspects of their research training. We follow with a summary of their insights, gained from their research efforts, regarding three key domains of change:

1. The development of teachers as qualitative researchers
2. The formation of new relationships with families
3. The redefinition of local households as containing important social and intellectual resources for teaching

We conclude with a discussion of the minimal conditions necessary to conduct this work in other settings. As we emphasize, we offer no "recipes" for replication elsewhere. Instead we suggest the importance of developing at each site a community of learners, where teachers are offered a format to think, reflect, and analyze with others and to produce the knowledge necessary to transform their teaching in positive ways. In describing such communities of learners, Ayers (1992) remarked that "people learn best when they are actively exploring, thinking, asking their own questions, and constructing knowledge through discovery" (p. 20). As teachers actively coconstruct the theory and practice behind research-based household visits, the challenging sense that knowledge is open-ended, active, and continuous can create new and meaningful environments of learning for all concerned.

THE RESEARCH PROJECT

A central goal of our project is to draw on the knowledge and other resources found in local households for the development of classroom practice. We can summarize our three main project components as follows:

1. *Community:* Featuring an ethnographic study of the origin, use, and distribution of funds of knowledge among households in a predominantly Mexican, working-class community of Tucson, Arizona
2. *After-school "lab" or study groups:* These are settings especially created to enhance the collaboration between teachers and researchers; to discuss research findings; and to plan, develop, and support innovations in instruction
3. *Schools:* Featuring classroom studies to examine existing methods of instruction and implement innovations based on the household study of funds of knowledge and conceptualized at the after-school sites

These three components allow us to conduct research simultaneously in several related areas and to shift our primary unit of study from classrooms to households or shift from a focus on teachers to a focus on the students, without losing sight of the interconnectedness of the settings or of the activities we are analyzing.

In terms of the community component, our emphasis has been on understanding local households historically. This approach involves understanding the sociopolitical and economic context of the households and analyzing their social history (see, e.g., Vélez-Ibáñez, 1988). This history includes their origins and development and, most prominently for our purposes, the labor history of the families, which reveals some of the accumulated funds of knowledge of the households. Funds of knowledge refers to those historically developed and accumulated strategies (skills, abilities, ideas, practices) or bodies of knowledge that are essential to a household's functioning and well-being (for details, see Greenberg, 1989; Vélez-Ibáñez & Greenberg, 1992). A key finding from our research is that these funds of knowledge are abundant and diverse; they may include information about, for example, farming and animal husbandry, associated with households' rural origins, or knowledge about construction and building, related to urban occupations; or knowledge about many other matters, such as trade, business, and finance on both sides of the U.S.–Mexico border.

We are particularly interested in how families develop social networks that interconnect them with their environments (most importantly with other households) and how their social relationships facilitate the development and exchange of resources, including funds of knowledge (see, e.g., Moll & Greenberg, 1990; Vélez-Ibáñez & Greenberg, 1992). A key characteristic of these exchanges is their reciprocity. As Vélez-Ibáñez (1988) has observed, reciprocity represents an "attempt to establish a social relationship on an enduring basis. Whether symmetrical or asymmetrical, the exchange expresses and symbolizes human social interdependence" (p. 142). That is, reciprocal practices establish serious obligations based on the assumption of confianza (mutual trust), which is reestablished or confirmed with each exchange, and they lead to the development of long-term relationships. Each exchange with kinsmen, friends, neighbors, or teachers in our case, entails not only many practical activities (everything from home and automobile repair to animal husbandry and music), but constantly provides contexts in which learning can occur—contexts, for example, where children have ample opportunities to participate in activities with people they trust (Moll & Greenberg, 1990).

PARAMETERS OF TEACHER PARTICIPATION

Another key feature of the project is the close collaboration of anthropologists and educators, especially in the work with classroom teachers. We have been experimenting with after-school teacher study groups (labs) as contexts for informing, assisting, and supporting the teachers' work—contexts, in other words, for the exchange of funds of knowledge between teachers and researchers (for details, see Moll et al., 1990).

These after-school settings function as mediating structures in forming strategic connections between the household fieldwork and classroom practice. After-school lab meeting locales alternate among the four schools and the university. Participants include the four teachers involved; a teacher-researcher who is on leave of absence from the school district and is pursuing graduate work in anthropology; university researchers in education, anthropology, and math education; and graduate students in education. Meetings take place every two weeks, although they are sometimes preempted because of school activities. Within the study group framework, a combination of ethnographic field methods are analyzed, and participant observation, open-ended interviewing strategies, life histories, and case studies are incorporated into the joint inquiry of household and community ethnography. In this way, the ethnographic experience becomes a collaborative endeavor, not based on a lone researcher venturing out into the field, but a multiauthored discourse constructed out of experiences as participant, field-worker, teacher, and anthropologist. Mentoring functions switch back and forth as researchers and teachers each manipulate their own sphere of expertise. As teachers enter the households as learners, so the researchers enter the teacher study groups as learners. As previously noted, reciprocity as a theoretical construct has formed the basis for the exchange between households and schools, and this construct has been paralleled to incorporate the relationships between teachers and researchers. Within this interactive and constitutive process, the role of the teacher is defined in nontraditional ways. The redefined relationship is that of colleagues, mutually engaged in refining methodology, interpretation, and practice (see González & Amanti, 1992). In this way, "curriculum, research and learning become matters of authorship rather than authority" (Woodward, 1985).

As is often the case with anthropological research, certain insights and conclusions came in a post hoc fashion, and the evolution of the teacher study groups is a case in point. The original prototype of the teacher labs consisted of the discussion of household visits and data. However, the actual fieldwork was not conducted by teachers, but by anthropologists. Ironically, although a participatory model of learning was advocated in work with children, the original teacher labs relied on a transmission model: Information was presented, and teachers received it without actively involving themselves in the production of this knowledge (see Moll et al., 1990). It became apparent that although worthwhile information about the forms and functions of the households was being transmitted to the teachers through the study groups, true ownership of the data was not taking place. Teachers were disconnected from the actual context of the household. The admonition suggested by Spindler and Spindler (1990)—that "learning about human cultures must occur empathetically and emotionally as well as conceptually or cognitively" (p. 108)—began to take on transcendent importance. The connection of the household and teacher could not come about through a field researcher as intermediary: The bond had to be formed interpersonally, evocatively, and reciprocally.

On the few occasions when teachers did accompany field researchers into homes, the teachers had a noticeably ready access to the households, which the anthropologists had to labor to achieve. For a child's teacher, entrée into the household in a position of respect and honor was the standard. The households evinced no suspicion of motives, nor mistrust of how the information was to be used, circumstances which had at times plagued the anthropologists. The common bond of concern for the child overrode most constraints. In addition, it was found that once the teachers were involved in a dialog with the households, they were effortlessly asking much better learning questions about the child's activities. It became apparent that for the teachers to know the households, a ethnographic method of approaching the households could be productive. Thus, the stage was set for the entrance of teachers as ethnographers into the households of their students.

THE TEACHERS

Four teachers were recruited to work as teacher-researchers. Recruitment of teachers was carried out through personal and previous research contacts. The number of teachers was purposely limited in order to maintain a small, tight-knit group which would remain together for a prolonged amount of time. Initially the four teachers represented two schools, but by the beginning of the second year, two had moved to new schools. All of the schools are located within working-class, predominantly Mexican neighborhoods. Two Mexican-origin and two Anglo teachers participated in the study, all of them fluent in Spanish.

Anna Rivera, a bilingual classroom teacher for 15 years, is presently an elementary school principal, although she was a bilingual first-grade teacher at the time of the study. She completed her doctorate in elementary education and has taught the full range from prekindergarten to graduate courses at the university.

Patricia Rendón has been teaching since 1969. She received her undergraduate degree in Ohio and taught there for 4½ years. With a background in languages, she moved to Medellín, Colombia, and later to Bogotá. She taught K–8 in different bilingual settings in Colombia for 9 years. Since moving to Arizona, she has been both a monolingual and bilingual teacher. She received her MA in 1991 and presently teaches fourth and fifth graders in a bilingual classroom.

Martha Floyd Tenery has been a teacher in various settings for 9 years. She has taught as an elementary classroom teacher, a bilingual resource teacher, an English as a second language (ESL) teacher for Spanish speakers, a teaching assistant in the Japanese Department, and as an English teacher at Anhui University in China. She recently completed her doctoral studies in language, reading and culture.

Raquel Gonzales has been a bilingual kindergarten teacher for 6 years. She is presently finishing her MA in counseling and guidance.

TEACHERS AS LEARNERS

Once teachers entered households as learners—as researchers seeking to construct a template for understanding and tapping into the concrete life experiences of their students—the conventional model of home visits was turned on its head. No attempt would be made to teach the parents or to visit for punitive reasons. This shift constituted a radical departure from household visits carried out in other programs that incorporate the home visit concept (Vélez-Ibáñez, Moll, González, & Amanti, 1992). The after-school labs were restructured to accommodate these shifts, and the ethnographic method, rather than household visits, emerged as the vehicle for participant observations. Within the lab setting, ethnography surfaced as more than techniques. It became the filter through which the households were conceptualized as multidimensional and vibrant entities. This new perspective reflected a corresponding shift in teachers' theoretical paradigms. As has been noted (Spindler & Spindler, 1990, p. 20), in teaching anthropology "a state of mind is more important than specific technique"; or as Segal (1990, p. 121) put it: "The question is: How can we go about teaching an anthropological imagination?"

Through the mediating structure of the after-school study groups, teachers were provided with the forum to engage in reflexive thought. Although specific techniques in participant observation, fieldnote writing, interviewing, and eliciting of life histories were presented, the focus was continuously on the discourse, on the joint construction of knowledge. Ethnographic fieldwork became not one lone researcher grappling with overwhelming data, but a collaborative and reflexive process in which teachers and researchers shared insights and information. However, reflexivity in fieldwork is not unproblematic. Indeed one of the missions of the study groups became overcoming the paradox of gaining understanding without falling into the trap of inaction. In the face of the sometimes overwhelming social and structural factors that face the students and their families, it would be easy to simply "give up." One teacher (Martha Floyd Tenery) voiced this sentiment as she reflected on her initial pessimism:

> I did not realize it at the time, but I used to believe that my students had limited opportunities in life. I thought that poverty was the root of many of their problems, and that this was something too big for me to change as a teacher.

Through the reflexive discourse of the study groups, this hopelessness was short-circuited. The teachers no longer felt isolated from each other, or the community, as this same teacher explained:

> This fatalistic obsession of mine has slowly melted away as I have gotten to know my students and their families. I believe this transformation is the most

important one I have made. Its ramifications have reached far beyond the classroom.

TEACHING AN "ANTHROPOLOGICAL IMAGINATION": TEACHERS AS REFLECTIVE PRACTITIONERS

This is not to say that the road has been smooth. Initially, teachers reported a struggle with shedding notions of educational research based on quantifiable variables that must be meticulously controlled. Yet a realization gradually emerged that reflexively oriented work needs to "begin with the understanding that systematic thinking about one's own experiences is a valid source of some knowledge and insight" (Segal, 1990). A reliance on anything but empirical data and a shift to reflexive observation, in many cases, left the teachers feeling overwhelmed with the sheer complexity of the task.

Anna Rivera reported feeling "like a private investigator—like you're watching everything. What are they cooking? How do you make this, how do you do that? The home visit was totally different from what I had done before." The myriad of details, of participating and observing, of interviewing and audiorecording and note taking, of being both the teacher and ethnographer, was at the outset of the first interview a numbing experience. This hesitance soon wore off as teachers became more and more comfortable with the process. Martha Floyd Tenery reported after her series of interviews:

> I remember at first I was scared to death. Would the family be skeptical? What would they think of me? Would they feel uncomfortable? I remember thinking all kinds of things. And now, it seems, like, what is the big deal? I can do this, and I can do it well.

When questioned about their own particular transformations, teachers overwhelmingly cited two factors: the orientation to the households as containing funds of knowledge and the reflexive process and debriefings after the visits. Anna Rivera affirmed that "most of the change had come during the study groups. I heard something, or I said something during the study group." Teachers in the study group affirmed their theoretical development as an aftermath of the actual practice of household visits. They reiterated that theory and practice are really two sides of the same coin, and one without the other is limited.

The reflexive mode injected into the study groups noticeably altered the ways in which participants viewed their own participant observation as it engendered an examination of underlying beliefs and rationalizations. As other qualitative researchers have stated, "people who have never before articulated their beliefs and customs now are asked to do so and what may never before have been examined has now become verbally objectified, so that it is at least present for examination" (Ely, 1991, p. 197). One teacher, commenting on the reflexive process, stated:

> That was the only time I had ever talked about how I was teaching and why I was teaching that way, and how that related to how I perceive children to learn. At all the other in-services or teacher meetings I had ever attended, I was talked at, I was fed information, and it was more technique, how to do something, not why.

The study groups offered a safe, nonjudgmental environment for thinking out loud about classroom practice as well as about household functions. Participants in the study groups were able to voice their changing ideas about households and the subsequent transformation that the observations and reflection provoked.

Throughout the study groups, anthropological inquiry was presented as more of a state of mind than a technique. However, the theoretical implications of technique became conspicuous in several ways, and an effort to systematize reflexivity emerged. As part of the ethnographic experience, teachers were asked to select two to three students from their classrooms. No formal attempt at representativeness was made. Households were visited three times, and the interviews lasted an average of two hours each. An interview of the target child was also conducted. Ages of the students ranged from kindergarten through fifth grade. Teachers were asked to tape-record the interviews (if the family was comfortable with it) and to conduct the interview as conversationally as possible. Teachers were paid (when possible) as project participants for their extra duty time.

Following their forays into the field, teachers were asked to write fieldnotes based on each interview, and these fieldnotes became the basis for the study group discussions. Teachers overwhelmingly remarked on the time-consuming nature of this process. After a hectic school day, taking the time to conduct interviews that often stretched two or three hours and to later invest several hours in writing fieldnotes was an exacting price to pay for a connection to the households. They cited this one factor as precluding wholesale teacher participation in this project. Yet, in spite of the strain of the task, the teachers felt that the effort was worth it. The reflexive process involved in transcription enabled the teachers to obtain elusive insights that could easily be overlooked. As they replayed the audiotapes and referred to notes, connections and hunches began to emerge. The household began to take on a multidimensional reality that had taken root in the interview and reached its fruition in reflexive writing.

Writing gave form and substance to the connection forged between the household and the teacher.

A second ethnographic technique involved the writing of a personal field journal. Not all teachers opted to do this. One teacher who kept an extensive journal noted:

> Transformation occurs over a long period of time and is quite subtle in its nature. Elements of my transformation would have been elusive had I not documented them along the way. I recognize this as I look back and cannot remember having those feelings/beliefs.

Another teacher lamented the fact that she had not kept the journal. She did not follow the suggestion and bemoans the fact in retrospect:

> I don't remember when I stopped feeling and thinking this way or that way. I don't think it was an overnight thing. I think all of that is just changing little by little. If I had kept a journal, I could go back and read and say, okay, this is where I first started thinking about it.

These comments highlight that an awareness of the documentation of the reflexive process began to take shape.

A third field technique involved questionnaires. Teachers felt that the use of questionnaires signaled a shift in approaching the households as learners. Entering the household with questions rather than answers provided the context for an inquiry-based visit, and the teachers considered the questionnaires a meaningful resource. They addressed such diverse areas as family histories, family networks, labor history, educational history, language use, and child-rearing ideologies. Within each topic, questions were left open-ended, and teachers probed and elicited information as the interviews proceeded. Interviews were, as teachers commented, more of a conversation than an interview, and one teacher noted that with the tape-recording of the interview she was free to be a conversational partner without the task of furious note-taking. Teachers used the questionnaire as a guide rather than a protocol, suggesting possible areas to explore and incorporating previous knowledge into formulating new questions. Interviews were not conducted as a unilateral extraction of information, as teachers were encouraged to make connections with their own lives and histories as they elicited narratives from the families.

These issues illustrate the critical effect that methodology had in learning a different way of visiting homes. Teachers often voiced the notion that "methodology helps to implant theory and represents its embodiment particularly in this project, which is very experiential." The theoretical orientation to the households as containing funds of knowledge was critical in teacher transformation. But equally as important in the transformative process was the reflection generated by the collaborative effort of a collective ethnographic experience.

FUNDS OF KNOWLEDGE AS TRANSFORMATIVE PRINCIPLE

Teachers voiced two underlying transformative potentials in viewing the households as repositories of funds of knowledge. The first concerns a shift in the definition of culture of the households, and the second concerns an alternative to the deficit model of households.

The first shift owes its genesis to the prevailing trends in anthropological literature away from an integrated, harmonious, univocal version of culture. It seemed to us that the prevailing notions of culture in the schools center around observable and tangible surface markers: dances, food, folklore, and the like. Viewing households within a processual view of culture, rooted in the lived contexts and practices of their students and families, engendered a realization that culture is a dynamic concept and not a static grab bag of tamales, quinceañeras, and cinco de mayo celebrations (see González, 1992). Instead teachers learned how households network in informal market exchanges. They learned how cross-border activities made "mini-ethnographers" of their students. And most importantly, they found that students acquired a multidimensional depth and breadth from their participation in household life (Moll et al., 1992).

Cathy Amanti, a teacher who participated in an earlier pilot phase of this project and is now on leave pursuing a graduate degree in anthropology (and is a researcher on the project), evoked what this realization signified (from González & Amanti, 1992):

> The impact of participating in this project went far beyond my expectations. My approach to curriculum and my relationship with my students are two areas where the impact was most profound. In the area of curriculum, as a teacher of predominantly Mexican and U.S. Mexican students, I believed in the importance of acknowledging and including aspects of my students' culture in my classroom practice. However, though teachers are trained to build on students' prior knowledge, they are given no guidelines for how to go about eliciting this knowledge. Also, the multicultural curriculum available in schools perpetuates an outdated notion of culture as special and isolated ritual events and artifacts, the kind featured in National Geographic. Its focus on holidays, "typical" foods and "traditional" artifacts covers a very narrow range of my students' experiences and ignores the reality of life in the borderlands, which often falls outside the norms of traditional Anglo or Mexican culture.
>
> Participating in this project helped me to reformulate my concept of culture from being very static to more practice-oriented. This broadened con-

ceptualization turned out to be the key which helped me develop strategies to include the knowledge my students were bringing to school in my classroom practice. It was the kind of information elicited through the questionnaires that was the catalyst for this transformation. I sought information on literacy, parenting attitudes, family and residential history, and daily activities. But I was not looking for static categories, or judging the households' activities in these areas according to any standards—my own or otherwise. I simply elicited and described the context within which my students were being socialized. What this meant was that if the father of one of my students did not have a "job" I did not stop the inquiry there. The format of the questionnaires encouraged me to continue probing to discover any type of activity that the father and mother were doing to ensure the survival of the household.

If we were simply eliciting labor history associated with categories of work in the formal economic sector, we would risk both devaluing and missing many of the experiences of our students and their families. This has clear implications for how we approach culture. If our idea of culture is bound up with notions of authenticity and tradition, how much practice will we ignore as valueless and what will this say to our students? But if our idea of culture is expanded to include the ways we organize and make sense of all our experiences, we have many more resources to draw upon in the classroom.

The second transformative effect of the funds of knowledge perspective deals with debunking the pervasive idea of households as lacking worthwhile knowledge and experiences. Teachers were particularly concerned about reiterating this theme, as they felt that many educators continue to hold an unquestioning and negative view of the community and households. Closely related to this point, teachers said that some educators approach the community they work in with an attitude of "How can they help *me*? This places the entire burden on the community to reach out to the school." One teacher (Martha Floyd Tenery) stated:

> It's never "How can *I* do this?" They feel if parents don't show up for school events it means they don't care. But there could be many reasons why the parents can't come to these meetings such as conflicts with work, or not knowing the language.

However, this same teacher recognizes that she still thinks and says many things that could be construed as emanating from a similar mindset. "You have to disprove what you've been taught," she said. Another teacher (Anna Rivera) remarked on "unlearning" her previous training in household visits: "Can you imagine what kind of subtle message comes across when someone comes into your home to teach you something?"

Each teacher, as she came to know the households personally and emotionally, came away changed in some way. Some were struck by the sheer survival of the household against seemingly overwhelming odds. Others were astonished at the sacrifices the households made in order to gain a better education for their children. They all found parents who were engineers, teachers, and small business owners in Mexico, who pulled up stakes and now work in jobs far below their capabilities in order to obtain a "better life and education" for their children. They found immigrant families living with 15 people in a household, with all adult men and women working, in order to pay for rent and everyday necessities. As Raquel Gonzales noted:

> I came away from the household visits changed in the way that I viewed the children. I became aware of the whole child, who had a life outside the classroom, and that I had to be sensitive to that. I feel that I was somewhat sensitive before the visits, but it doesn't compare with my outlook following the visits.

What follows are four brief case study examples[1] based on the teachers' experiences in doing research in their own students' households.

The Estrada Family (Anna Rivera)

I have been in contact with the Estrada family since August 16, 1991. During the last year and a half I have visited the family during five formal interviews, two birthday parties, one *quinceañera* (an adolescent girl's debutante party), and several informal visits. I summarize here what I have learned about this family, describe how I used that knowledge in my teaching, and reflect on what changes I have undergone.

My first contact with the family occurred before the first day of school. I was preparing the classroom for the first day of school when I heard a knock at the door. In walked a family who wanted to introduce themselves to their new school. Mr. and Mrs. Estrada wanted their third-grade daughter to become acquainted with the school and her teacher, me. In Spanish, they shared that they believed education to be important and that they decided to visit their third-grade daughter's classroom and their kindergarten daughter's classroom in order to make the transition to a new school a positive experience. They had in tow a 4-year-old son because they wanted him to know what was expected.

Through the interviews, I learned that the family was quite extensive. I met the middle-school-age son, two high-school-age daughters, a maternal grandfather, and a maternal uncle, all of whom shared the same household. The trailer they lived in was located among 14 other trailers in a recently developed trailer park.

---

[1]The first two examples were authored by the teachers; the final two were narrated to Norma González. All household and family names have been changed to preserve anonymity.

The living room included a bookcase of reference books in Spanish. The father had been trained in Hermosillo, Sonora, Mexico, as an electrical repairman. He worked on refrigerators, air conditioners, and other appliances while in Hermosillo. In Tucson, he works for a local tortilla factory delivering tortillas to grocery stores.

The living room bookcase also includes recipe books and craft books. The family had owned and operated a small convenience store in Hermosillo. Mrs. Estrada was in charge of managing the store, including ordering, bookkeeping, and selling. In fact, they had named the store in honor of the third-grade daughter.

They moved to Tucson because they wanted to improve the opportunities for their children. Mrs. Estrada had family in Tucson and had lived here for a while as a child. Mr. Estrada came in search of a job and living quarters and then made arrangements for his family to join him about 6 months later. The children left their schoolmates and moved here in 1988.

During my visits, I have observed each family member take responsibility. The three older children are assigned the care of a younger sibling. The two sisters in high school are each responsible for one of the two younger sisters, and the brother in middle school is responsible for the youngest brother. The family is very resourceful. Everyone helps with the household chores, including producing tortillas for eating and for selling. The males are the ones in charge of maintenance, and the father shares his tools with the sons.

During a birthday party, I observed that the family had choreographed their duties. The father and the son in middle school took care of the piñata, which meant that the son had to stand on the roof of a van to hold one end of the line while the other end was attached to the roof of the trailer. The daughters organized the children for the piñata breaking. Each family member served food and beverages. What do these observations have to do with my teaching? Specifically, I used the knowledge about owning and managing a store to create a math unit on money. For three weeks, we explored the social issues of money, along with mathematical concepts about money.

Beyond that, I used the information I learned about the home in incidental matters that color the curriculum. I knew where my student lived and who her neighbors were. I made connections in class: "I want you to practice hitting a softball. I bet you can use that empty lot near your home to practice with your classmate who lives across the street"; and, "How about if you work on your science project with your classmate who lives next door to you?"

The knowledge I gleaned also had an impact on the student. She knew I had been at her home to talk with her parents. She understood that her parents and I communicated. This influenced the other students also. They recognized me in the trailer park. They came over to chat with me. They knew I knew where they lived and played.

What changes have I undergone? Fundamentally, I have redefined my conception of the term home visit. I was trained during my first years of teaching (some 15 years ago) that my goal during a home visit was to teach the parent. I had an agenda to cover. I was in control.

Now I go to learn. I have some questions I want to explore, I might want to learn about some particular home activities like what the family does for recreation. However, these questions are open-ended. I start an interview and follow the conversation to wherever it might lead. I am an active listener. I am a listener who returns to pick up the conversation from the last visit.

Most significantly, I am becoming a listener who reflects. During the last year and a half I have made time to do the visits and have made time to reflect about what I have learned. I have firsthand knowledge that I have gained through my research with the families. I use this knowledge as background when I am reading about minoritized families in books or articles. I read an article and compare what it states to the knowledge gained from my work. I contrast and sometimes confirm, but more often challenge what I read.

I must admit that this whole process is a demanding one. I am choosing to place myself in situations where I have to listen, reflect, communicate, act, and write. I believe I am learning, developing, and creating, and that is what makes this research worthwhile.

Reflecting on Change (Martha Floyd Tenery)

As I reread some of the early journal entries I made for this project, I realize how I have changed my views of the households. As I read these entries, I realized that I had discussed my students in terms of low academics, home-life problems, alienation, and socioeconomic status, and that I was oriented toward a deficit model. I no longer see the families I visited that way. Since I am looking for resources, I am finding resources, and I recognize the members of the families for who they are and for their talents and unique personalities. We now have a reciprocal relationship where we exchange goods, services, and information. I have also dispelled many myths that are prevalent in our region.

One example of a dispelled myth is that Mexican immigrants have poor educational backgrounds. To the contrary, I discovered that some schools in Mexico were academically ahead of the United States, and discipline was stricter. Instead of finding parents who do not emphasize education, parents wanted more homework, more communication with the schools, and stricter discipline. All five families (that I interviewed this year) informed me that education was one of the reasons they came to the United States. Another myth dispelled by the interviews is that Mexicans have limited work experience. The parents of my five students had held the following occupations: grocery store owner, bank executive, carpenter, mechanic, dairyman, grave digger, military, factory supervisor, farm worker, international salesman, mason, and domestic worker.

Strong family values and responsibility are characteristics of the families I visited. In every case, the household included extended family membership. Fifteen family members lived in one house, including the student's grandmother, mother, two aunts, and their husbands and children. My students were expected to participate in household chores such as cleaning house, car maintenance, food preparation, washing dishes, and caring for younger siblings. I learned what this insight meant when one of my students was unable to attend school drama and chorus rehearsals one day. In my journal entry detailing this project, I noted the following incident:

> Wednesday (11/25/92). The music teacher commented (to me), "You know, Leticia has missed two chorus rehearsals." Before I could answer, the school drama teacher stepped in to add, "Oh, she's very irresponsible." She had signed up to be in the Drama Club and had only been to two meetings. I said "Wait a minute. . . ." The drama teacher corrected herself, and said, "Well, she's acting irresponsibly." I then told her how Leticia's younger brother was being hospitalized for a series of operations, and when the mother had to leave, she left Leticia in charge of caring for her two younger siblings. In fact, her missing after-school rehearsals was an act of responsibility, obedience, and loyalty to her family.

I believe that this episode, and many other similar occurrences, help me to separate truths from myths by relying on what I have seen and heard from my students.

The Ramírez Family (Patricia Rendón)

The reason I chose this family was basically because the mother was available during school hours so that I could visit during school time. When I was free, and my student teacher was available, I was able to walk over there and meet with her, so my criterion for choosing the family was more for practical reasons than anything else. Once I got there, I really enjoyed sitting and talking to her. She was very eager to talk and very open about sharing her experiences, her family history, her impressions about what she has gone through. I felt it was as therapeutic for her as it was informative for me. I believe that these are visits more than interviews. I didn't have a clipboard writing everything down. Once the tape recorder is on, it is easy for the interview to flow.

I found out during the interview that she had undergone radical changes in her life. She had been born in Nogales, Sonora, and came here as a married woman without very many rights. Apparently her husband was quite dictatorial, and whenever there was a decision to be made, he made it, and that was it. When her husband decided to go back to Mexico, she decided to stay, I feel, because she had a need to become her own person.

Another interesting characteristic that I noticed about her was that her daughters were more like her peers. She values their company and their ideas. A case in point is an incident that occurred when her older daughter was about 10. A neighbor went on vacation and left Mrs. Ramírez in charge of her house and gave her the keys to the car, assuming that she knew how to drive. Mrs. Ramírez took this opportunity to teach herself how to drive. She made the statement that she saw many elderly women driving, and she thought to herself, "If they can do it, I can do it." She put all the girls in the car with her oldest daughter in front and started to teach herself to drive. The daughters know how to read English, so she depended on them to help her read the signs and to know where to go.

She also takes her daughters' ideas into consideration when they make a decision as a family, and she is very careful that they have the right kind of care. Mrs. Ramírez was working for a while when her children were younger, but the woman who was caring for them was not doing an adequate job, and so she had to quit her job. She did this even though it meant that she would have to go on food stamps and welfare. She felt that her daughters' care was more important than her having a job.

At the time of the interview, Mrs. Ramírez was looking for a job but was not able to find one, and she thought it was because of her lack of English skills. She was looking around for some English classes to take nearby, and she would also go out every day, walking and looking for work that she could do. Mrs. Ramírez had several requirements for her job: She did not want to take care of children or to clean houses, and she wanted something that was close by where she would not have to drive too far. She was limiting herself to a certain extent, but she was being exclusive in the kind of work that she could do because she felt that her job should be one where she could improve herself. She chose assembly types of work to apply for, and the last time I spoke to her, she had gotten a job at a lock assembly plant. Her youngest daughter is 8, so she feels that the children are now able to be alone after school until she gets home at 6:00.

Mrs. Ramírez is on welfare at this point in her life, but definitely does not want to stay in that position. This is the reason why she was so discriminating about the kind of job that she wanted to do. She felt that if she did work like watching children or cleaning houses, she would never be able to better herself. She feels that the job she has now is a step to something higher. I think that this is a common thing in many women's lives, where they are dependent on government aid but do not want it to be a permanent situation. She also commented that many women in her situation link up with a man just to have financial security, and she refused to do that, because she feels that it is not a good example to her children. Visiting her validated my respect for many Latin women. Mrs. Ramírez is one of those people who knows what she wants and is patient, trying to accomplish it. Sometimes people will say that the Latin culture dictates that you let fate or providence dictate your actions, but I feel that she is an example of a person who takes the bull by the horns and does not sit back and wait for things to happen.

Finding a Colleague (Raquel Gonzales)

I was very affected last year when I found out that the mother of one of my students had been a teacher in Mexico and that approaching the household as if I were going to "save" them would have been a gross error. She came in to volunteer in my classroom, and I felt that she was a little uncomfortable. I said something to her about, "Well, you're a teacher, you can show us how you do it." She said, "Let me watch a couple of days and see how you do it." The next day, she had her own little group, and she took it over. I feel that by establishing the relationship with her, she was able to function up to her potential. We talked in the study groups about a theoretical interpretation of confianza and the theory gave me an orientation of what to look for.

These case studies illustrate the multidimensional facets that the students take on when teachers become aware of household networks, survival strategies, and procurement of resources. Even more important, the case studies can be read with an eye toward the theoretical development of teachers. Teachers were not given predigested methods to use unreflexively. Emerging from the teachers' own theoretical understanding of ethnography, home visits became participant-observation, and insights from the households were tied into broader regional, social, economic, and gender-related patterns. An anthropological imagination paved the way for teachers to probe beyond the surface issues of welfare, missed appointments, and overcrowded living conditions to inspect the underlying constructions that rendered the surface structures meaningful and understandable. In addition, as teachers came to view their students as competent participants in households rich in cognitive resources, they came away with raised expectations of their students' abilities.

PROBLEMATIC AREAS

We have highlighted many of the affirmative and constructive aspects of our project. However, this is not to say the project has been unproblematic. Teachers have encountered a number of obstacles that impinge on the implementation of field research. The most often cited dilemma is, of course, time constraints. During a typical day, teachers are barraged on a number of fronts with demands on their time and energy. Adding to this already overloaded schedule, an effort to visit students' households, write fieldnotes, and meet in study groups can be an exacting price to pay for making a connection to the home. Once the connection is made, other problematic situations can arise. Some households have felt the *confianza* between teacher and household grow to such an extent that the teacher has (although rarely) been placed in the role of confidante, furnishing advice and resources in times of crisis.

One of the more important connections to be made concerns the tapping of the funds of knowledge for use within classroom pedagogy. Although all of the teachers are convinced that these funds exist in abundance, extracting their potential for teaching has proven to be an intricate process. Curriculum units based on the more conspicuous funds, such as ethnobotanical knowledge of medicinal herbs and construction of buildings, have emerged, but developing a tangible, systemic link to classroom practice has been more elusive (however, see Moll et al., 1990, 1992). The general consensus is that teachers are in need of time and support to move from theory to practice, or from field research to practice. They strongly affirmed that the labs or study groups provide an important way of maximizing time and combining resources and of conceptualizing the pedagogical connection between classrooms and households.

A final dilemma concerns the evaluation of the project. The assessment of the ethnographic process, the study groups, and the curriculum units cannot be carried out along conventional (experimental or quasiexperimental) lines. Transformation does not have a time frame. Qualitative evaluation methods have been most amenable to the methodology, and teachers were willing to document their own intellectual journeys through the use of personal journals, debriefing interviews, analysis of fieldnotes, study group transcripts, and classroom observations. In sum, how to provide convincing evidence of positive change is a constant project issue.

CONCLUSION

At the end of a presentation in a local school district, one educator remarked cynically, "We don't need teachers to learn to be anthropologists. We need them to learn to teach." We suggest that the point is not whether teachers learn to become anthropologists or good ethnographers. The teachers themselves have made this very clear, as Pat Rendón comments: "I don't want to be an anthropologist. I want to use what resources I can to become a better teacher." The issue is how to redefine the role of teachers as thinkers and practitioners. We have argued in this article that it begins by teachers themselves redefining the resources available for thinking and teaching through the analysis of the funds of knowledge available in local households, in the students they teach, and in the colleagues with whom they work.

As the teachers' field research has evolved in such a way as to provide ownership of the process, they have been able to construct themselves as agents of change. In significant ways, these teachers have begun to fuse the role of technicians in their practice as educators. As Giroux (1985) indicated, educators as transformative intellectuals can recognize their ability to critically transform the world. In a parallel fashion, as teachers have transcended the boundaries of the classroom walls, so have parents transcended the boundaries of the household. In a few but significant instances, parents have come to view themselves as agents capable of changing their child's educational experiences. As parents responded with personal narratives concerning their own unique and singular life course, a heightened historical consciousness began to emerge. The welcome communicative event of articulating the trajectory that brought parents to be where they are facilitated an awareness of the historical character of their experiences. In this way, the notion of dialog as an emancipatory educational process (Freire, 1981) was injected into the households. As other researchers (Lather, 1986; Savage, 1988) have stated, ethnography can be seen as a tool for social action that can enable persons to transform the confines of their circumstances. In the powerful dialog that this ethnographic interview can engender, parents can and did find a passageway to the schools. As the teacher validates the household experience as one from which rich resources or funds of knowledge can be extracted, parents themselves come to authenticate their skills as worthy of pedagogical notice. Most significant, teachers have reported that parents have felt an increased access to the school. No longer is the institution viewed as an impenetrable fortress ensconced on foreign soil. Rather, the teachers' incursion into previously uncharted domains has been reciprocated by the parents. Parents have felt the surge of *confianza* which has unlocked doors and overcome barriers.

Clearly the project's payoffs are multifaceted and complex. The emergence of teachers as qualitative researchers is clearly one by-product. A second involves the increased access to the school felt by parents. A third is the changed relationships between teachers and the students whose households they visited. A fourth, and for our purposes, a significant goal, is the emergence of curriculum units based on the household funds of knowledge. Teachers have been able to sift through the household resources and have found multiple elements that can be used as the bases for math, science, language arts, or integrated units. The classroom application is an evolving portion of the funds of knowledge inquiry. We have opted not to focus on this aspect in this report because of its multiple dimensions. However, teachers have invariably noted that each household contains an array of activities, strategies, and topics that can form the kernel of units to engage students. For example, teachers have formed mathematical units based on construction knowledge, ecology units based on ethnobotanical knowledge of the home, a unit titled "Sound and Its Properties" based on music, and a comparative history of clothing, including topics such as inquiry into absorbency of fabrics, among other instructional activities.

For teachers interested in developing a similar project in other locations, we propose the following minimal conditions based on our experiences, and as discussed in this report:

1. *Theoretical preparation:* The theoretical concept of funds of knowledge provided a new perspective for the study of households as dynamic settings with abundant social and intellectual resources.
2. *Home visits as participant observers:* The key is to enter the homes in the role of "learner," willing to interact and prepared to document what one learns, to produce new "firsthand" knowledge about the families and community.
3. *Study groups:* These meetings become the centers for discussion, reflection, and analysis of the household visits and a catalyst for ideas about teaching.
4. *Voluntary participation:* All teachers agreed that participation in the project must remain voluntary, so that teachers have maximum control over the project and the work does not become an undesirable imposition on teachers.

The teachers identified other aspects of the project as being important to its success, although not necessarily essential, such as the use of questionnaires to help guide the household interviews and observations, the collection and elaboration of fieldnotes, and collaboration with anthropologists or other educational researchers. There was also consensus that the project must be reinvented anew at each site, in relation to its social and historical conditions.

We suggest that these minimal conditions can engender a dialog of change and collaboration among teachers, parents, students, and researchers. The dialog of the ethnographic interview can provide a foundation for the development of critical consciousness. The discourse that the interview sparks highlights the theoretical assertion that knowledge is not found but constructed, and that it is constructed in and through discourse (Foucault, 1970, 1972). As the participants in this project become colearners and coconstructors of knowledge, environments for a probing disposition of mind can be meaningfully and effectively created.

REFLECTION QUESTIONS

1. How were these four teachers affected by the process of ethnographic interviewing?
2. How can a funds of knowledge approach be transformative?
3. How can we become colearners and coconstructors of knowledge?

REFERENCES

Ayers, W. (1992). Work that is real: Why teachers should be empowered. In G. A. Hess, Jr. (Ed.), *Empowering teachers and parents: School restructuring through the eyes of anthropologists* (pp. 13–27). Westport, CT: Bergin & Garvey.

Ely, M. (1991). Reflecting. In M. Ely, M. Anzul, T. Friedman, D. Gardner, & A. Steinmetz (Eds.), *Doing qualitative research: Circles within circles* (pp. 179–226). New York: Falmer.

Foucault, M. (1970). *The order of things: An archeology of the human sciences.* New York: Pantheon.

Foucault, M. (1972). *Archeology of knowledge and the discourse of language.* New York: Pantheon.

Freire, P. (1981). *Education for critical consciousness.* New York: Continuum.

Giroux, H. (1985). Teachers as transformative intellectuals. *Social Education, 2,* 376–379.

González, N. (1992). *Child language socialization in Tucson U.S. Mexican households.* Unpublished doctoral dissertation, University of Arizona, Tucson, AZ.

González, N., & Amanti, C. (1992, November). *Teaching ethnographic methods to teachers: Successes and pitfalls.* Paper presented at the Annual Meeting of the American Anthropological Association, San Francisco, CA.

Greenberg, J. B. (1989, April). *Funds of knowledge: Historical constitution, social distribution, and transmission.* Paper presented at the Annual Meeting of the Society for Applied Anthropology, Santa Fe, NM.

Lather, P. (1986). Research as praxis. *Harvard Educational Review, 46,* 257–277.

Lytle, S., & Cochran-Smith, M. (1990). Learning from teacher research: A working typology. *Teachers College Record, 92,* 83–103.

Moll, L. C., Amanti, C., Neff, D., & González, N. (1992). Funds of knowledge for teaching: Using a qualitative approach to connect homes and classrooms. *Theory Into Practice, 31,* 132–141.

Moll, L. C., & Greenberg, J. (1990). Creating zones of possibilities: Combining social contexts for instruction. In L. C. Moll (Ed.), *Vygotsky and education* (pp. 319–348). Cambridge, UK: Cambridge University Press.

Moll, L. C., Vélez-Ibáñez, C., Greenberg, J., Whitmore, K., Saavedra, E., Dworin, J., & Andrade, R. (1990). *Community knowledge and classroom practice: Combining resources for literacy instruction* (OBEMLA Contract No. 300-87-0131). Tucson, AZ: University of Arizona College of Education and Bureau of Applied Research in Anthropology.

Savage, M. (1988). Can ethnographic narrative be a neighborly act? *Anthropology and Education Quarterly, 19*, 3–19.

Segal, E. (1990). The journal: Teaching reflexive methodology on an introductory level. *Anthropology and Education Quarterly, 21*, 121–127.

Spindler, G., & Spindler, L. (1990). The inductive case study approach to teaching anthropology. *Anthropology and Education Quarterly, 21*, 106–112.

Vélez-Ibáñez, C. G. (1988). Networks of exchange among Mexicans in the U.S. and Mexico: Local level mediating responses to national and international transformations. *Urban Anthropology, 17*, 27–51.

Vélez-Ibáñez, C., & Greenberg, J. (1992). Formation and transformation of funds of knowledge among U.S. Mexican households. *Anthropology and Education Quarterly, 23*, 313–335.

Vélez-Ibáñez, C., Moll, L. C., González, N., & Amanti, C. (1992). *Funds of knowledge for educational improvement. An elaboration of an anthropological and educational collaborative dissemination project* (Report submitted to the W. K. Kellogg Foundation). Tucson, AZ: Bureau of Applied Research in Anthropology.

Woodward, V. (1985). Collaborative pedagogy: Researcher and teacher learning together. *Language Arts, 62*, 770–776.

Part **II**

TEACHERS AS RESEARCHERS

In this part of the book, we hear the voices of the teachers who have participated in one or more stages of the Funds of Knowledge project. This is, we believe, the heart of the book. Each of the perspectives presented is unique in voice and the context of the school, school district, and school community. Each presents thoughtful and perceptive reflections on how teachers have connected theory to their own practice.

It is interesting to note how the teacher-researchers in these chapters have incorporated the families' expressions and language into their narrative (*nana, tata, carambola, campo, confianza*), activating their own linguistic resources. As mentioned in the introduction, the research in particular communities could not have been conducted monolingually.

In chapter 6, Martha Floyd Tenery presents an unvarnished and richly detailed retelling of her experience of visiting the households of her students. This chapter, written as part of her graduate studies, amplifies the role of teacher as qualitative researcher. Initially apprehensive and insecure, she soon finds that she is an insightful ethnographer. Because of her own theoretical development, she is able to notice easily overlooked objects and practices and relate these to her own classroom practices. She uses ethnography as a tool to enhance her own professional development.

In focusing on one of her households in particular, the image of an economically marginalized household, poor in material resources, takes on a multifaceted aura, as Floyd Tenery is able to view the strategic choices that the household makes in procuring its subsistence. Trips to Mexico are not just for recreation, but have definite purposes and functions in the exchange of goods. Floyd Tenery is able to locate the family within a larger sociopolitical context, a context that is complex and multilayered.

However, she must invest out-of-school time and effort in order to reap these benefits. Her visits are conducted after school hours and on weekends. Her role as teacher-researcher took her beyond the school ground campus. We might ask, how can schools provide blocks of time in which teachers can make these connections? Does the teacher have to go above and beyond the call of duty in order to make deep and meaningful connections to students' lives? Or should professional development incorporate these principles into a vision of continuous learning?

This chapter highlights the process of theoretical interpretation as one tool of many that teachers can use. As the author conveys, she was able to make sense of the visit as she theorized practices. Practices that may have been opaque or obscure took on new meaning as she came to understand the context within which the household was embedded. In this way, every visit has possibilities for instruction, as the transformations are limitless.

In the next chapter, Cathy Amanti chronicles her own use of an anthropological perspective which sees culture as dynamic, interactive, and in flux, a departure from the National Geographic approach sometimes common in schools. She presents both a critique of images of culture, as well as an alternative practice, which emerged from her own experiences in visiting students' households. Recognizing that each of her students' households encompassed a unique merging of funds of knowledge, she recounts how her perspective on culture was pivotal in helping her to identify commonalities across students' households she visited, which later provided the theme for a learning module she implemented in her classroom on horses.

We can see in the details of her language arts, science, and math curricula that the topic can be extended over a wide range of content areas. Most importantly however, she uses students' familiarity with a known topic to teach the abstract, the scientific, and the unknown. She takes students from where they are, and connects them with a wider range of knowledge bases. In doing this, she validates their funds of knowledge and places that knowledge in an academic context.

Through the process of becoming a teacher-researcher and gaining confidence in her ability to develop engaging and meaningful learning experiences based on her students' funds of knowledge, Amanti also reflects on how her perceptions about her role within the educational hierarchy have changed. As a competent professional, she validates her own funds of knowledge, resisting the pressure to become a technician implementing scripted guidelines.

Next, Marla Hensley presents a compelling case study of how a teacher who was willing to listen and validate knowledge outside the classroom can impact parents. In her chapter, Hensley recounts how her conceptualization of her students and their families was transformed. Through her home visits she developed a growing awareness of her assumptions about the resources, talents, and skills encompassed in her school's community. She becomes increasingly sensitive and invested in the educational success of her students whose homes she has visited. At the same time, as she draws one particular father into her classroom to help create an original musical, we see him become engaged and his talents affirmed. This leads him to step into a leadership role in the school's parent–teacher organization. Finally, Hensley gives examples of the meaningful ways she involved parents in the development of her curriculum based on their funds of knowledge and areas of expertise. She also provides additional ideas for tapping into this knowledge in ways other than making ethnographically oriented home visits.

Next, Patricia Sandoval-Taylor presents excellent examples of curricula that build on the mathematical resources of communities, and how drawing on these resources can support articulated growth in various areas of the curriculum. In this chapter, Sandoval-Taylor recounts the development of a learning module in collaboration with others working on the project. The process of developing this module, as well as its implementation, was extensively documented. The chapter is written in a manner that tries to capture the complexity of the process of creating an optimum learning situation by weaving pedagogical theory with community knowledge, student knowledge, student interests, and teacher experience. Throughout the process, Sandoval-Taylor guided and grounded the planning discussions in her knowledge of her students' abilities, interests, and developmental level. The chapter documents a series of meetings that took place prior to the implementation of the curriculum unit, highlighting the translation of community knowledge to content area standards and other academic practices and goals. The process that is described is not a unitary lamination of one on the other, but a richly textured and nuanced acknowledgment of the real time investment of teachers in planning and reflection.

In the next chapter, Anne Browning-Aiken presents an extended example of her visit to the place of origin of a student's family that she studies. Following the family's trajectory, she spent time visiting Cananea, a small mining town in Sonora, Mexico, where many families in Tucson schools originate. Although Browning-Aiken has been a classroom teacher, she began this study first as a project for a field methods class and then later as part of her dissertation research in anthropology. This chapter provides a case study of how teachers can access family and cultural history to obtain a clearer understanding of their students' backgrounds and at the same time apply this information to construct classroom curricula. Browning-Aiken demonstrates how teacher contact with one household opens a door to understanding how individual family history is part of a larger cultural interchange that has been occurring along the U.S.–Mexico border for centuries.

This chapter begins with a description of the socioeconomic background of the population served by a Tucson Southside middle school. It then demonstrates how ethnographic interviews with a family serve as an incentive to explore related family histories on both sides of the U.S.–Mexico border and the local history and role of Mexicans in the development of Tucson. This combination of local and family history proves particularly fruitful for constructing a curriculum around copper, a natural resource that has provided a livelihood for borderlanders for the last century and a half. This economic aspect of border history becomes particularly significant once social and kinship networks in Arizona and Sonora reveal that a 1906 miners' strike helped set the stage for the Mexican Revolution.

Browning-Aiken explores the interview materials and identifies themes about education, social networks, and the impact of social memory of the past on the present. These themes provide a rich cultural understanding of border history and its impact on the lives of U.S. Mexicans. The chapter builds on this cultural fund of knowledge about family and regional history to construct a multidisciplinary middle school curriculum model that potentially fulfills many language arts, social studies, science, and math objectives. This curriculum concept model, "Arizona Connections: Mining and People," is designed to stimulate students' curiosity about their own environment and the relationship it has to their families' economic survival and history.

The chapter concludes with some recommendations about doing ethnographic interviews and interprets the pedagogical significance of the themes of education and networks across borders. The ethnographic methods described in this chapter can be used by anyone. They are simply tools to make teaching more effective, more creative, and more comprehensive.

In the final chapter of this part, Jacqueline Messing, a graduate research assistant for the project at the time and also a former teacher, writes about the interviews she conducted with some of the teacher-researchers at the end of the project, and the commonalities that underlie their experiences. Her interviews yielded narratives, which are excerpted. Messing presents an analysis of the perspectives of several teacher-researchers she interviewed. Teachers describe how this project changed their views toward their teaching, their students, and their students' families. The author takes up the anthropological view that schooling is a social creation to argue that educational research should offer new roles for its participants. These new roles lead to questioning assumptions, increased understanding, communication, and exchange, and, ultimately, to educational change.

It is in the words of these teachers themselves that we can begin to comprehend the transformative power of this type of professional development for teachers. These teachers have researched, analyzed, and theorized both community and school. Rather than practicing theories, these teachers are theorizing practices, learning, and developing as researchers, as educators, and as persons.

Chapter 6

La Visita

Martha Floyd Tenery

As I got out of my Honda Accord holding a manila folder, I wanted nothing more than to be inconspicuous. Instead, I stuck out like a sore thumb. A tall, blonde-haired, blue-eyed Anglo teacher set in the middle of a Mexican barrio. With permission from the school district, I had arranged an interview with the parents of one of my students.

I left school, alone, at 3:30 p.m., armed with an address and map of the neighborhood for my first home visit. I had never before ventured outside the school into this neighborhood, and I was nervous. Making matters worse, I could not find my student's street and trailer, as spaces were out of numerical order. I stopped and asked, unsure which language to use in addressing community members. As I finally approached the address, a middle-aged Mexican woman in a sleeveless cotton dress pulled back a blue homemade curtain and looked out her window. Two children, my student and a younger child, took turns peeking out.

I wondered what the family would think of me, and whether they would be suspicious of my motives. I worried I was imposing on their family time and wondered what to say. This meeting was simply to get to know them better. I planned to follow up with more interviews later.

By the time I reached the house, the door was already swinging open, and the mother smiled as she invited me in. I introduced myself and consciously allowed the parents to start the conversation. Our talk flowed naturally and centered on background information, medical problems, salaries, and their personal lives. I was impressed with how openly and warmly they

119

received me. Two men were seated in the living room and they stood to greet me and shake my hand. We exchanged introductions and I explained that I hoped to be a better teacher from what I learned from them. The men participated peripherally in the conversation for about five minutes then excused themselves and left. I took general notes of what my student's mother said to enable me to reconstruct the interview when I got home.

This first visit differed from subsequent visits in my level of anxiety. Being a teacher going outside her comfort zone, speaking a foreign language, being a learner, and fearing the unknown, all produced anxiety. This anxiety is similar to that which immigrant families encounter as they face unfamiliar people, customs, and activities. It is only by experiencing the same type of unease that someone from the outside can understand the family's daily anxiety. The fact that teachers are willing to move outside their comfort zone is key to the unusual relationship that developed between parents and teachers in this project.

DETAILS OF A HOME VISIT

After having completed three visits to the first family, I began to visit a second student and her family. Now, on my first visit to the second family, much of my anxiety had dissipated. On my way to the second family's home, I stopped to pick up a cake at a tiny market near the trailer court where my student lived. Bringing food seemed an appropriate gesture of reciprocity, considering I was frequently offered food on home visits. A man at the counter greeted me as I walked in the door. Immediately, I was struck by the high prices marked on the goods: $.69 each for fresh fruit, a small bottle of Coke for $1.39, and the package of sweet rolls I purchased for $3.14. I wondered if the family I was visiting shopped there, and, if so, how difficult it might be for them to purchase a loaf of bread at the high prices.

I returned to my car and made my way across an intersection without traffic lights. The trailer court was depressingly run down. A metal fence topped with rows of spiked barbed wire surrounded the area. There was broken glass in front of María's trailer, so I made a U-turn and pulled up on some grass. An abandoned brown station wagon without tires was parked on the strip. When I opened the car door, I could hear chickens clucking from a coop in the yard across the dirt road.

Noticing the household setting, I saw 10 feet of hard ground and occasionally wire or wooden fences separating the trailers. Screwdrivers, tires, bicycles, and boards were more common than vegetation in the yards. Just outside the front door of María's house was a two-square-foot bed of *hierbabuena* (peppermint). The wooden steps leading to the door seemed unstable, and when I bent over to look at the steps, I noticed blankets, boxes, clothes, and a television set stored under the trailer. I knocked on the door and waited. A Chevrolet pick-up truck was parked beside the home with its door ajar. As I looked more closely, I noticed that María was inside the truck with some papers and a pencil. She had been watching me and giggled as she stepped down from the truck to greet me. She walked into her house and told her mother I had arrived. From a back room her mother answered "*pase*" (come in).

I proceeded into the home and 11-year-old María motioned for me to sit down as she explained her mother was in the shower. I sat in the living room on one of two sofas, which faced each other. On the floor were four small rugs covering the red carpeting. The sofas, a console television, a smaller portable television, a stereo with a cassette player, and a radio were all packed into one small area. Across from me were a five-drawer chest and a small cloth-topped table covered with knickknacks. The kitchen, visible from where I sat, held a refrigerator, a double sink, counter top, stove, and kitchen table, and upper and lower cabinets and a floor cabinet. A hallway off the kitchen led to a bedroom and bathroom.

The walls were decorated with paintings of Jesus Christ and the *Virgen de Guadalupe*, nestled amidst velvet paintings of leopards and posters of bikini-clad women on motorcycles. One corner displayed three school certificates the children had earned for completion of English as a Second Language (ESL) and for reading programs. Hand-crocheted doilies, glass figurines, and a carved wooden armadillo with a bobbing head all adorned the tops of tables, counters, drawers, and the television. Ribbons, a papier-mâché parrot, wire baskets full of garlic, and an Easter basket hung from the ceiling.

In one corner of the living room a curtain closed off a small loft where a boy about 15 years old was sleeping. My entrance had awakened him, and he pulled the curtain open, revealing a cassette case, a wooden crate, clothes, and high-top tennis shoes stored behind him. Emerging from his three feet by four feet space, the boy presented me with the wooden crate, which contained cassette tapes of *ranchera*, rap, and *norteña* music. He asked me what I wanted to hear and I chose a recent release by Bronco called *A Todo Galope*, which he put into the family stereo. His 12-year-old brother, a former student of mine, joined us in the living room. The two boys told me about school, one in his first year of middle school and the other his first year of high school. The elder boy showed me his schedule, which included five classes, two periods of beginning ESL, sewing, shop, and health. He told me that he needed a notebook with 100 pages for his health class where they were currently studying the ill effects of drugs on the body.

Just then, María's mother, wearing a simple shift dress and thongs, emerged from the hallway combing her wet hair. I stood up to greet her, both of us having met previously at school. She said that she was preparing dinner and hoped I would stay. She explained that she was behind schedule because she had taken her youngest son to the doctor for a cut on his leg and had to wait for hours there. When the doctor finally saw her, he said to take the boy to Kino hospital on Monday where they would sew a small piece of skin onto his leg. The accident had actually occurred over a month ago in Mexico when her son fell from a car. After one month, the wound had not healed, so she agreed to consult a doctor. She asked her son to show me the wound. It was unprotected, but the boy assured me it did not hurt.

María's mother walked into the kitchen and uncovered a large pot on the stove, revealing a dark sauce with visible roots and herbs floating in it, next to a pot of steaming rice, and a whole chicken. She explained that the sauce was *mole*, a traditional dish from her hometown of Puebla. The family comes from a largely indigenous village, which is quite different from my other immigrant students, who come from our neighboring state of Sonora. I asked her how she made the dish, and she launched into an animated discussion. As she spoke, she pulled herbs out of tin cans, opened the refrigerator to expose vegetables, and even unfolded a dry, salted fish from inside a newspaper. She showed me three kinds of festive bread, two kinds of tea, *ayocotes* (kidney beans larger than the common sort), *pescado tenso* (stiffened, dry, salted codfish), *chile negro* (black chile), and *ajonjolí* (sesame)—terms which María recorded on my folder. María's mother explained that she brings large quantities of ingredients up with her from Mexico and stores them for use throughout the months. Three-tiered brass baskets hanging beside the stove contained some of these herbal secrets.

About 30 minutes later, María's uncle and aunt arrived with their newborn baby and two school-age daughters. María's father and a 2-year-old child belonging to another brother accompanied them. The older children began playing with the younger children, and took them to the back room, where they sat on the bed and played catch with a plastic ball.

María's father, after introducing himself, began telling me about a palace his brother had built in Cholula, just eight blocks from their house. He told María to find the *Selecciones* (*Reader's Digest*) magazine that featured her uncle. María went to the chest of drawers and rummaged through papers, notebooks, books from Mexico, a *Lengua Española* book, an English workbook, all kinds of worksheets, before coming across the magazine her father had requested. The feature in *Selecciones* told of a palace with 15 rooms and several staircases built over a period of six years by a man of striking resemblance to María's father. I skimmed the article, which told of the man's eccentric lifestyle that included 10 wives and 26 children. Our conversation evolved into a discussion of other areas of interest in Puebla, tourist sites and bars in Mexico, import and property taxes, and an elaboration of his job. He purchases televisions, radios, stereos, appliances, and clothes—either on sale or used—in Tucson and sells them in Mexico. Consequently, he travels frequently between Mexico and Tucson.

Just then, María's mother announced that dinner was ready. We pulled the kitchen table into the living room and ate there. The rice was served separately, followed by the *mole* and chicken. Radishes and jalapeños were served as condiments. María and her mother remained in the kitchen, heating corn tortillas on the gas stove and running them to the table. The children used their folded tortillas as spoons for the main dish, accompanied by iced Coke. The women made sure their husbands had plenty, serving them several heaping portions of *mole*. María's mother ate last.

After dinner, María's father brought out two books on astrology, one from the Chinese and the other from Japanese perspective. He asked me what sign I was born under and began to read me my fortune according to the stars. María's mother brought out an album that contained pictures from their hometown in Mexico. There were school pictures, pictures of birthday parties, and scenes from their home. The home had a dirt floor, chipped and plastered walls, and a bare light bulb hanging in the middle of the room. In one picture, María was holding a puppy. Her mother explained that was what their house looked like when they were poor. Since her husband is now making good money, the house has been remodeled.

When I left, I was given a care package of mole for two people, which the mother explained was customary for special guests. The children accompanied me to the car with big smiles on their faces as I thanked them. Still making the visits alone but now more experienced, I came away with data about household tools, books, electronic devices, products used by members of the household, and interactional patterns. Other information illustrated how the family developed networks and skills, dealt with health and economic exigencies, their multiple uses of literacy, and so forth.

DISCUSSION

Having presented a home visit in detail, the following section analyzes characteristics of that household visit from a comparative perspective. While recognizing that an analysis of a single household is limited in scope, I believe that this household is representative of other recent immigrant households I visited and is significant in terms of illustrating characteristics of the strategizing household.

The Strategizing Household

According to Vélez-Ibáñez and Greenberg (this volume), one of the keys to understanding Mexican origin children lies in the historical struggle of Mexican origin households for control of their labor, resources, and for economic security. Strategies for survival are omnipresent in the everyday lives of members of these households. The need to sustain the household economically, socially, and culturally manifests itself in behaviors, activities, and customs exhibited in households such as pooling resources, sharing household chores, trading goods and services, traditional economic activities, and shopping in informal markets.

For example, for María's household, the impact of immigration policies is critical to their survival in the United States. Transborder travel and commerce sustain this family economically and socioculturally. They own and maintain homes in Mexico and the United States and travel frequently between the two for religious ceremonies (*quinceañeras*, baptisms, weddings), vacations, and business.

The Spanish language is maintained orally and through written materials such as books, magazines, newspapers, and business documents. Clearly, this family's survival strategies for social, cultural, and economic stability impinge not only on what they do in the United States, but also on their activities across the border.

Domains of Knowledge

In contemporary Mexican origin households, unemployment, displaced workers, unstable employment, and the resulting low socioeconomic status influence households. Consequently, a vast spectrum of knowledge, skills, and talents commonly exist within these households and within the larger Mexican community network of nonmarket exchange. In this home visit example, knowledge of cooking and herbal remedies was demonstrated by María's mother and suggested by the *hierbabuena* growing outside the home. The reliance on home remedies prior to medical care suggests that the family may have developed this domain of knowledge in response to subsistence living. The knowledge of household repairs was evidenced by the hand-constructed stairs and makeshift loft bedroom as well as by the existence of boards, nails, tools, and construction parts spread throughout the yard.

Immigrant households typically contain transnational domains of knowledge. In this case, extensive knowledge of U.S.-Mexico international commerce, tourism, and taxes was demonstrated by the uncle and father. These families, and others I visited, made frequent trips across the border to visit relatives, take vacations, celebrate holidays and special occasions, visit doctors and dentists, and purchase goods and services. Frequent cross-border travel exposes children to Spanish language and literacy, games and songs, international commerce, biculturalism, and many other bodies of knowledge. This household's knowledge centered primarily around customs, traditions, and experiences in Puebla, but the domains of knowledge occasionally extended outside Mexico as in the example of Japanese and Chinese astrology.

Such bodies of knowledge can serve as the foundation for learning modules or thematic units developed by teachers. Teachers can combine standard curriculum objectives and teaching methods with local knowledge, resulting in lessons of familiar content to minoritized students. For instance, a unit could be developed on international commerce between the United States and Mexico that could include reading, writing, math, social studies, and science objectives.

Student domains of knowledge evidenced in the homes about such subjects as farm animals, pets, plants, and bicycles can be elaborated on and shared with others in school. Parents' domains of knowledge, such as knowledge of household repairs, construction, tile work, auto mechanics, and international trade can be developed into hands-on school activities on measurement, money, mathematics, and electricity.

Interactional Patterns

Some patterns of interaction observed in the homes can be attributed to adaptive responses to sociohistorical processes. The existence of extended families, clustered households, temporary houseguests, and nonconsanguine members of households could be responses to difficult economic conditions. It is common to find three or more adults residing in a single residence in order to maintain the household. In the case of one of my families, five adults, including one grown son, contributed to the financial pool to sustain the household. Because these families depend on their social networks to cope with unemployment, immigration, discrimination, and other consequences of the borderland's complex political and changing economic environment, they are willing to invest considerable energy and resources in maintaining good relations with their members. Children are exposed to relations with members of various age groups and learn to relate at a variety of levels with the adults and others in their lives. They may live with their parents, grandparents, stepparents, uncles and aunts, and may relate to them as family, friends, confidants, or acquaintances. Extended families provide financial support, childcare support, and assistance in cleaning, cooking, and running errands. They provide moral support because someone is always home, and can contribute to a feeling of love and belonging in children.

Children play important roles in sustaining the household, as well. In the earlier example, María performed adult-like roles of cooking, cleaning, babysitting, translating, and carrying out cultural rituals such as baptismal celebrations. She naturally followed her mother's lead in entertaining guests and caring for younger children. Her brothers contribute to the household by helping adult males in household repairs, construction, car maintenance, yard work, and other chores. These abilities could be highlighted in school through cooperative grouping, projects, joint presentations, and the development of leadership skills. For example, teamwork, cross-age interaction, and apprenticeship roles are direct reflections of household interactional patterns observed in the homes.

Cultural Practices

Changing immigration policies, seasonal labor, language policy, and discrimination have precipitated changes in thought, as well as behaviors and practices. At the household level, cultural practice is manifested in linguistic, literacy, religious, and cultural traditions or events. Such events provide families with a sense of belonging, solidarity and ethnic identity. For example, family rituals such as birthdays, *quinceañeras*, outings, and *visitas de respeto* provide a sense of belonging to the family, and reaffirm family solidarity by bringing relatives together frequently.

Maintaining Spanish language and literacy skills is a strategy used in María's household to maintain a link to Mexico and relatives living there, as it is in other homes I visited. For example, María's father referred to literature in Spanish (*Selecciones*, horoscopes) for both entertainment and information. María was often observed reading, writing, and speaking in Spanish. The family album, a visual reminder of their life in Mexico, and the way it was presented to me, indicates a strong sense of pride and memories from Mexico, and is a marker of the family's socioeconomic mobility.

Religion plays an eminent role in the families by helping them cope during difficult times, by providing family members with a sense of commonality and a sense of connection to tradition through rituals and ceremonies, and by producing a sense of belonging in the larger scheme of life. Paintings and ornaments exhibited throughout the home indicate strong reliance on Christian beliefs. Attending church, reading the Bible, and other religious activities contribute to a sense of security and play a deciding role in family customs, priorities, decision-making, interactions, lifestyles, and sense of safety. Retaining customs, religion, and language is a conscious effort.

Temporary sacrifice for the betterment of the family is another adaptive behavior demonstrated in the households. All parents in my study expressed that they came to the United States for better opportunities, namely for their children. Men often work more than one job, and women work to provide supplemental income. The parents do this so that their children will not have to endure the hardships they have endured. This motivation by obligation to the children is similar to what Suarez-Orozco (1989) discovered in his study of immigrants from Central America, only the children in his study incurred an obligation to repay their parents.

Many parents I visited had not completed school beyond sixth grade in Mexico. One father had finished second grade when he was forced to work to earn money for his family. He worked odd jobs such as picking up bones from cattle that had starved and gathering firewood so they could eat. To go to school meant paying for uniforms, papers, pencils, and books. This cost was too much of an expense for some parents, and the children had to stop going to school. One of the student's homes burned down and he did not have clothes to wear to school for the rest of the year.

Parents develop strategies to compensate for their own limited literacy skills. They become very resourceful about networking with others as the need arises. For example, when letters from school arrive, they will find a neighbor to read or translate. Older siblings often help with homework in English.

Naturally, these practices have applications to the classroom. Stories, songs, and written materials encountered in the homes can be used as the basis for literacy, history, music, or social studies lessons.

The language use observed in households, such as particular dialects, regional lexicon, and patterns of speech have enriching possibilities in the classroom. Students could share characteristics of their home language orally and through writing. Teachers can use language data from household observations to make lessons more pertinent to students.

TEACHER AS MEDIATOR

Through my experience as a classroom teacher visiting students' homes, I came to view the role of the teacher as that of a mediator in multiple contexts. Mediation has been a recurrent, albeit implicit, theme throughout the Funds of Knowledge project. Teachers are perceived as active agents of mediation from the conception of involving teachers in conducting household visits, to the theoretical assertion that knowledge is socially constructed and ethnographic methodology transformational. The strength of the research is the involvement of teachers in all aspects of the project. Consequently, teachers are positioned to mediate between homes and school as well as between communities and the university.

Throughout the process of qualitative research, teachers also mediate the roles of teacher and researcher. Never abandoning one at the expense of the other, they remain at one time both objective and subjective, professional and intimate. Although the undertaking of both teacher and researcher is logistically complex, teachers have particular insights and advantages over nonteaching researchers. Such advantages include rapport with informants; an insider's perspective into schools; access to official records, students, and parents; credibility among community members; and an intimate relationship between the researcher and what is studied. Ethnographic research conducted by teachers represents a voice that lies somewhere between self and other, teacher and learner, insider and outsider. In this sense, the term *teacher as mediator* is used to describe this voice.

Mediating Between Home and School

The importance of home–school collaboration has been well documented in educational literature. Regrettably, though, teachers have rarely been directly involved in parent involvement programs or community research. This oversight has resulted in research and program findings that fail to result in meaningful change in the relationship between parents and teachers. Teachers are in an ideal position as agents of change because they have the training, knowledge, and access to interact personally and consistently with students and their families. Neither outside researchers nor community liaisons are afforded this fortuitous opportunity.

Because of the changing needs of students and society, teachers must continuously develop methods that enable them to mediate strategically between homes and schools. Ethnographic home visits are designed to establish a relationship of mutual trust while eliciting personal narratives from members of households. Both the relationships established and the information gathered in households are useful for teachers in designing instruction based on strengths found in the homes to better fit the needs of minoritized students and facilitate formal intellectual development.

Characteristic of learning modules created through the project is the creation of new knowledge. In effect, what happens in the classroom is a reflection both of the themes and language of students' lives as well as the teachers' goals for student learning. Students in U.S. schools coming from non-mainstream backgrounds can appropriate school concepts and incorporate them into their present understanding without relinquishing their home language, culture, and values. Students should be encouraged to express their own voice and to challenge hegemonic power relations, including the standardized school curriculum, that "parade as universals" (Giroux, 1992), which in reality represents a Eurocentric perspective.

Mediating Interpretations

The ethnographic research process causes teachers to become more aware of the multidimensionality of students and their families. A parent may at one time be a father, an uncle, a brother, a laborer, a Catholic, a baseball coach, and a household repairman. A student may be a teacher, caretaker, friend, musician, champion Nintendo player, and family interpreter. Ethnographic observations in the home and school allow teachers to widen their knowledge base and perspective about each student. On many occasions, information acquired through home visits prevented teachers from jumping to erroneous conclusions regarding school behavior.

SUMMARY

The characteristics of the families described in this chapter contradict many stereotypes of Mexican origin families. Stereotypes such as lacking morality, having broken families, not valuing education, and demonstrating low skill levels are invalidated by the data. In fact, observations in Mexican origin households suggest that the harder their lives, the more coping and survival skills they develop. Strategizing households are rich resources for learning, as skill domains of knowledge and cultural practices may be utilized in the classroom to conceptualize mathematics, comprehension, and composition lessons.

Furthermore, relationships established between teachers and parents during household visits have positive consequences on student learning in the classroom. The experience of interacting socially with minoritized families of low socioeconomic status provides teachers with an appreciation of cultural systems from which Mexican origin children emerge. Oral histories and narratives told by family members, in combination with expressions of cultural identity and solidarity, build an appreciation for the individuals and what they have endured. This empathy, or caring attitude, transfers to the classroom, as teachers perceive students within a cultural and historical framework. Additionally, personal contact with community members establishes a line of communication and an invaluable relationship of *confianza* among parents, students, and teachers. In all, an analysis of *la visita* portrays Mexican origin households as resourceful, connected, and full of life experiences.

REFLECTION QUESTIONS

1. Why might teachers be hesitant to visit their students' homes? What conditions would facilitate teacher home visits?
2. Anthropologists often find it difficult to study their own culture—"to make the familiar strange." Describe one room in your home in detail and write what you think a stranger would learn about you and your funds of knowledge from observing that room.
3. What are some of the resources Tenery found in her students' homes that can be drawn on to facilitate her students' academic success?

4. What advantages and drawbacks are there to teachers doing educational research?

REFERENCES

Giroux, H. (1992). *Border crossings: Cultural workers and the politics of education.* New York and London: Routledge.

Suárez-Orozco, M. (1989). *Central American refugees and US high school: A psychosocial study of motivation and achievement.* Stanford, CA: Stanford, University Press.

Chapter 7

Beyond a Beads and Feathers Approach

Cathy Amanti
Tucson Unified School District

The typical approach to culture embodied in most multicultural curricula taught in public schools today is static, normative, and exclusive. Culture is portrayed as homogenous and frozen in time, such as when teachers engage their students in learning about the holidays, food, typical costumes, and art of their own or other cultures. This special event approach to culture ignores and devalues the everyday experiences of many minoritized and immigrant students in our country, who may not practice all of the traditions of their cultural past. This is also how stereotypes of other cultures are created.

Educators need to be aware that all cultures, not just their own, change over time. In fact, just as the culture an individual teacher practices will be a mix of old and new, traditional and modern, so is the culture of other groups in this country. This includes recent immigrants as well as people that were here long before the arrival of Europeans. All cultures are heterogeneous, and practices within a group will vary according to such factors as gender, religion, class, and geographic location. This has major implications for the way educators should think about multicultural education.

I gained an appreciation for the complexity and importance of understanding how the idea of culture has been contested and transformed while I was pursuing a master's degree in cultural anthropology. Our assumptions about culture shape what we consider to be important information about ourselves and others, and how we interpret and judge human behavior. With that in mind, in the Funds of Knowledge project we have been in-

tent on including in our classroom practice the actual lived experiences of
our students rather than a traditional or stereotyped version. As Renato
Rosaldo pointed out:

> From the pirouettes of classical ballet to the most brute of brute facts, all hu-
> man conduct is culturally mediated. Culture encompasses the everyday and
> the esoteric, the mundane and the elevated, the ridiculous and the sublime.
> Neither high nor low, culture is all pervasive. (1989, p. 26)

As educators, we must stop giving our students the idea that culture comes
in a neat package.

To tap into the lived cultural experiences of our students in this project,
we use ethnography. That is what our fieldwork experience of visiting our
students' homes is all about. It allows us to gain firsthand knowledge of our
students and their families rather than accepting the second- or thirdhand
accounts of researchers. Researchers often focus on knowledge and cultural practices that families may lack rather than appreciate the extensive
knowledge and practices to be found in working class, minoritized, and immigrant communities. Classroom teaching and learning that developed
from the Funds of Knowledge project has included the knowledge encompassed in our students' homes and lives. This process—of developing curricula based on local knowledge—is the reverse of the typical Anglocentric
curriculum developed by education specialists usually located at a great distance, spatially and conceptually, from the classroom.

In this project, we challenge the status quo by asserting that local knowledge has a legitimate place in our educational institutions for both our students and our pedagogical knowledge as teachers. We also say that no matter what background our students have, there is knowledge in their home,
that can be tapped into and used in the classroom.

Thus, when I began my fieldwork as a pilot phase teacher-researcher, I
discarded preconceived notions I had about communities sharing my students' community's demographic characteristics. I had no idea what knowledge I would find in my students' homes or how I would use that knowledge
in my classroom practice. I only had the expectation that I would find pedagogically viable funds of knowledge in my students' homes and that I would
be able to find a way to draw on that knowledge to create meaningful learning experiences for my students once I got back to my classroom.

There is a tension inherent in this "practice" approach to culture. On
the one hand, it makes us cautious not to make assumptions about anyone
based on their ethnicity, gender, class, religion, and so forth. On the other
hand, some commonalities will be shared within groups because of shared
histories, and it is these commonalities that provide the richest themes for
the classroom teacher. So despite unique characteristics of the households

I visited, once I began visiting my students' homes it was not long before I found that a number of my students that year had extensive background experiences with horses, which later became the theme for a learning module I implemented. The fact that many of my students had extensive experiences with horses is no accident. Although this topic may appear to be an unusual component for a multicultural curriculum, horses have played an important role in the southwestern United States where I live and work. Cattle ranching became an important industry soon after the Spaniards arrived in the Americas, and its importance in Northern Mexico continues. A number of my students had relatives living in rural areas and on ranches in Northern Mexico. Some of my students had their own horses on these family ranches where they visited on weekends, holidays, and school vacations. One of my students even had three horses at his urban home a few blocks from school. This came as a surprise to me when I visited his home early in the school year.

Excerpts from field notes I wrote after visits to three of my students' families follow (all of the names used are pseudonyms and the addresses have been changed):

Student 1: The Alfaro family live at 7 W. Lincoln Ave. They have a chain link fence around their home, which is locked at all times. The Alfaros live in a several room home which has a shelter attached to it. This shelter is home to three horses and a goose.

Mr. Alfaro is teaching all his sons how to care for and ride horses. He himself is teaching his horse to dance. The horse is five years old. My student, Daniel, is in charge of feeding the horses and brought the two different kinds of feed to show me while he explained the daily feeding schedule. While Mr. Alfaro was showing me the maneuvers he has his horse go through, Daniel and his brother rode the other smaller horses inside their barn-like shelter. The boys would like to be in a rodeo and their father is teaching them how to rope. Mr. Alfaro participated in rodeos in Mexico. The boys have practiced to participate in a rodeo on occasion. The family also has many friends with ranches around Tucson and they visit them frequently. . . . The family also goes to horseraces at Three Points, in the rural area surrounding Tucson.

Student 2: The grandparents of my student, Fernando, live in Colonia Tres Alamos, Chihuahua. They have a ranch there where the children go spend their vacations. Fernando spent a month there this summer and his brother spent two months. While at their grandparents' ranch, they help care for their grandparents' horses, cows, and burros. The children really enjoy riding horses. . . .

Fernando's mother reports that she likes things that are related to the *campo*. She grew up on a ranch in Trinchera, Sonora. When she was young, she went camping with her school. She studied Indians and they looked for flints. The whole family likes being on a ranch the best.

Student 3: Mrs. Rivera's brothers learned to do construction through observation and participation. Sometimes they take my student and his brother to work with them on Saturdays. Mrs. Rivera's father and brothers also know a great deal about horses. When I arrived, I knocked on the door of the house at the front of the property. When I announced who I was and who I was looking for, I was asked to wait. A video was showing on the television of horse races in Sonoyta, Mexico, which one of my student's uncles had taped. This uncle goes to Sonoyta almost every other week and has horses there. Mrs. Rivera says this tape and a tape showing the butchering of a bull could be brought in to show at school.

The type of horseracing shown in the video at the third home I visited was like the *carambolas* of historic Sonora. The races in the video took place on long stretches of flat ground. Some of the horses in the videotape belonged to my student's uncle who did the taping. I borrowed this video to show as part of our horse study. The students learned about this particular aspect of horses from the video. It also made a statement to the value of the cultural experiences of my students. Many of them have attended similar horse races in parts of Northern Mexico. I never would have known this video existed unless it had been playing the day I went to visit this student's home.

The three students from the families whose field notes I excerpted above were not the only ones I found who were familiar with horses in my multiage, bilingual classroom. Here is a sample of what some of my other fourth and fifth graders wrote about their experiences with horses:

I have ridden a horse. It is fun. I ride horses at my friend's house and at my *nana's* house. My *nana* has horses at her house. We like riding horses. My *nana* has a ranch and she has horses, cow, chickens, and a lot of other horses. My *nana* lives in Mexico.

Yo no tengo caballo pero mi tío si tiene unos en su rancho. Mi tío Alberto tiene un rancho en Chihuahua.

(I don't have a horse but my uncle has some on his ranch. My uncle Alberto has a ranch in Chihuahua)

I know how to ride horses but nobody in my family has one. I ride horses when my dad goes to his friend's house on weekends.

I ride horses whenever I go to my *tata's* ranch.

Yo monto a caballo cuando voy a México. Yo monto a caballo en México por las milpas. Alguien en mi familia tiene caballos. Es mi tío y mi tata. Mi papá tenía uno en el pasado y ahora tenemos uno pero a lo mejor mi papá va a comprar otro.

(I ride horses when I go to Mexico. I ride a horse in Mexico in the fields. My uncle and my grandfather have horses. My father used to have horses and now we have one. Maybe my dad will buy another one.)

I rode a horse when I was in Cuba. I rode in front of my uncle's house. Nobody in my family has a horse. No one in my family has or had a ranch.

¿Cuándo montas a caballo? Los fines de semana.
¿Dónde montas a caballo? En el rancho de mi tío.
¿Tienes tu propio caballo o alguien en tu familia tiene caballo? Tengo mi propio caballo.
¿Alguien en tu familia tiene un rancho o tuvo en el pasado? Tuvo en el pasado en Nogales.
(When do you ride horses? Weekends.
Where do you ride horses? At my uncle's ranch.
Do you or anybody else in your family have their own horse? I have my own horse.
Does anybody in your family have a ranch? Or have one in the past? In the past we had one in Nogales.)

Yo monto a caballo cuando me voy a México. El pueblo donde monto a caballo se llama Tres Alamos. Yo voy a Tres Alamos cuando salgo de vacaciones. Yo tengo mi propio caballo para montarlo. En mi familia mi tata tiene un rancho.
(I ride horses when I go to Mexico. The place I ride horses is Tres Alamos. I go to Tres Alamos during vacations. I have my own horse to ride there. My grandfather has a ranch.)

Knowledge of, and experience with, horses was widespread among my students this particular school year.

DEVELOPING CURRICULUM BASED ON FUNDS OF KNOWLEDGE

Once it became clear to me that a substantial portion of my class had background knowledge and experiences relating to horses, and once I decided to implement a module on this topic, I began collecting resources such as books and videos, and contacting guest speakers, including my students' parents. I did not want to plan too many lessons in advance because, like many other teachers participating in this project, I believe that students should participate in determining the direction their learning should take. Also, I want to give students themselves a chance to tell me what they know about a topic in order not to waste time reteaching students material they already know. The Funds of Knowledge project is not about replicating what students have learned at home, but about using students' knowledge and prior experiences as a scaffold for new learning.

Before I participated in the Funds of Knowledge project, I began new learning modules with a whole-class brainstorming session to explore my students' prior knowledge on the module's theme. I continued to do so as a participant in the project. But the brainstorming took on a whole new meaning because of the work I had done to get to know my students and families in an ethnographic sense. I also give my students the opportunity to formulate questions they would like to explore as part of a module. After the initial session of brainstorming and question generating is when I create ideas for lessons and activities that we will do during our module study. The following are a sample of some of the questions my students had about horses at the beginning of the horse module. They reflect both the knowledge my students already had about horses as well as the potential for in-depth learning to take place.

- How strong are horses?
- Why don't mares ever make a mistake in identifying their foals?
- Why do horses get diseases?
- How many bones and teeth do horses have?
- How can you tell how old they are?
- Can horses have more than one baby?
- How many miles can a horse run?
- Where do horses come from?

The following is a brief outline of the horse unit I implemented in my classroom, organized according to areas of the curriculum:

I.   Preparation: Collect books and materials related to theme from libraries and resource center to display and have available
II. Brainstorm what students already know and think about horses and what questions they have about the topic
III. Social Studies Topics
     - Spanish explorers and missionaries and their role in bringing horses to the Americas
     - Speaker on history and comparison of saddle types (English vs. Western)
     - Movies: "Vaqueros and Cowboys" and "Transporting Arizonans"
     - Early history of horses and their domestication
     - Horseracing in Mexico—home video
     - Laws pertaining to animals in the city
     - Different uses of horses

IV. Language Arts Topics
- Horse vocabulary in English and Spanish
- Stories from readers—"Fierazo," "La Vigüela," and "George Mc-Junkin Cowboy"
- Story analysis of video "Rodeo Red"
- Thank you letter to resource teacher for taking students to see horses and horse shoeing
- Online search of the public library catalog to find resources for research paper
- Library research
- Writing and oral presentation of research projects (to answer questions from brainstorming)

V. Science and Math Topics
- Horse anatomy
- Cells and multicelled living organisms
- Horse behavior: View movie "Horses and How They Live"
- Horse shoeing—live demonstration
- Field trip to see resource teacher's horses
- Field trip to home of student whose family had three horses in the neighborhood
- Individual interview of zookeeper on zebras for research report
- Converting hands (horse unit of measure) to inches and feet—table and graphs
- Life size graph of heights of different horse breeds
- Horse training: View movie "Black Stallion"
- Horse evolution
- Gestation, herd behavior
- Bipeds vs. quadrupeds

Again, one of the benefits of tapping into my students' background knowledge as a basis for classroom pedagogy is that I do not have to spend a lot of time teaching facts students already know. Instead, I can go on to more abstract and critical learning within a very short time period. The type of educational practice often prescribed for working-class and minoritized students is rote learning in small, incremental steps. I find this type of teaching to be stifling and unnecessary. My students are as capable of developing and carrying out their own inquiry-based research projects as students of any other background. In addition, when learning incorporates topics central to students' own lives, they become more confident and engaged learners, as I witnessed during the implementation of the horse module.

I am not advocating that all teachers of Latino students include the study of horses as part of a culturally inclusive curriculum. Most of my students are Mexican or Mexican origin. Their experiences are different, for instance, from those of Puerto Rican Americans or Cuban Americans. In that respect, this project cannot be packaged or standardized for export. What I do advocate, however, is that teachers become acquainted with their students through an ethnographic, not just a teacher, lens in order to get beyond a superficial and stereotypical familiarity with them. Through this process, which is the aspect of this project that can and should be replicated, ideas and themes will emerge for integrating students' cultural experiences into different areas of the curriculum, which go far beyond the current standardized routines. More importantly, this process gives students and their families a sense that their experiences are academically valid. For far too long, the homes of working class and minoritized students have been constructed as deficient and lacking in sufficient stimulation for academic success. It is time to rethink this construction and reevaluate how we teach. This runs counter to the practice of teaching the same curriculum and applying universal assessment criteria to all students—the "one size fits all" approach. It also runs counter to the tendency of many educators to view multicultural education as an "add-on" to the standard curriculum (Reissman, 1994).

IMPLICATIONS FOR THE ROLE OF TEACHERS

As I reflected, along with other participants in the Funds of Knowledge project, on whose knowledge should be used in the construction of curricula and assessments, that of my students or that of middle- and upper-class mainstream students, I also came to reflect critically on whose knowledge should control classroom practice—mine, or that of others in more powerful positions within the educational hierarchy. The traditional structure of a teacher's work being shaped by often politically motivated research, and by curricula developed by "specialists" further up the educational hierarchy, has been perpetuated by a number of factors, chief among them being the asymmetric distribution and valuation of the knowledge of individuals according to their location within the educational hierarchy. In undergraduate courses, and later in teacher in-services, the pedagogical knowledge teachers are exposed to is largely ahistorical and stripped of theory or details about its production. It is scripted and prescriptive, and teachers are rarely encouraged to critically analyze or question what they are taught. Even the knowledge teachers produce themselves through research is often labeled atheoretical and confined to short-term goals. The knowledge learned and produced by education researchers, administrators, specialists, and consultants, on the other hand, is considered to be more theoretical and is therefore more highly valued. Those at this level of the educational hierarchy control the "conception" of teachers' work, leaving teachers only to "execute" what has already been planned (Apple & Teitelbaum, 1986). The above factors are complicit in the suppression of the voices and experiences of teachers and contribute to the weakening control teachers have over their classrooms and their practice.

Anthropology provided me with conceptual tools to rework and improve my teaching. To what extent I will be able to use these tools is another matter, as I am situated within an institution that both devalues my knowledge and mandates most aspects of my daily practice. I am expected to structure my practice according to research, curricula, and means of assessment developed by individuals who have no firsthand knowledge of my students. One need only take a look at current textbook teachers' guides to realize that there is literally no need for teachers to think about their practice if they are so inclined (or so instructed). All teachers need to be able to do is follow the directions.

THE IMPORTANCE OF RELATIONSHIPS
IN THE SCHOOL SETTING

Participating in this project has had a profound impact on my thinking about multicultural education, teaching, and schools. It is difficult to summarize in a few words the impact it has had, especially when many others in this volume have done so, so well. It is not so difficult, however, to explain why I am still practicing many aspects of this project—especially the ethnographically oriented home visits. I am committed to this work because of the unique personal relationships that are established one at a time as I get to know my students' families. These relationships stand as symbols of opposition to all the rules and regulations and bureaucratic practices that try to confine and define the student, the teacher, and the parent roles within educational institutions. Through home visits, we become real people to each other rather than shadow figures occupying our different niches. I stay involved in this project because of the rewarding personal relationships I can develop with my students' families that this process allows in an otherwise very impersonal context.

The impact and importance of personal relationships in the educational setting goes unrecognized. As I visit my students' homes and interview them and their families, layers are added to our relationships. With each home visit, we teachers become more a part of the socially dense contexts within which our students are growing up (see Vélez-Ibáñez & Greenberg, this volume). Parents whose homes we visit drop by our classrooms to make social visits or to extend invitations to our students' birthday parties or First Communion celebrations. New babies are brought by for us to meet.

It would be a tragedy to overlook or ignore this aspect of the Funds of Knowledge project. Because of the deeper relationships we develop with our students and their families, all of us become more invested in and committed to the educational process. I go out of my way to do things for students whose homes I have visited. This act on my part is reciprocated in many ways by those students and their families in their dealings with me, both within and outside the classroom. The students whose homes I visit are the students I will never forget.

Why are these bonds so important? Because you can know the academic standards inside and out, and write the most creative lesson plans, but if positive, affirming, and mutually respectful relationships are not the norm in our classrooms, no learning will take place. Even academic knowledge must be distributed through social relations.

This fact stands in stark contrast to the current trend to assume that all teachers need to know about their students for effective instructional planning is contained in test scores. These days, staff development has been narrowed to the study of test data on which pedagogical choices are to be made. Educational decisions are "data-driven." But test data are only part of the picture and do not provide teachers with enough information to effectively instruct and engage their students. Coming to know their students intimately, as participating teachers in the Funds of Knowledge project do, is the piece that is missing in education planning today.

REFLECTION QUESTIONS

1. How would you define multicultural education? How does this compare with what you believe Amanti's definition to be? (see Ovando & Collier's chapter on "Culture" in *Bilingual and ESL Classrooms: Teaching in Multicultural Contexts,* 1998, for a good discussion of multicultural education, as well as González's chapter in this volume).

2. What do the media say about the community in which you work? Does your experience in the community support or refute the media image?

3. What are some of the funds of knowledge present in your students' homes? How could you draw on these funds to enhance your classroom practice?

4. How does the parent–teacher relationship change when teachers visit their students' homes to discover their students' families' funds of knowledge?

REFERENCES

Apple, M., & Teitelbaum, K. (1986). Are teachers losing control of their skills and curriculum? *Journal of Curriculum Studies, 18*(2), 177–184.

Ovando, C. J., & Collier, V. P. (1998). *Bilingual and ESL classrooms: Teaching in multicultural contexts.* Boston: McGraw-Hill.

Reissman, R. (1994). *The evolving multicultural classroom.* Alexandria, VA: Association for Supervision and Curriculum Development.

Rosaldo, R. (1989). *Culture & truth: The remaking of social analysis.* Boston: Beacon Press.

Chapter 8

Empowering Parents of Multicultural Backgrounds

Marla Hensley
Cavett School, Tucson, Arizona

Parents in the neighborhood where I teach in Tucson, Arizona, are sometimes viewed as lacking. They are viewed as lacking in parenting skills, lacking in education and lacking in knowledge. When I began this project, I thought I knew the community where I taught. I had always made an effort to welcome parents into my classroom and validate them and their opinions. Yet when I look back, I realize that even with the efforts I made, there were many funds of knowledge to be tapped.

I will give an example of how my experience in conducting ethnographic research helped me reach this untapped potential. This is really a case history of Jacob, the African-American father of one of my kindergarten students, Alicia. The change that occurred in Jacob was phenomenal and yet the talents were there just waiting to be channeled in a new direction. I had chosen Alicia's family for my first interview. I had some difficulties with Alicia's behavior and thought working with the family would help.

I had made home visits many times over the prior 10 years, but the focus had always been a teacher agenda. I wanted to know what the parents and I could do to help the student whose home I was visiting. If you contrast this with the actions of being an ethnographer, the whole atmosphere changes because you let the parents do the talking. A rapport develops that puts everyone at ease.

Prior to my home visit, Alicia's dad, Jacob, had brought their pet rabbit to school when we were studying pets. I found out he was a groundskeeper. I was looking for some expertise to start a garden with my kindergarten class and he was the perfect person to do just that. Jacob helped us prepare and plant a vegetable and flower garden. As far as I was concerned I had already tapped into a fund of knowledge and my project was a success. If I had not gone to the home I would have thought that gardening was the most important fund of knowledge Jacob had to offer. By the end of my second home visit and interview, however, I had discovered that Jacob had impressive communication skills. He would ponder each question and respond in an articulate and eloquent fashion. His communication skills were another fund of knowledge.

During one of my visits to Jacob's home, I noticed a guitar propped against a closet and discovered Jacob played guitar and keyboard and also wrote songs and poetry. I might have discovered this resource if I had sent a survey home, but I would have probably only asked Jacob to come in to play for us. Instead, I asked him to write children's songs and create a musical based on the story of The Little Red Hen. It would tie in both his knowledge of music and of gardening. When Jacob came to class after writing his first two songs, it was amazing. The kids loved the catchy words he had written and tunes he played on his guitar and his keyboard. We began to get down to the business of putting the musical together and practicing on the stage.

By this time I had started to interview my second family. Wanda was an African-American single mother raising her son and was a foster parent to many other children. It turned out she had a background in dance so I asked her to help choreograph our musical. She worked full time but was able to come in on her days off.

The preparations for the musical Jacob had written were in full swing! I organized costume-making workshops and several of the parents participated. The children learned seven songs for the play, with two of the songs related to spin-off topics. Since the Little Red Hen story involves bread-making, we did a multicultural unit on bread and I asked Jacob to write a tortilla song. A Navajo parent came in to help us make fry bread and my teaching assistant's *nana* and *tía* (101 and 102 years old!) came to school to make tortillas with the children. I would not have thought to have these two tortilla-making experts come if I had not actually been seeking further funds of knowledge. The children sang the tortilla song over and over.

The class performance of the musical was an incredible experience. We performed it five times for the parents and for other classes in school. The talents Jacob shared with the class were great, but the other results for him were far more important than presenting the musical to the parents. These results included:

- He realized he loved working with children and coming to the school. He experienced enjoyment!
- He had control! He was empowered. His skills were needed.

- He was interested. He wanted to be there and was engaged.
- Jacob realized that his musical talents could be shifted to children and writing children's songs, which he had never done before. He felt success! He could see the children's reaction to his songs.
- His self-worth increased, as he felt valued. No one judged him by the way he looked, the clothes he wore, or the amount of his education. He was accepted for who he was and what he had to offer.

Jacob was not the only one to benefit from this experience. The children and parents benefited by seeing a parent bring a new avenue of learning into the classroom. Parents could see that they were valued and that their talents could be utilized. In a community where parent participation is often poor, more parents participated as we needed costume makers, stagehands, and make-up experts. Some parents made up their own ideas for the costumes and created very unique designs. That increased their self-esteem and confidence because the teacher did not impose the costume designs! We even had all but one family at the performance for the parents!

The children changed dramatically, too. When they first went on stage some were shy and would not sing. But by the end, we had a class full of soloists and performers. They gained a tremendous amount of self-esteem. The parents saw the growth in their children as a result of this performance, and many of them were moved to tears. The play gave the class a special bond that they will remember for the rest of their lives.

Alicia was especially proud of her father, and that made her proud of herself. She adjusted better because she knew me as a person rather than just a teacher.

WHAT OTHER IMPACTS DID THE MUSICAL HAVE ON JACOB?

Jacob ended up writing a musical for his son's fifth grade class as well. This second musical focused on the issues of drugs, violence, and gang pressures. The children helped him write it. You might think that was the end of the story but it was only the beginning.

That year, Jacob had rarely attended any Parent–Teacher Association (PTA) meetings and was turned off by the negativity of the meetings. His involvement with the musicals brought out his concern with the PTA leadership so he decided to run for, and was elected, president.

The next year, Jacob was extremely involved at school. He conducted the PTA meetings with sensitivity and led them in a positive direction. This positive focus inspired much greater attendance and a more balanced ethnic representation among attendees than in the past. That year an issue came to the forefront concerning the right of our school's students to attend their neighborhood middle school instead of being bused across town to comply with court-ordered desegregation mandates. Jacob rallied the parents around this cause and he spoke to the school board about the injustice. His speech was featured on the news that evening on all three channels. Currently the issue is being brought before a federal judge.

Jacob's involvement was a catalyst for change and empowered the students and parents. Parents who never attended meetings before were suddenly not only coming to the meetings, but also speaking out, asking questions, demanding answers, and addressing officials who were brought to the school to listen to their concerns.

Jacob was obviously an untapped gold mine of funds of knowledge. He was not just a knowledgeable gardener; he also had musical talents, the ability to relate to children and adults and a desire to make a difference in people's lives. He just had not realized how to do this. His ability to express himself while listening to others and empowering them made him a great leader.

HOW ARE TEACHERS, PARENTS, AND CHILDREN CHANGED WHEN TEACHERS TAP INTO FUNDS OF KNOWLEDGE?

Through these in-depth case studies of families, the teacher-researcher begins to tap into a wide range of resources he or she previously may not have realized were available. The teacher develops ideas and strategies to utilize these skills. The fact that teachers are enthusiastic when they discover these talents is critical in motivating parents and children. If the teacher places value on this knowledge, then the parents suddenly feel important. They feel empowered. This alone can dramatically change the climate of the teacher–home relationship. The parents feel equal. The barrier between the professional and the home caregiver is broken. A friendship develops and the relationship becomes ongoing and permanent.

Back in the classroom, the teacher shares the discoveries she has made about the students' families with the children. The child hears the teacher extolling all the skills and knowledge her parents have, and the child's perception of her own parents improves as well as the child's perception of herself. This often creates a special bond between the child and the teacher, which helps them cope better when there are conflicts.

After making visits to a student's home and discovering all its resources, the teacher views that student differently. The teacher has seen the child in her home setting, which helps in understanding the whole child. The teacher is able to relate classroom experiences to situations the child has experienced. The teacher listens more attentively and is more enthusiastic and sensitive with this child. A ripple effect also occurs—the teacher, to some extent, is more sensitive to all the children and their parents, even if there has not been a direct home visit.

Once a teacher has spent time in a child's home, the teacher can, to some degree, have a better feel for the home lives of all students. Homes are different, and it is beneficial to visit each family as time permits. But connecting with just one family creates an awareness of parents as people. These are people with skills to offer, with successes and struggles, and with goals and dreams. Teachers take more interest when children discuss happenings in the home and ask more questions. For example, a child recently came to school wearing a T-shirt with a handpainted cactus. Prior to being involved in this project, my response to this shirt might have been to say, "Isn't that a cute shirt!" Instead, I wanted to know where he got it and who made it. When he told me his grandmother painted it, I was ecstatic. I knew I had found a fund of knowledge that I could use. I decided to have my class decorate T-shirts. More than half the parents in my classroom helped to raise the money to buy the shirts and supplies with a bake sale, and then they helped the children paint the fronts of their shirts.

I interviewed another family recently and discovered that the father was exceptionally artistic. I told the class that Crystal's dad was an artist. Normally, I would not have noticed that talent but just noticed that he was a custodian at a school. Crystal beamed with pride. All that day she sang, "My dad's an artist. My dad's an artist!" It boosted her self-esteem and made her proud of her dad. That night I took the T-shirts to their house because we were doing decorative lettering and designs on the backs of all the T-shirts. The dad smiled as I told him about the song Crystal had sung. Normally, I would not have had any contact with this family since the parents both work full-time. This project allowed them to participate outside the classroom.

I feel so comfortable with this family now and I know they feel comfortable with me. Crystal has really bonded with me. At the beginning of the year, she was intensely sensitive, but the home visits have helped her adjust better.

FROM MATH TO FUNDS OF KNOWLEDGE TO QUILTS

Another experience I had integrating funds of knowledge into my curriculum was through studying quilts as part of a math investigation. A child mentioned that his grandmother made quilts. Previously I would have just said, "Wow, that's great!" This quilting resource gave me the idea to have every child make a family quilt. Each family drew pictures of the members and special events on quilt squares and intermingled them with scrap material squares. Parents who did not have time or knowledge were helped by parents who did. I discovered many parents made quilts, so this project tapped into the talents of many families.

OTHER SPINOFFS

Identifying the funds of knowledge of my students' families has led me to reflect on my own funds of knowledge. Recently, I wrote some songs for a musical about the desert. I discovered I could write songs as well! I have funds of knowledge that I have not yet tapped.

As another example, during our fall conference one year, Wilma, a grandmother, told me she was very busy and would not be able to volunteer very often. I asked her what she did and she said she made African American clothes with material she ordered from Africa. She displayed them in fashion shows. I asked her if we could put on a fashion show with our class in the spring, when it fit into her time schedule. She said "yes," but months went by without any more mention of it. Finally, we talked about it again and I started to request donations of material from the parents.

I ordered some solid, bright-colored material from the school warehouse and got a multicultural book from the library for parents and students to see designs from different cultures. I asked a parent to cut sponges in the shape of some Ashanti symbols from Ghana. While I still envisioned Wilma sewing outfits for the whole class, I knew this would be extremely time consuming.

The project got underway with two mothers and their daughters who worked in the classroom while the class was outside. They used acrylic paints and each made different designs on their large piece of fabric. One was very structured with a large lizard and the prints in squares, and the other had prints and dots all over it. As the parents were talking, I discovered that one of the mothers, an African American woman, had a sister who also put on fashion shows. Evelyn had learned (from her sister) how to wrap the large material into a dress. That was the answer for most of the girls' outfits. No sewing was needed. Parents could come in, do designs on the fabric, and the outfit was ready.

Wilma then brought in her own material to school, and about 10 kids painted on the fabric. She took the fabric home and sewed a dashiki top with a gathered skirt that was stunning. I began to display all of the outfits as they were created. Grandfathers and grandmothers, mothers and fathers (including two who had not participated all year), aunts and uncles, all came to help their child print and paint their outfits. The boys used a simple V-neck Ghanaian dashiki design that only needed a small amount of stitching on each side under the arms. Various parents sewed these.

Once we had the outfits, we arranged the fashion show. I decided to teach the children an African rain dance, and we made rainmakers from toilet paper rolls filled with macaroni. We included an authentic rainmaker stick that a parent had loaned us. We collected both African and traditional instruments to use in the production.

At the same time all this parent participation was going on, I received a fabric kit from the University of California at Berkeley Lawrence Hall of Science's Full Option Science System (FOSS) science program, a program our district has adopted, which was perfect. We investigated fabrics. Some parents brought in different fabrics, and we made a display of the weavings (using cross-age helpers). We did additional investigations such as taking material apart to learn about its construction. Students compared and tested fabric for absorbency and experimented with stains and ways to remove them. The children could really see the stages of the project, "From Fabric to Fashion," which covered the walls with the science work and clothing designs.

As I have mentioned, this particular success did not stem from a single home visit; rather it was inspired by my experience making home visits. I learned many things from the home visits that enabled me to recognize a fund of knowledge and expand on it. I am more tuned in to parents now because of my experience with the Funds of Knowledge project. It is important to perceive the parent as someone with expertise, and this helps create a trusting relationship between parents and teachers.

WHAT CAN TEACHERS DO TO DISCOVER THE FUNDS OF KNOWLEDGE OF THEIR STUDENTS' FAMILIES?

I have found that the following ideas have been helpful to me when seeking to discover the funds of knowledge of my students' families:

- Go on at least one or two home visits with the sole purpose of learning about the family and their talents.
- Listen actively to your students and they will continuously give you clues about their interests and the talents of their parents and grandparents.
- Look for homemade articles the children are wearing and ask questions about these articles.
- Have your students interview their parents at home about their talents and bring the information to share.

- when parents come to visit at school, build a rapport with them and be interested in their activities and projects. Field trips are a great format for these casual conversations. Talk to parents while on the playground or when children are having free choice.
- At an open house, have the parents pair up and briefly interview each other to find out what they enjoy doing and what they feel they do well. Have them write down these skills for you to refer to later. Then introduce the parents to the group and mention their special talents. This will help them get to know each other and recognize common threads in the group.
- Projects that need individual help from parents provide an incentive for participation.
- Incorporate the occupations of the parents in your thematic planning.
- Find out where parents work and arrange field trips to visit their work, even if only to the outside.

CONCLUSION

I feel there is a tremendously heightened sensitivity and curiosity about students and their families that is awakened by participating in this work. This enhances my teaching as I allow children and parents to feel valued and use their knowledge in developing the curriculum. The children and parents feel more ownership in their school, build their self-esteem, and develop a stronger comfort level with the school. New teacher–parent relationships transcend the typical teacher–parent connection and foster a friend-to-friend interchange that creates a new bond of closeness and purpose. The families that participate enjoy being involved. They are empowered to use their skills and talents. The parents and children are interested because their ideas are used in the curriculum. Parents feel success with their efforts. They make a contribution and a difference. Finally, they feel pride in themselves and their accomplishments and feel valued and equal.

If teachers include parents and families in the formula for educating children and seriously listen to and value their funds of knowledge, we will turn the key that unlocks the door to a bright future for children and their parents.

REFLECTION QUESTIONS

1. How do home visits in the Funds of Knowledge project differ from traditional teacher visits to students' homes?

2. What does the author of this chapter mean by "parent participation is often poor"? How can the Funds of Knowledge project increase parent participation in schools?

3. What are some of the different models of parent involvement in schools?

Chapter 9

Home Is Where the Heart Is: Planning a Funds of Knowledge-Based Curriculum Module

Patricia Sandoval-Taylor
Tucson Unified School District

The year that I participated in the Funds of Knowledge project, I was a teacher at Booker Elementary (pseudonym), and I had moved up with my first grade class to second grade. Booker is located on the outskirts of a Native American reservation, where about 40% of my students were Native American (Yaqui) and about 50% were Hispanic. Because the Yaqui people have roots in the northern Mexican state of Sonora, and because of our borderland context, many of the Yaqui students are also Spanish speakers. Yoeme, the Yaqui language, was also included in our classroom language practices in certain contexts.

I had visited my students' homes during the time that they were in first grade, and using some of the information gathered from this ethnographic fieldwork, I decided to create a learning module based on the concept of "construction" for my second grade bilingual education class. This was a topic that came up frequently when I did my home interviews the previous year. Since I was going to have the same students in my class for a second year, I used the fieldnotes from the previous school year when I taught first grade.

During my fieldwork I observed that many of the families interviewed had building and construction experience. I noticed a lot of construction in their homes, such as bricklaying and concrete work. I observed that some of the children had their own building tools. One of them had a miniature trowel; others had their own hammers.

Since I was tied to the Funds of Knowledge project, I was invited to meet with project consultants to share my ideas and plan the learning module. In a series of meetings over the summer, Norma González, Cathy Amanti, Marta Civil (a math professor at the University of Arizona), and I developed a construction module for my second grade classroom for implementation in the fall. Prior to the meetings I went through my fieldnotes and the fieldnotes of other Booker teachers who had participated in the pilot project. I also read two books—*Learning and Loving It: Theme Studies in the Classroom* (Kwak, Hutchings, Altheim, Gamberg, & Edwards, 1988) and the National Council of Teachers of Mathematics' (NCTM) book on math assessment—because I wanted to emphasize mathematics in the module. In the remainder of this chapter I recount both the planning process and the thinking that went into the development of the construction module as well as my experience in implementing it.

THE PLANNING PROCESS

At our first meeting, I began by reviewing what I hoped to accomplish during this unit, which is something I do when planning any classroom activity. I wanted the module to be inquiry-based, focused on my students' prior knowledge, and I also wanted the children to make the decisions and negotiate the curriculum. This would allow students to use their knowledge as a starting point from which to grow. I also wanted to prove that these children would achieve academically, which I hoped to demonstrate through a holistic assessment component. We began by brainstorming ways that we could tap into the knowledge that my students already had.

We also brainstormed ideas about how we could include all of my goals for this module. Math became an area of focus during our brainstorming because I saw the mathematical potential of a construction module's theme and it was one of my goals. During the brainstorming, we put together a list of activities that could become part of the module. For instance, I wanted students to survey their parents to see what they had built and have some of the parents come into the classroom to be expert consultants. I also wanted to have my students compare and contrast their homes with those of their grandparents. I hoped to have my students learn about diameter, perimeter, volume, and fractions (for instance, as relating to mixing concrete). In addition, I wanted to have them take some field trips related to the unit. We brainstormed many other activities that could be included in the learning module.

In planning the activities for this module, I revisited a medicinal plant module I had implemented during the pilot phase of the project, in order to draw from the strengths of that experience. From this experience, I knew that students would become experts, teaching each other about areas of construction based on their own background. This issue came up as we discussed the type of teaching I would be doing—what my role would be as a teacher. We talked about to what degree the unit should be teacher- or student-directed. My plant module had been very student-directed. We also talked about how much factual knowledge students should be acquiring and whether students should be taught the processes for finding out information (e.g., how to use a dictionary to spell a word) or taught the information itself (learn how a word is spelled so that you can spell it when writing).

At our first meeting we also talked about my goals for the assessment component. We discussed how to show that the children had grown in reading, writing, and mathematics. We decided that one way we could assess students would be by interviewing children in pairs. We designed a pre- and a post-interview that would be given to six students where we asked them one simple question: "How do you build a home?" In addition, we decided the entire class would respond to the same question in writing as a pre- and postassessment.

As for how long the construction module would last, I did not want to set any limits because I thought that would betray the goal of students taking ownership of the learning process. I took a thematic cycle approach to curriculum construction so that issues students brought up during the construction module could become topics for cycles that would follow. This is where the connections are made to new learning. I wanted to be sure this unit would help my students later on. I also wanted this unit to be motivational, to engage students in ongoing and broader goals such as increased reading, writing, and math proficiency.

During the first meeting we brainstormed the following possible goals for the construction learning module:

1. Students will learn about estimation, measuring, fractions, and geometric concepts such as area, patterns, perimeter, and volume.
2. Students will become familiar with research strategies. These may include collecting information and identifying what they need to know and how to get it.

The final work we did at our first planning meeting was to make a rough outline of what would happen in my classroom during the first days of the construction module:

Day 1

- Read "The Three Little Pigs" to the class.

- Web student ideas related to: What building is being done around your home? How many of you know how to build or have seen someone build?
- Ask and record, "What are some things you would like to know about building?" Ask other questions to help provide some direction for later lessons to meet some of my other goals for student learning.
- Homework would be for each student to draw their own home and tell about it the next day in class.

Day 2

- Students share their own drawings of their homes in small groups.
- Ask students if they have any additional questions about building. Prioritize student questions with their help.
- Select five of the questions for students to begin answering.
- Have students form cooperative groups to answer questions in which they are interested.
- Have groups brainstorm ways to research answers to their questions.
- Share brainstorming with the rest of the class.
- Have students write their own group's question on a sheet of paper for homework so they can ask their parents if they have any information to help in answering the question. Students will write what parents have to say on this sheet for homework.

Day 3

- In groups, students share findings from homework assignment with whole class.
- Begin compiling a class construction dictionary (three-ring binder with dividers on which topics are written so that the dictionary can be added to during the module; topics will be alphabetized).
- Repeat process of answering other questions through homework assignments if there are enough appropriate questions.

Days 4 through 6

- Have parents come in as experts to speak on construction topics. Students may use parents as a resource to answer the questions they have generated.
- Continue adding new information to construction dictionary.

Day 7

- Brainstorm with students something they would like to build.

This was as far as I wanted to go in planning the construction learning module, although we also came up with a list of other possible activities to include in the module later on (see Table 9.1). I wanted to see what my students' interests were to help guide the direction the module would take before making further decisions. It seemed contradictory to do too much planning in advance. I thought it might be a good idea to do the rest of the unit planning at the end of the first week of implementing the module after I'd been able to assess my students' knowledge and interests as well as the knowledge of their parents.

I met with the project consultants the next day to continue planning. First, I talked about a chapter I had just read in *Learning and Loving It* (Kwak et al., 1988) that talks about a theme study on construction for five and six-year-olds. It reinforced what we had talked about the day before when we had discussed teaching factual knowledge versus process. The teachers in the book felt they needed to teach some things separate from the theme

TABLE 9.1
Ideas for Related Activities to Construction Study

- Free exploration—Build with lumber scraps or other materials such as spaghetti and gum drops, sugar cubes, etc.
- View other children's structures and reflect on their own structures.
- Build major structure of student's choice (e.g., animal home, loft, playhouse).
- Build model playground or neighborhood (scaled to toy figure).
- Research how animals build their homes.
- Study what different kinds of building materials are used to make structures.
- Compare how homes differ in material in different climates and regions of the world.
- Discuss what materials are good for different purposes.
- Invite a draftsperson to give a talk to the class about his or her work.
- Look at the blueprints for Booker School and discuss.
- Make "how-to" instruction books related to module theme. Information could be researched or recalled from a talk by a visitor.
- Do surveys to answer some of students' questions. Possible other surveys may include kinds of homes students live in (i.e., brick, wood, mobile, etc.).
- "Construct" something by sewing it (e.g., make a quilt with each student designing a panel, or curtains for a loft if that is what students decide to build).
- In pairs have students design an ideal room in a house. Make a model of it with an architectural, top-down view.
- Measure bricks. Compare and make a chart or graph.
- Build structures out of cookies.
- Make a three-dimensional diorama of a room in a shoe or other box, including furniture. Have students bring in figurines to use for scale.
- Estimate the volume of a given container. Have students fill a jar of water and estimate the number of jars needed to fill the container (to simulate the pouring of concrete).
- Make plaster walls for building a model home. Have students pour plaster into flat containers and then use them to build a small structure.
- Explore choosing a strong mixture for bonding materials. The students could observe different types of mixtures and decide which is best to use as mortar.

study. I wanted to use some of the activities from the book but I wanted to tie my activities more strongly to my students' community.

We reviewed the ideas we had come up with the day before and added to the list new ones we had thought of in the meantime. We talked about where the module planning had stalled. One of the problems was deciding the how and why of incorporating strategies for building homes into the module. The discussion went back and forth on this issue, and it was decided that Day 7 would be changed from a brainstorming day for a student construction project to a day of free exploration with materials such as pattern blocks, Legos, and other math manipulatives. I talked about one activity from *Learning and Loving It* in which students drew homes and the tools used in construction. From this, we thought of other ideas for classroom activities that my class could do during the module. The revised seventh day activity would be as follows:

Day 7

- Students will explore building structures using different manipulatives (unifix cubes, pattern blocks, Legos, and Cuisenaire rods) located in stations. There will be a maximum of four students per station at a time. They will build houses, reflect on their structures, and talk about them. Possible additional extensions to this activity will include written descriptions of their structures, including measurements of height, length, and perimeter, estimation, and counting of number units used in construction (e.g., bricks in a wall).

Next, we talked about whether it was a good idea to include a major construction activity as part of the unit. After some discussion, we went back to the idea that the unit should be designed so those topics that crop up spontaneously during the actual implementation can be integrated into the module. In terms of doing a big construction project, which might make a good culminating activity, I thought that an appropriate final project or activity that would bring closure to the unit might not emerge until the unit was under way. The solution to this problem of how much planning to do ahead of time was resolved by the idea of having a teacher's activity menu which could be drawn on according to the direction the unit was going.

We met again five days later. During that time we had all given some thought to this project. I decided to talk to an expert in construction to become familiar with the process and to make a list of tasks involved in building so that I could point out the process to my students as it emerged during the unit. We returned to discussing the idea of having a menu of possible activities prepared to accompany the unit ahead of time. I wanted to be able to do mini-lessons on topics when my students brought them up.

For instance, if a parent visited the class and brought up estimating how many nails are needed for a certain task, I wanted to be able to follow this with a mini-lesson on estimation. The parent would provide the focus, and the set would already be there for this lesson. I had also been thinking about the idea of having students compare their homes with their grandparents' homes. We had not talked about this since the first planning day, but I wanted to elaborate and use this idea.

Once again, I brought up the fact that I wanted my students to be involved in shaping the module's culminating activity. I explained that I believed my role in this activity should be having the resources available to facilitate its implementation. An example of this might be bringing my father in to help the students construct something if that is what they are interested in doing.

Our discussion returned to the issue of assessment of the learning taking place during the unit. Thinking about what my students would be learning prompted me to think about what tasks are involved in building something. We talked about the pros and cons of individual versus group assessment as well as what form the assessment should take. In the assessment, it would be important to look for whether students' writing is well thought through and makes sense, and whether the students use mathematics in a meaningful and organized way. A pre- and postwriting assessment for the unit was easy to come up with. It was not as easy to come up with a math assessment. Designing the specific student task was difficult. We agreed that the pre- and posttest would begin with posing a problem to all students. They would first respond individually, either orally or in writing, discussing how they would go about solving that problem. I would select six students to interview orally about their solution—two with high oral skills, two with average oral skills, and two with low oral skills. At each level I selected one student dominant in Spanish and one dominant in English. After they responded to the problem individually, they would respond to the problem as a whole group. This would take into consideration the student as an individual learner and a group learner. I preferred individual assessment so that I could assess individual growth. Norma González brought up the fact that in cooperative work, learning is participatory and can be assessed as well. I pointed out that in group assessment, learning is still taking place as students share ideas; that students will perform better in cooperative assessment.

We returned to a discussion of the specific prompt that I would use for the assessment. Marta Civil suggested using one of her ideas from a previous planning meeting in which students would be asked to build a proportional model of a chair for a doll. The posttest could involve students making something else for this doll. I was not sure that learning about proportion would emerge during the unit. From my experiences in my students' community, I thought that the unit focus would more likely be on constructing buildings. I thought this might be a better focus for an assessment prompt. Students could be asked, for instance, how to build an additional room on their homes.

We talked about how general or specific the prompt should be and whether the students should be asked to perform a task during or after the assessment. During the assessment they could write or talk about the steps they would take and why. After the assessment, students could confirm or check whether what they wrote would work.

The meeting ended with no agreement on what prompt I should use for the math pretest. I felt that I needed to leave things the way they were and think about them for a while. I was satisfied with the assessment procedure but still felt that parents would contribute additional knowledge that would help students on the posttest, and I wanted to reflect this in the assessment task. I knew students would grow when parents came in and particularly when students used them as resources to answer their own questions.

We met again three weeks later. Since the last meeting I had read about student assessment in *Learning and Loving It* (Kwak et al., 1988). Something I found in the book that I liked was the idea of making checklists of what students are learning as the unit develops. I thought I could develop a checklist at least in the area of mathematics then use it to assess what students had learned. Other areas mentioned which could be assessed in this way were social studies and social skills. The authors of this book felt that you could teach thematically but not assess thematically. This might have contributed to the difficulty we had conceptualizing how to go about assessing student learning during the learning module's implementation.

Another idea I had about assessment was that I would like to have a general pre- and posttest that would allow students to bring in more of what they had learned than they would if they were given a specific task. I wanted to do this because a general assessment task was more compatible with what I envisioned for the pre- and posttests, and a specific assessment task was more appropriate to measure learning within the unit. I was concerned with emphasizing process over product in assessment, especially in the general assessment task. I wanted to make sure that my students had the opportunity to show what they know and have learned, using a holistic assessment rather than criterion-based assessment, because there is often an underestimating of what students can do.

I also wanted to encourage my students to evaluate themselves and what they had learned during the unit implementation. My role in this would be to question the students about their work and ask them to reflect on it as they went on. This would be a more spontaneous type of assessment.

At this point, I was satisfied with the amount of planning that had been done ahead of time for the construction unit. The rest would be done after school started. The first week of school I planned to call the parents I wanted to invite to my classroom during the module. I also planned to invite my father to become involved. In addition, I thought I would call and ask Brown Construction Company (pseudonym) to send someone who had helped build Booker Elementary to my class during the module. I did not plan to begin implementing this module until the second or third week of school.

IMPLEMENTATION

During the module's implementation I used many of the activities I had brainstormed in our meetings over the summer. I added some new ones as well. I tried to let the children take the module where it needed to go, but I still included pieces of literature that I needed to cover as part of the curriculum. I went through my required curriculum to find out where pieces could fit.

Because I wanted this module to be literature-based, before beginning to teach the module I collaborated with the school librarian in collecting a set of literature related to the theme of construction. I wanted to read one of these books to my students every day before beginning work related to the construction module to provide context for the learning that would occur.

As I was implementing the construction module, I had to deal with the normal everyday pressures of teaching. Certain holidays were coming up and I did not want to take away from activities that would have normally occurred. So I modified them. For example, when we started learning and talking about what it takes to build a home, the idea of blueprints came up. It was Halloween, and we were making a haunted house out of shoeboxes, so I had my students draw a blueprint of their haunted houses first. Then they replicated their blueprints when they built their houses. Each student created his or her own room, but we put the rooms together to make one big haunted house. We taped the blueprint on the sides. People could see that they followed the blueprint.

Other activities we did during the actual implementation of the unit included reading the story of the "Three Little Pigs." After reading the story we discussed the different methods the pigs used to construct their homes. We compared and contrasted the three little pigs' homes. I asked my students which they thought was stronger and why. We read the poem "Home is where the heart is" by Jack Prelutsky. He was our author of the month when I read the poem. We did sequencing activities with the poem, and the students wrote their own poems about homes.

One day I showed my students pictures of different kinds of houses. We discussed the different styles of buildings. We looked at a trailer, a glass house, and so forth. My students had to discuss why they liked a particular house better than the others.

We took a walk around the school looking for geometric shapes in our new school building. Then I asked my students to draw a house with just one geometric shape. I showed my class a picture of a geodesic dome made only with triangles. My students used manipulatives to create a dome in cooperative groups and then drew it.

We integrated our study with our computer lab work. The students drew pictures of houses using Kid Pix, then that same day they wrote about what they had drawn. The writing helped me understand how my students were thinking.

For one activity, I had the students work in pairs and take turns constructing a house using different math manipulatives. After one student built a home, the other one had to replicate it exactly. The students had to think mathematically in order to replicate what their partner had built. The students building with the unifix cubes, for example, had to pay attention to certain attributes of the cubes in order to build a home like their partner had built. It was challenging for them. As a teacher, I wanted to challenge them—I wanted them to think. I was concerned with process. The central question was: What does it take to get there? I was trying to encourage the children to problem solve. In the real world, I am sure builders do this.

LOOKING BACK

The planning of this module was often frustrating. I knew my academic objectives, but I was not exactly sure how I would make them fit into this theme. It was not a common theme to work with. There were more resources readily available to teach themes like weather or plants. Also, I was letting go of the reins of teacher-directed instruction because a lot of the curriculum was being negotiated. I felt that I was in a state of uncertainty, yet I still had to cover certain areas of the curriculum. I had to make sure that my students learned the strategies and skills to be academically successful.

In looking back I realize that, given the current context of high-stakes testing and scripted curriculum, my students were catapulted to higher levels of literacy and numeracy during this module because I had provided them with multiple access to the content. In the words of Jim Cummins, "we provide the scaffolding [for content learning] by embedding the content in a richly redundant context where there are multiple routes to the meaning in addition to the language itself" (2003, p. 6). I felt I had accomplished this in this module.

The creation and implementation of this thematic module was an event that led me to a higher level of teaching. My students flourished in ways that I did not expect. I believed my students had internalized what they were learning because what they brought from home surrounded and supported their learning. The context was provided and I was able to teach additional content within this realm. The feeling of uncertainty I had felt in the beginning was now gone with the progress and products the students had made. While there are some who might see the in-depth planning process as being unworkable and too time-consuming, I found that the investment in planning yielded a more productive and integrated learning experience for the students. The planning became the heart of the experience.

◆ ◆ ◆

Patricia Sandoval-Taylor implemented her construction learning module during the fall of 1992 with her second grade bilingual students at Booker Elementary School. Her progress was documented and six of her students were given an oral pre- and posttest, as planned. In addition, her whole class was given a written pre- and posttest. Her students exhibited significant growth in knowledge and vocabulary during their construction study. The results of the written pre- and posttests follow. During both the pre- and posttest, students were asked to write down how they would go about building a house. Sandoval-Taylor encouraged her students to invent the spelling of words that are in their vocabulary but whose written form may be unfamiliar to them. (Editor)

◆ ◆ ◆

Lola's Pretest
October 1, 1992
Do you no how to bild a home. I do wache and see. You hafe to groe ii frist. En then you hafe to pant it. En then you bild it. Then you have some piple living in ther.

Lola's Posttest
November 30, 1992
How to Build a house
First you make the blue print. Secend you dig up a hole with a mashing. Thrd you make the wall's. Forth you get redy to stand up the wall's. Fift you put plaster on the wall's. Six you frame the house. seven you copy the Blue print. Eite you get 2x4 then you hammer The 2x4. Nine you put the mud betin the bikse. Ten you paent in side and out side. Eleven pepel move in a prty buteful so prty house.

Arnulfo's Pretest
October 1, 1992
you need sum wood. you need sum Pantu. you need sum shegos. you need a hamer and Naos. and you need a sol.

Arnulfo's Posttest
November 30, 1992
Fast you put cement. and Then you Smove out The cement. Then
Thay put The floor. and put Then a boy put's 2x4's Then The
Carperner's Thay put Windol's and door's and Thay put a roof
win Thay put The roof Thay put Tar and win Thay put Tar Thay
put shingligo's. Then the electr put's wier's for the electrician win The electrician Then Thay put's lith and fan's and
a fidjerwayter win The Hosue Is Finesh Thay Pait The Hosue

Rosa's Pretest
October 1, 1992
how to Bieald a house
If you want to bieald a house you have to buy fiberglas. you
need Lot's of wood you need shieat roxk and sideding, a flor.

Rosa's Posttest
November 30, 1992
How To Build A House
Were the hill is thats ware the house is going to be build
first dig up the hill make a holl. Thin mesher the holl Thin
trace the holl with cement Thin make a woodin floor with
pliewood and niel it down Thin put wood sill. what woodsill is
it comes in a can and it helps your floor for if you spil
smomting it wont rot the wood Thin put the carpet down Thin
get 2x4's and nial them down And thin you lift up the wall And
Lift up the oder wall And then we build the roof
Building the roof
The roof
   First we nial the bords Flat or in a traingel thin you put
pliewood and woodsill and shigngols The wall thin put pliwood
on the wall and put primer And paint it
doors and widows
   Thin get doors and widows And scow in the widows And put
hinges so the doors will open and close and you put difrent
primers

Roberto's Pretest
October 1, 1992
Como puedes construir una casa con bloces i tablas i con
semento i Fierro i con virdio i con puerta's i con plastico i
con goma es todo lo ce puedo desir

Roberto's Posttest
November 2, 1992
Primero pones el cemento en el suelo y clavas los 2x4's y
pones madera encima de los 2x4's y entonses pones el techo y
clavas las ventanas y pones goma en rededor y viene el plomero
y el pone los tubos de agua y el carpintero pone las puertas y
las ventanas. y en el Fin pintan las casa. y viene el
electricista y pone los enchufes en la pared y viene los

```
planos para la casa y entonses pintan La casa y el techero
pone los tejamaniles
```

REFLECTION QUESTIONS

1. What resources did the author draw on in planning her learning unit?
2. In which areas of the curriculum did the author's students exhibit growth from their pre- to their posttests?
3. How can the type of articulated, reflective teaching exemplified in this chapter be supported in schools?

REFERENCES

Cummins, J. (2003). Supporting ESL students in learning the language of mathematics. *Research says: Trends in mathematics.* Parsippany, NJ: Pearson/Scott Foresman.

Kwak, W., Hutchings, M., Altheim, J., Gamberg, R., & Edwards, G. (1988). *Learning and loving it: Theme studies in the classroom.* Portsmouth, NH: Heinemann.

Chapter 10

Border Crossings: Funds of Knowledge Within an Immigrant Household

Anne Browning-Aiken

The funds of knowledge and experiences within immigrant families can become educational resources for curriculum development and provide insight into more effective pedagogical practice. The use of these funds in practice can also affirm the cultural identity of students and enhance relations between teachers, students, and their parents.

The purpose of this chapter is to show how ethnographic methods can lead to the development of a curriculum module responsive to the interests of students and to the pedagogical objectives of teachers, a curriculum that draws on community and regional resources. More specifically, this chapter demonstrates how teachers can extract from ethnographic interviews and participant observation a clearer understanding of their students' cultural backgrounds, their families' educational philosophies, and the funds of knowledge within the households, all of which can serve as inspiration for curriculum design.

The study discussed in this chapter was undertaken as part of the studies I did while working on a doctorate in cultural anthropology at the University of Arizona. It reflects my lifelong interests in both education and anthropology. Before pursuing a doctorate in anthropology, I taught English, American literature, and composition for 13 years in North Carolina, Greece, and Michigan, in private and public schools and at Athens College. I have always loved working with students from multiple cultural backgrounds and generally used their backgrounds as a resource in my teaching.

167

As a doctoral student in anthropology, ethnographic interviews with an immigrant family and brief visits with extended family across the border opened a window onto the richness of the family's background within the border region. What this family learned from border crossings and how it shared this knowledge with its children provided me with inspiration for an interdisciplinary teaching unit for secondary schools. This unit teaches students the value of human ties across the border and the importance of the border environment in their families' lives. As this chapter demonstrates, a single household can offer an opportunity for educators to understand and access the kind of education that is an integral part of the Mexican-American culture.

This case study of one immigrant household, the Aguilar family, living in Tucson, Arizona, as well as other studies of Mexican-origin households, suggests that this family's knowledge and life experiences are probably shared by many other families living in the 10 U.S.–Mexico border states (Moll, Amanti, Neff, & González, 1992; Vélez-Ibáñez & Greenberg, 1992; González et al., 1992). To begin with, their experiences furnish the basis for understanding part of the cultural system from which other Mexican-origin children emerge. Using such knowledge within the curriculum can help build constructive relationships between teachers, students, and parents—the kind of relationships "needed to improve the educational quality and equity in schools that serve the U.S.-Mexican populations" (Vélez-Ibáñez & Greenberg, 1992, p. 313).

Advocates of the integration of home culture within classrooms have also pointed out the benefits of producing "a more comfortable and productive learning environment through a wide range of learning alternatives" (Delgado-Gaitán, 1987, p. 358). Moreover, innovations in teaching that draw on the knowledge and skills in local households can implement levels of classroom instruction "that far exceed in quality the rote-like instruction these children commonly encounter in schools" (Moll et al., 1992, p. 132).

My critical assumption is that educational institutions underutilize the cultural resources and experiences of their working-class minority students, but that teachers possess the skills and creativity needed to draw on this knowledge to enhance their curriculum and their home–school relationships. In this respect, using household funds of knowledge within the classroom, as discussed later, provides an alternative to the deficit model of instruction.

In addition, immigrant households such as the Aguilar's place high value on *educación,* a concept that stresses knowledge not only in an academic sense, but also in terms of moral respect for adults who act as teachers. These instructive adults are found within the household network of relatives and friends, across the state and over the border, as well as in the classroom. From these adults, children learn skills such as tending a small store and managing household tasks, and these sources of knowledge have provided inspiration for curriculum units on math and the market economy.

From their family network, the Aguilar children have learned about the nature of copper mining and about the importance it has had in the economic and political development of southern Arizona and northern Mexico, for many of the men in the family have worked in the mines on both sides of the border. Copper mining itself provides firsthand opportunities for middle school children to learn about the nature of their environment, the complex relationship between industry and state economy, the international exchange of technology and trade, and the rich history in which miners have taken part. To the Aguilar family, their network of family and friends in Arizona and Sonora, and to members of the copper mining industry on both sides of the border, I owe the idea of a multidisciplinary teaching unit that brings the home into the school and the school out into the basin and range.

This chapter is divided into five parts. First I describe the research context and objectives. Second, I present the Aguilar family household and its familial and social networks. The third part contains the interview themes and their implications for educational pedagogy, and the fourth is a curriculum module for middle school students. I then conclude with an evaluation of using ethnographic methods to create curriculum units.

RESEARCH CONTEXT AND OBJECTIVES

Border Crossings began as a field methods project at the University of Arizona. The purpose was to interview a family with school-aged children in order to determine their family background, philosophy of education, expectations for their children in terms of their behavior and learning at home and at school, labor and educational history, migrations, and the nature of their social and family networks. Another purpose of this interview was to discern the family's funds of knowledge—their "historically accumulated and culturally developed bodies of knowledge and skills essential for household or individual functioning and well-being" (Moll et al., 1992, p. 133). This knowledge was to be the basis of a curriculum unit or module, which could be used in local schools.

In this case, the curriculum module was developed for a particular school setting, an inner-city middle school in Tucson, Arizona. This school was only a little more than an hour from the U.S.–Mexico border. It served a population of students whose parents were mostly employed at the local air force base, in construction, or other inner-city services. The student make-up was 45% Hispanic, 13% African American, 1% Native American, 1% Asian, and the remaining 40% Caucasian. According to the assistant principal, these children were exposed to at least some drugs and violence, and 75–85% of them received free or reduced lunch. All classrooms, except English as a Second Language (ESL), had limited access to books. Each subject area only had one set of 30 books to use with 150 students. The school also acted as a receiving school for ESL middle school programs in the city. That means that for a large part of the 45% Hispanic student population, English is a second language. The administrators reflected the nature of the population they served in that one assistant principal out of two was fluent in Spanish and the other was an American Indian. Parents, teachers, and administrators act as representatives for site-based management which convened twice a month in open meetings. Parents were also present in the school as tutors and monitors.

In one of the language arts classrooms I met Myriam Aguilar, whose parents agreed to be interviewed for the project. I met with the family four times for 90 minutes in their Tucson home, and then three times in Cananea as they visited relatives in Sonora, Mexico. My role was primarily that of an interviewer, since I was still learning Spanish and needed Myriam or one of her brothers to act as translator much of the time. By the time I went to Cananea to visit the family the following summer, I could understand her mother well enough so that my role had developed into that of a participant–observer during social visits and interviews with other family members in Cananea.

Family photographs and stories about Cananea during the interviews in Tucson piqued my curiosity about the copper industry in the border region and the history of Cananea. I visited five Arizona copper mines and the ones in Cananea to learn about miners' work and how copper mines functioned. I spoke with representatives of the copper industry at different levels to determine the connections between copper, the regional economy, and the involvement of Mexican-origin workers in copper mining.

A geologist at one of the local copper mines proved to be a particularly helpful instructor. What I learned was that geology has never had the propriety to conform to political boundaries or vice-versa. A map of Southwestern porphyry copper deposits in Arizona and Sonora revealed that Cananea, Tucson, and Phoenix were situated near large copper deposits located on a northwest trending belt. Arizona mining authorities claimed that these deposits were part of the greatest copper-producing region of the world. Cananea and its neighbor Nacozari produced 95% of Mexico's copper (Flores, 1993, p. 106), while Arizona copper mines produced 67% of U.S. copper (Ridinger, 1994, pp. 1–2).

Mining engineers and other mine workers currently employed in Arizona confirmed that the Aguilar family's experiences in the mining industry were shared by many others who maintained their connections on both sides of the U.S.–Mexico border. They also stated that Mexican-origin workers in southern Arizona accounted for as much as 50% of the mining employees from management to miners. In Arizona in 1993, copper mines employed 11,800 people, including those in service-related industries attached to the mines. In addition, copper mining contributed $123 million in taxes and $864 million in goods and services to Arizona's economy (Leaming, 1999).

Family stories about border crossings and of friends and relatives who have come to Arizona to settle or visit led me to investigate the role of immigrants in Tucson and to inquire how the copper industry affected the flow of population back and forth over the border. Thomas Sheridan's *Los Tucsonenses: The Mexican Community in Tucson, 1854–1941* (1986), and Patricia Martin's *Songs My Mother Sang to Me: An Oral History of Mexican-American Women* (1992) gave a sense of the prominent role Mexicans had in the growth of Tucson and brief glimpses into Mexican-origin miners' lives in Arizona.

It was essential also to consult Myriam's teachers and an assistant principal to discover what curriculum objectives they were trying to fulfill, what budget constraints they were operating under, and how they were meeting the needs of the Mexican-origin population they were teaching. Although some of the eighth grade teachers met as planning teams, not all could because of scheduling difficulties. Unfortunately, Myriam's teachers did not meet as a team, so my work with them was done individually.

The home interviews consisted of a combination of life histories and more open-ended questions about attitudes toward education, child rearing, and discipline and accounts of survival strategies used while moving from one culture to another. As family members became more familiar with me, they began sharing more and more of their life histories in Mexico and Tucson. Likewise, as a participant–observer, I could use their photo albums, trophies, wall hangings, or a chalcocite sample (variety of copper core) as a stimulus to further conversation.

My task was to compare or match these sources of information with what Myriam's family knew of mining in both southern Arizona and Cananea to see whether this combination could be used to build a middle school curriculum or to improve school–community relations. The description of the Aguilar household, with their social and kinship networks, and the interview themes below indicate that such a connection existed.

THE AGUILAR FAMILY AND THEIR SOCIAL AND KINSHIP NETWORKS

The Aguilar household consists of Myriam, age 13; her mother María, age 47; her brothers Juan Carlos, age 11, and Bernardo Jr., age 14; and her father Bernardo Sr., age 50. Originally from Cananea, Sonora, they moved to Nogales, Sonora, where Myriam's father worked in a general store, and they lived about 75% of the time. After a year, the family moved to Tucson to provide better educational and employment opportunities for their children and to be closer to relatives living in Tucson and Phoenix.

Myriam's mother had been a nurse in a doctor's office in Cananea. In Tucson she worked as a volunteer home nurse and as a monitor in Myriam's school. Bernardo Jr. worked in his father's store in Nogales and did yard work for relatives in Tucson. While Myriam and Juan Carlos did not have paying jobs yet, they were responsible for specific tasks in the home and at their uncles' houses in Cananea. In Cananea, three of Myriam's uncles on both sides of the family worked or had worked in the copper mine. Those who were no longer working in the mines received settlements from them after the mines closed. However, two other uncles had been working in Arizona copper mines between Tucson and Phoenix.

In Tucson, Myriam had a maternal cousin with four children close in age to her and her brothers. The two families participated in frequent visiting back and forth, joint activities, and provided mutual support in child-raising and household concerns. Her mother also had a friend in Tucson whom she regarded as a sister, and a sister-in-law in Cananea whom she described as her best friend. Myriam's family returned every summer to visit her mining relatives in Cananea and had been on mine tours with them. In addition, conversations about family photographs and about travel back and forth across the border revealed a familiarity with past problems in the mining industry, such as wage disputes and hazardous working conditions. Myriam and her brothers were familiar with the role the 1906 Cananea miners' strike against the American mine owner William Greene and against the economic policies of Porfirio Díaz played in the Mexican Revolution.

INTERVIEW THEMES

Several themes became apparent during the interviews: the value of education and knowledge, the need for maintaining a network of relatives and friends across the border for emotional and sometimes economic support, and the impact of the social memory of past experiences and expectations on mining families in the present. Although these themes may have been shaped in part by the interview questions themselves, the direction in which the Aguilar family took them was their own. At the same time, the themes were probably common to other immigrant families who came out of similar Mexican backgrounds to cross the border into the United States with fervent hopes and dreams for their families.

The Value of Education and Knowledge

Reese, Balzano, Gallimore, and Goldenberg (1991) described *educación* as a cultural concept that encompassed academic learning and nonacademic moral training such as learning the difference between right and wrong, respect for adults, and good manners (pp. 6–7).

María's actions and those of her children demonstrated that the acquisition of knowledge and moral values was a key objective in their lives and a matter of pride. In the first place, the move to Tucson from Mexico was made so that the children could go to what the parents considered better schools, with good prospects for employment after graduation. All three children were A/B students in what was a second language, yet they continued studying Spanish in school and used it in their discourse at home, with considerable switching between the two languages. Myriam won two Spanish spelling trophies from Tucson citywide middle school contests. Her mother continued to read Spanish medical books from the public library, especially on diseases, and to practice as a volunteer at Woman to Woman, a home health service. Her interest in current events and the political history of Mexico were also indications of her lifelong interest in knowledge acquisition. Finally, her volunteer work as a library assistant and a hall monitor in her daughter's school showed her commitment to supporting her children's education. As McCarty, Wallace, Lynch, and Benally (1991) have indicated, knowledge can be considered a personal possession, "more prized than material possessions since it can be endlessly expanded and it neither diminishes nor can it be taken away" (p. 51).

Both Myriam and Bernardo Jr. want to attend the University of Arizona. But in addition to this emphasis on the value of learning and high educational aspirations, María's concept of *educación* carried a strong emphasis on moral behavior. She repeatedly emphasized that respect for other people was the most important thing she could teach her children. She pointed out as a bad example a student at school who talked back to her while she was a hall monitor. She believed that learning responsibility for one's actions was partly taught by assigning household responsibilities at an early age. As her children grew older, she worked to keep the boys away from gangs by encouraging sports after school or going to the public library if they could not get a bus home from school right away. For the same reason, she wanted Myriam home as soon as possible after school and encouraged her friends to come to the apartment. She believed that how she raised her children really made a difference in the quality of their lives as adults.

The Importance of a Network of Family and Friends

Reciprocity among relatives and friends was especially evident from the family photo album. Each of the pictures revealed a network of family and friends who exchanged *quinceañera* cakes, advised children or each other, shared farm tasks, and maintained second-generation friendships despite problems of time and distance. These activities and exchanges demonstrated how the networks established enduring social relationships and social interdependence. The practical reason for this interdependence, as Vélez-Ibáñez and Greenberg (1992) indicated, was "because many Mexicans work in highly unstable labor markets, in their struggle to make a living, they are not only forced to crisscross national boundaries, but they must also depend on one another to gain access to resources found on each side" (p. 316).

Family photos and María's reports of picnics and other excursions with her cousin's family in Tucson, the Aguilar family's summer visits to their uncles' families in Cananea, frequent trips to the border town of Nogales to see their father and other relatives, and occasional visits to the mining families in southern Arizona, as well as the visits of many of these families to the Aguilar home, suggested long-term relationships based on both reciprocity and *confianza,* a sense of trust and faith in the support of one's friends. As Moll et al. (1992) described, each exchange visit "entails not only practical activities . . . but constantly provides contexts in which learning can occur—contexts, for example, where children have ample opportunities to participate in activities with people they trust" (p. 134). Thus Bernardo Jr. had learned how to repair tires and sell goods at a general store, while Myriam knew how to tend the little neighborhood store in Cananea because of her aunts, how to take care of the farm animals in Cananea from her uncles, and how to get homework help from her older cousin in Tucson. Likewise, María occasionally took care of and instructed her Tucson cousin's younger children, while her cousin took María and her family to places in her car.

Mining as an Impetus for Border Crossings

Finally, the historical theme of border crossings of mining families and of the economic significance of the copper mining industry in both Sonora and southern Arizona to Mexican-origin families became increasingly significant. Five to six members of Myriam's family had worked in copper mines on both sides of the border for many generations. Vélez-Ibáñez and Greenberg (1992) indicated that, historically, the population flow that Myriam's family demonstrated was much more fluid during the 19th and early 20th centuries: "the dynamic qualities of the border region have their roots in the introduction of large-scale technological and capital-intensive investments . . . [that] created binational labor markets that proletarianized rural populations and pushed persons back and forth across the border" (p. 315). Mining was one of these investments, especially after new technologies were introduced into the borderlands arena.

Los Tucsonenses further confirms that labor and union problems were shared on both sides of the border from the 1870s to the 1930s and that the repatriation and deportation policies of the 1930s along the Arizona–Sonora border resulted in the border guards and mining employers being more strict about immigration papers. In the 1920s, Mexican *braceros* provided the backbone (60%) of the U.S. mining industry (Sheridan, 1986, p. 209). More recently, the 1986 Immigration Reform and Control Act attempted to stem undocumented immigration, but, according to Vélez-Ibáñez and Greenberg (1992), it "has had no striking impact on the labor sectors of which Mexican undocumented workers are a part." It has, instead, "legalize[d] Mexican immigrants, guarantee[d] their permanent settlement, and increase[d] the flow of individual workers and families back and forth to the United States with newly acquired legality" (p. 316).

María's own knowledge of the Cananea mines, passed on to her by older members of the family, revolved around the 1906 strike, when Esteban Baca Calderón led strikers in protest over working conditions and pay. Although a number of workers were killed, the miners' protest eventually led to an American mine owner, "Colonel" William Greene, losing the mine because of his New York financiers' loss of confidence in him (Sonnichsen, 1974, pp. 207–219). María's more recent knowledge of the Cananea mine included her extended family's experiences with the 1989 military closing of the mine due to bankruptcy and loss of power among union workers.

BORDER CONNECTIONS CURRICULUM MODULE

The knowledge of geology and mining had not been taught systematically to the Aguilar children. But such knowledge became useful within a school curriculum as a means of stimulating and motivating students' curiosity about their environment and local history in a context that was relevant to their lives. It could also help students restructure their existing knowledge and build new knowledge emphasized by curriculum objectives.

Within school systems where there was an unequal distribution of funds and where materials and textbooks were limited, the use of a pedagogy that drew on the students' own cultural knowledge and the educational resources available within the area made good sense. In middle school science, for example, an understanding of geological processes could be built on existing familiarity with mining and geography. The mining industry, specifically the Arizona Mining Association, offered free rock kits and educational materials about geology, ecology, and mining processes, including physics and chemistry at multiple grade levels. Geology and mining exhibits were available in Tucson at the Desert Museum and the Arizona Historical Museum and in Phoenix at the Arizona Mining and Mineral Museum. Mining companies were generally interested in increasing public awareness of mine ecology and mine operations. Geologists offered their services during local school visits or took busloads of students on mine tours. Funds to defray the costs of such tours were often available from either the mines or the Arizona Mining Association.

In addition, Wiggenton's (1985) concept of students' gathering and writing of family history and anecdotes about events and people who work, in this case, on the basin and range land or in related service industries can be applied to a curriculum module or unit. Accounts or demonstrations of the use of skills—from first aid and safety tactics to construction, cattle ranching, or tire repair—can be used to better understand individual heritage and household funds of knowledge in the context of local history and human ecology. As the curriculum module below suggests, this approach can fulfill objectives in both social studies and language arts. Furthermore, building on students' existing knowledge, in part acquired from their households on both sides of the border, is a way of recognizing and acknowledging the value of cultural identity.

The goals for this curriculum module are (1) to stimulate and motivate students' curiosity about their basin and range environment, geology, mining and local history, and ecology in a context that is relevant to their lives and (2) to facilitate learning experiences that help restructure students' existing knowledge and build new knowledge and skills. This concept model (see Fig. 10.1) evolves out of discussions with middle school teachers and media specialists, the Arizona Mining Association, the Arizona Department of Mines and Minerals, the Arizona Historical Society, and the Arizona Geological Survey. Likewise these sources can be consulted in establishing a more detailed scope and sequence chart, a content-process matrix with activities and assignments, and an assessment plan.

The concept model included in this chapter offers an overall view of the interdisciplinary nature of this unit. It is designed to provide some answers as to the question of how the geology of southern Arizona has affected the lives of the people who have come here. Stripped to the main subheadings listed under each arm, it can also be used to assess students' prior experiences, knowledge, expectations, and preconceptions about Arizona mining, history, geology, and ecology in an initial brainstorming session. It can be used as well for a general postassessment of what new material has been learned in the unit. Otherwise it stands as a guide that can be modified by teachers to suit more closely their own needs and interests.

CONCLUSION

In evaluating ethnographic interviews as a tool to improve classroom pedagogy, it is important for educators to recognize that a school system and individual teachers must commit themselves to the time required to carry out the interviews and to learn how to conduct them. They should also commit time to sharing their results with other teachers, such as a middle school grade level team.

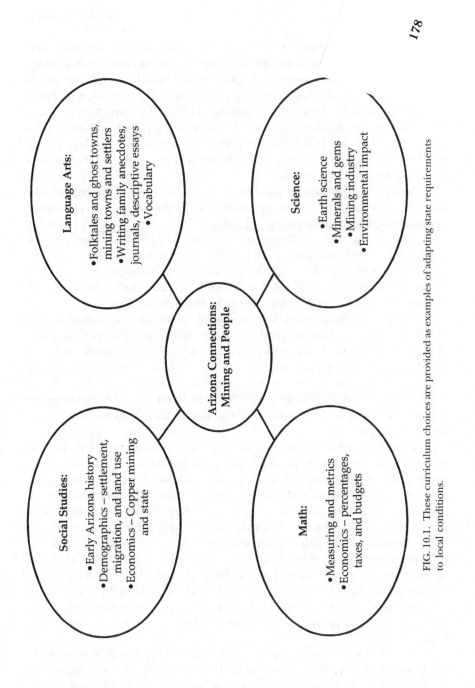

Language Arts:
- Folktales and ghost towns, mining towns and settlers
- Writing family anecdotes, journals, descriptive essays
- Vocabulary

Social Studies:
- Early Arizona history
- Demographics – settlement, migration, and land use
- Economics – Copper mining and state

Arizona Connections: Mining and People

Science:
- Earth science
- Minerals and gems
- Mining industry
- Environmental impact

Math:
- Measuring and metrics
- Economics – percentages, taxes, and budgets

FIG. 10.1. These curriculum choices are provided as examples of adapting state requirements to local conditions.

Learning how to conduct the interviews could be done in four after-school or workday workshops with the help of video models, role playing, and a discussion of chapters from Spindler and Spindler's *Interpretive Ethnography at Home and Abroad* (1987) and Wolcott's *Transforming Qualitative Data: Description, Analysis, and Interpretation* (1994). This preliminary training would enable teachers to set interview goals, write factual and open-ended questions, act as participant–observers more than recorders, recognize their cultural biases, keep reflective field notes, and evaluate the thematic content of their interviews.

Although it is not always possible to learn the home language of students, it is advisable for ethnographers and teachers with a large second language student population. In any case, students can act as translators for their parents, but they must sometimes be encouraged to help you explore a particular answer, and their presence may shape some of their parents' responses. However, in this case, the presence of Myriam and her brothers was always an asset. They liked talking about their family's background and frequently added their own comments to those of their parents.

The interviews themselves should probably take four visits of one to one-and-a-half hours and be matched with grade level team discussion sessions after each. If four to six teachers on a team with 120–150 students visit only two students' families a year per teacher, that team could visit 8–12 families and together could create two new curriculum modules per year. Some teachers might also want time to gather further background information in order to see how the knowledge of the family they interview fits into a larger, regional picture.

This ethnographic experience with just one immigrant family has revealed a number of themes that directly affect the nature of school–home–community relations and have the potential for improving academic achievement on the basis of the use of more knowledgeable pedagogical practices and educational policy. For one, this family placed extremely high value on *educación,* which is indicated in their daily efforts to acquire academic knowledge as well as to exhibit moral respect for adults who acted as their teachers. Learning was something that occurred at home and in the community, not only in school, in the form of gradually increasing household responsibilities and in the businesses of the people in their family network on both sides of the border. Knowledge appeared to be prized more than material possessions since it was the key to future economic well-being.

Together, the themes of *educación* and networking across borders have implications for curriculum changes and for the nature of pedagogy within the classroom. They suggest that teachers and administrators need opportunities for learning what funds of knowledge exist among their students.

Cultural knowledge and local resources provide a viable alternative to deficit model education and are an essential part of teaching methodology when textbooks and library resources are limited. On the other hand, when such resources are available, the funds of knowledge approach can also be considered a form of enrichment within the curriculum. In either case, becoming aware of the cultural resources that exist within the U.S.-Mexican community enables educators to become more creative in their teaching and to build on that knowledge in their fulfillment of curriculum objectives.

Finally, through the process of ethnographic interviewing, discovering the nature of local resources, and of sharing and planning with colleagues, teachers arrive at a clearer sense of how their students' lives, and even their own, fit into a regional, and in this case borderland, context. Teachers can acquire an overall sense of the cultural and historical continuity existing within a population that has flowed back and forth across the border for economic and family reasons for centuries. The border in this sense is not just an arbitrary geographical line or fence for keeping people in or out, but it is a bridge for people trying to maintain their ties in two countries and to have the best of both worlds.

POSTSCRIPT

Four years after I carried out the initial project both Myriam and her older brother had applied to and/or been accepted at the University of Arizona. Their mother María had learned to speak English and continues her volunteer work as a nurse. The family maintains cross-border ties by making frequent trips to Cananea and Nogales.

I lived with a mining family in Cananea for a year while studying the impacts of Mexican mineral policy changes on the lives of the miners and their families. I found the importance of a good education, both the teaching of moral values at home and a secondary education at preparatory and technical schools, to be one of the most frequently mentioned values in more than 100 interviews with active and retired miners and their families. Over the past 30 years the unionized miners have advocated increased salaries and student grants through the collective bargaining process. Because of their efforts, an average of 4–5 children in every mining family of six children received a technical or university-level education and became professionals in the last two generations of miners. Peso devaluations and inflation since the 1980s have made advanced education less affordable, but Cananean miners continue to regard it as a major life goal for their children.

REFLECTION QUESTIONS

1. How do you or other teachers in your school obtain information about the cultural background of your students? What kind of information about students and their family backgrounds would you like to gather from ethnographic interviews?
2. Is there a fund of knowledge in your classroom that might fit the curriculum concept model presented in this chapter (or one like it)?
3. How have natural resources or the natural environment helped to shape the development of your community? What do you know of the local history of your community? Are there industrial or technological developments that have had an impact on the social or economic nature of your community?

REFERENCES

Delgado-Gaitán, C. (1987). Traditions and transitions in the learning process of Mexican children: An ethnographic view. In G. Spindler & L. Spindler (Eds.), *Interpretive ethnography of education: At home and abroad* (pp. 333–361). Hillsdale, NJ: Lawrence Erlbaum Associates.

Flores, V. (1993). Mexico. *Mining Journal Annual Review,* 106–107.

González, N., Moll, L. C., Floyd-Tenery, M., Rivera, A., Rendón, P., Gonzáles, R., & Amanti, C. (1992). *Learning from households: Teacher research on funds of knowledge.* Educational Practice Report. National Center for Research on Cultural Diversity and Second Language Learning.

Leaming, G. F. (1999). *The economic impact of the Arizona copper industry, 1993.* Marana, AZ: Western Economic Analysis Center.

Martin, P. P. (1992). *Songs my mother sang to me: An oral history of Mexican-American women.* Tucson, AZ: University of Arizona Press.

McCarty, T. L., Wallace, S., Lynch, R. H., & Benally, A. (1991). Classroom inquiry and Navajo learning styles: A call for reassessment. *Anthropology and Education Quarterly, 22,* 42–59.

Moll, L. C., Amanti, C., Neff, D., & González, N. (1992). Funds of knowledge for teaching: Using a qualitative approach to connect homes and classrooms. *Theory Into Practice, 31*(2), 132–141.

Reese, L., Balzano, S., Gallimore, R., & Goldenberg, C. (1991, November). *The concept of educación: Latino family values and American schooling.* Paper presented at the Annual Meeting of the American Anthropological Association, Chicago.

Ridinger, D. (1994). *1993 impact of copper industry on Arizona.* Phoenix, AZ: Arizona Mining Association.

Sheridan, T. E. (1986). *Los Tucsonenses: The Mexican community in Tucson, 1854–1941.* Tucson, AZ: University of Arizona Press.

Sonnichsen, C. L. (1974). *Colonel Greene and the copper skyrocket.* Tucson, AZ: University of Arizona Press.

Spindler, G., & Spindler, L. (1987). Teaching and learning how to do the ethnography of education. In G. Spindler & L. Spindler (Eds.), *Interpretive ethnography of education: At home and abroad* (pp. 17–36). Hillsdale, NJ: Lawrence Erlbaum Associates.

Vélez-Ibáñez, C. G., & Greenberg, J. B. (1992). Formation and transformation of funds of knowledge among U.S.-Mexican households. *Anthropology and Education Quarterly, 23*(4), 313–335.

Wiggenton, E. (1985). *Sometimes a shining moment: The Foxfire experience.* Garden City, NY: Anchor Press.

Wolcott, H. F. (1994). *Transforming qualitative data: Description, analysis, and interpretation.* Thousand Oaks, CA: Sage.

Chapter 11

Social Reconstructions of Schooling: Teacher Evaluations of What They Learned From Participation in the Funds of Knowledge Project

Jacqueline Messing
University of South Florida

Anthropologists describe schooling as socially constructed (Levinson & Holland, 1996), which is an important idea, opening up the possibility of educational change of the kind that has taken place through the Funds of Knowledge project. The social context of the education of culturally and linguistically diverse students in the United States today too often includes a wide gap between home and school worlds. The Funds of Knowledge project has offered a method to conceptualize schooling so that these worlds are integrated, and it uses ethnography to challenge participants to question assumptions behind common roles and create interaction between students and teachers, teachers and parents, and teachers and researchers.

The teachers in this project have undergone a process of professional and personal transformation as a result of their participation in this collaborative project. Their insights are documented in this chapter. As Moll and González (this volume) point out, all project participants underwent a change of perspective through our collaborative work. I focus on the teachers' process of change in the way that they approach their teaching and their students and families. This chapter has emerged from conclusions drawn by the teachers themselves about what they have learned and how their perceptions of their students and families have changed over time through the Funds of Knowledge project experiences.

The study and practice of ethnography that is central to a funds of knowledge perspective has created a dialectic—between the teachers and researchers and between teachers and students—which has led to a questioning of established roles and understandings. It is this questioning that has the potential for leading to educational change. As ethnographers, the teachers have engaged a meta-dialectic between established roles and understandings of teachers and students that, through the experience of ethnography, are challenged.

This analysis is based on interviews I conducted with the teachers and is informed by my experiences during the 2 years I served as a graduate research assistant on the project, where I worked closely with both teachers and researchers. At the project's conclusion at the end of 1995, I conducted exit interviews, asking the teachers to reflect on their experiences for the purpose of project evaluation. Each interview lasted from 1 to 2 hours. The views of seven teachers are included here in the form of actual excerpts from transcripts of recorded interviews and quotes or references to their publications. The interviews were a formal way of capturing the teachers' evaluations, and the results are based on an established rapport between the teachers and myself. I approached my work on the Funds of Knowledge project as a student of interdisciplinary collaborative research and linguistic anthropology, but also as a participant–observer and former high school teacher now in graduate school.

During the interviews, I was in the role of the ethnographer, seeking to learn from the teachers what the impact of this work had been. In this chapter I present an analytic description of the teachers who formed the backbone of the Funds of Knowledge project. I have chosen to present narrative excerpts because I want to share with the reader the teachers' voices, through their articulate and passionate narratives that describe their experiences with this unique collaborative effort.

As Norma González points out in the Introduction, as project participants, we are all learners. For the teachers, the shifts in perspective all began with the premise of the teacher as learner idea, central to the Funds of Knowledge project and the goal of fostering home–school links and understanding. The idea of approaching one's own classroom practice as a learner, as an ethnographer, opens up the possibility of new forms of understanding, which is at the heart of ethnography, in which the anthropologist enters a new culture or social context, observes and participates in daily life, and documents some part of the patterns of life that he or she experiences. The anthropologist may undertake fieldwork in his or her own back yard as well, trying to consider a familiar context with the new eyes of a trained observer, as the teachers did.

"TEACHER AS LEARNER" AND THE THREE COMPONENTS OF THE FUNDS OF KNOWLEDGE PROJECT

Many project teachers have spoken or written about the ideas of what teacher as learner and teacher as researcher mean to them. The first phase of training in ethnographic theories and methodologies led the teachers to more open-ended home visits than is the norm, teacher study groups, and curriculum development based on student–family funds of knowledge. These three components of the project come together to incite a shift from a "deficit view" of "linguistically and culturally diverse" students, to a positive view that considers the wealth of household knowledge that is too often overlooked, with little or no connection for the child in the classroom.

Teachers must also be recognized for their knowledge as professionals in a constantly challenging vocation. The simple premise of respect for each participant's funds of knowledge was the modus operandi of the project. One teacher explains her view of parents as experts, a perspective she developed through participating in the Funds of Knowledge project:

> We're taking a whole new focus. The parent involvement that [other programs] had was—Yes, they come into the classroom and they participate, and that's very strongly encouraged. And yes, they go on home visits, but the home visits are always "here's a little math game that you can play at your house, here are some ideas that you can use." And the parent workshops are always what the *teacher* has to offer the parent. And this is totally changing the whole role. And I think that these teachers are very excited about that, and interested in how I've used *their* ideas [the parents], and made *them* feel like *they're* the experts. I think that that's really exciting for them and *for me* to see that. And it also makes me change *my* attitude. I mean I just don't think about parents as not knowing things. I think about them as being very knowledgeable and having amazing skills.[1]

This teacher's changing attitudes toward parents have been prompted by her home visits and the analytical discussions with the other teachers and researchers in the study groups. The idea of the teacher going into a home as a learner has a strong impact on all of the participants. These are a different kind of home visit than what the teachers had previously experienced, as we see in the following excerpt:

---

[1]Transcription conventions: Italics indicate vocal emphasis, and additional information is enclosed in brackets.

Before, when I was a PACE [pre-school] teacher for five years, and we went into the homes . . . we, the teachers, were more the imparter of the knowledge type person. So we would bring games into the homes. And we would bring activities the parents could do with the students, and there was a lot of reciprocal communication, and the parents are very, you know, open and we would end up finding out some information about the family, but we really didn't look at the whole situation as a *learner.*

And with the funds of knowledge program, if I went into the same home— well in this case I did—the same home . . . I saw things in a totally different light. And I was trained more in *observational* skills; instead of me doing all the *talking,* I would do more of the *listening.* It's amazing what you can find out, *when you listen and observe* [laughs]. And you know, reflect on what people say, and I remember the family I visited—the Campbells. Mrs. C was talking to me about her job in the original home visits when her son was in the PACE program. I knew she was a nurse, but that's as far as it went. I didn't *know* that she had *all* these other things that she did with her leisure time. And um, she was a wonderful cook. And she did sewing and she did crafts and I found out a lot of other things about the father, besides his job. So I think the whole outlook was different for me and I gathered more information. I looked at the students in a different light, because I started seeing them as a contributor to the curriculum. You know, what the student could bring *to* the class. And the other focus was what *I* could give the family. Like, *me* developing curriculum for them to do at home. So it was a totally different approach.

Seeing the students and families as a source of knowledge, and the potential application of this knowledge in the classroom, has been a topic of much discussion and analysis in the study groups, where the teachers can engage with the theories they are reading, with each other, and with the researchers. Teachers begin to view households as repositories for knowledge that can be drawn out to shape classroom curriculum. As Luis Moll points out in the Introduction, these study groups were key to the success of the project.

When I taught high school, I remember feeling as though I were teaching on an island, that my colleagues and I never had the time or the opportunity to sit down and discuss our work. The study groups are important for brainstorming, to provide a time, place, and forum for colleagues with common interests and experiences to reflect and share ideas about teaching theory and practice. The teacher quoted below described her view of the teacher study groups in fulfilling this need for teacher communication:

One complaint teachers have is we don't necessarily get much time to plan together and to *talk,* you know, and to share ideas. And sometimes that camaraderie—when you just have another person that's been through similar experiences, you get very excited about implementing ideas when there's another person that you can bounce ideas off of. And I think everyone needs *support*, and *encouragement*. And that's what that did for me. And I would get new ideas every time I went. I'd see *another* way a *different* teacher would look at the knowledge that came from the household and develop curriculum that maybe you'd never thought of. So it was really helpful.

The training in ethnographic theory and method went hand in hand with the study group discussions where the teachers could, in a workshop format, recount and analyze their experiences with their household visits, their interviews, and their field note write-ups. This follow-up allowed for the group participants to make articulations between the theory they were reading and their experiences with conducting ethnographic interviews in a way that was directly meaningful to them—in the context of their students with their families:

> And what was great was the little study groups, and we got to share information with each other. And, the actual—the, you know sometimes we would have speakers that would teach us specific skills—observational skills. But what I liked, we'd go out and practice and we could come back, and meet together and share our experiences. So I thought the training was very helpful.

The development of curriculum specific to a teacher's classroom and community context is a main goal of the Funds of Knowledge project. This is fostered through the exchange of ideas that takes place in the teacher study groups. This exchange is exemplified in this teacher's description of what happened when she told the study group about a student who had brought in his uncle's small coin collection:

> ... and I just offhandedly mentioned it in one of our teacher study groups. And one of the teachers picked up on that right away. She said, "well, why couldn't you do a study on money?" So then I—that turned the light bulb on and we thought, "Oh yeah, that would be great. It would fit into social studies, it would fit into math, it would fit into language arts." And so we went ahead and did this study—the study of money that worked out really well. We got into the barter system, how an economy works. The money itself, how it's produced, how it's made. We got into exchange rates. It was just a really interesting course of study. And it was all based on the collection.
>
> And then other kids brought in collections that they had. They shared their experiences about going across the border, and spending the pesos, and each day the peso was worth less, because it kept being devalued, and we got into some political issues. It was just very, very all-encompassing. I really enjoyed that.

The creativity of individual teachers leads to many different curricular applications of funds of knowledge from the student households. The following teacher began by visiting the home of a student who was having a challenging time in the classroom. Not only did the student improve in class, but the teacher also found a rich source of ideas from the household that provided the seeds for a successful classroom project that benefited all participants:

> The second student I visited was a young girl. And what was interesting about that situation is that she was a discipline problem in the classroom at first. Minor discipline problem—she had a little, um, attitude you might say. But she was very bright and creative and through her home visits I—it was a different situation. I didn't feel as accepted—the father didn't really talk to me until after the third visit was over. But what happened was that that little girl also— she became a real leader in the classroom. And what happened with the knowledge I gained from that household—she was doing a lot of clapping games I noticed at P.E.
>
> So really, what we based the curriculum on wasn't something I gathered from the home, although she learned the games in the home. I didn't really see them during the visit, but I saw them in the school playground and she did a lot of singing and clapping games. And what we did was we had a program and invited the parents. And her father came, even though he hadn't been very verbal in the visit. He came and he took off work. And so did the other father of the student that I was visiting. And both mothers came, and we had a little performance. And this little girl taught everyone in the class the clapping games. And she put them on charts with a group—she ran a language arts group. So again they were using the reading, the writing, and movement and singing, and then they did the performance on the stage and we invited the principal. And it helped with not only her academic skills, but also her social skills and she had a way to channel her creative energy. And the rest of the year I had no problems with her—with her behavior, discipline. . . .
>
> It's interesting because I didn't think, at the time, that doing those games—the written dart games, and then the verbal clapping games—would make such a difference in these . . . children, but it really did. . . . The little girl I did pick because I saw such wonderful qualities in her and I wanted to see if this would help our relationship, which it did.

This teacher's home visit to learn about this family improved her communication with the parents, and her increased skills of observation led her to notice the games the child played outside of class. The decision to include the games she observed on the playground in her classroom curriculum further opened doors between the teacher and her students because she created a student-centered curriculum unit based on her new knowledge.

The applicability of a funds of knowledge approach to special education classrooms is also fruitful, as discussed later, because the teacher's connections to the students' families can have a very positive effect in challenging situations:

The next year when I did the same funds of knowledge project with my special education children that had severe emotional problems, I did pick two of the students that were having most of the difficulties. . . . I had made home visits when I taught special education before but not in the same light. So what I did was in this situation, I picked the toughest kid in the class, and if you look at the outcome of it, it was interesting for him. The way you'd measure success I guess would be, he—we only had to call the police on him once and the year before they had to eight times. So that was quite a reduction. That was one little measurement that—objective measurement.

But his home visits proved to be really amazing—what happened to this student. And um, he came from a very, um, real abusive environment. And when he started doing all the leadership roles of planning our African American studies—that's what he did. He just really—it just really helped his behavior, you know he felt, he was already kind of a leader in the classroom, when he was in control of his anger. And he was a very, very bright student. And he was—he just blossomed and he even went into the sixth grade class that he was mainstreamed—they were integrating it for social studies.

The teachers suggest that the main components of the Funds of Knowledge project have challenged them to learn new things about their students and students' families and therefore about their own roles as teachers and their practices. The ethnographic interviews and observations challenge them to see their students as children with lives outside of the school and become less judgmental of their students' parents.

TEACHERS' PROCESS OF CHANGE

The teachers interviewed discussed having gone through a process of reflection on their teaching and reconsideration of their own often previously unacknowledged assumptions about their students. This reflective process is observable in the following teacher's statement:

I think that's one thing that we as teachers—I think we're guilty of judging the kids and maybe even looking down on them—not seeing them as equals but as inferior to us because of the kinds of—the class of society that they may come from. I never intentionally judge the kids, not doing it intentionally and this helped me so much to realize that kids are kids—no matter what socioeconomic level they're from and that we need to encourage them in every way. And these visits helped to do that. It gave credence to what *they* do at home. I learned to value everything that they did at home. The intentions of the parents many times were very good, but they were so overwhelmed with day-to-day survival that they didn't have time for things that my mother did all the time. You know, it was just very eye opening and humbling for me to be able to go into their homes and share with them.

This teacher needed the experience of going into a household as a learner to realize that she had been unconsciously judging the students in her classroom, and that this judgment was based on a lack of understanding of the family's day-to-day reality. The home visits made evident the class and cultural differences between the teacher and her students, which she had not been able to see before. The candidness with which she now discusses her own lack of tolerance is characteristic of many project teachers who have come to similar realizations. The same teacher goes on to explain how her shift of perspective began with her first home visit:

> But it's just amazing how my perspective changed after having been able to make the home visits. I was much more tolerant, of things that I noticed. Before I would be very critical of things that I would see in the classroom. And when I would then go into the homes I would realize, I need to be much more understanding, because my background is very different from their background. I can't expect them to have the same kinds of values or understandings that I had when I was their age because their upbringing is very different from mine. And it was very nice to go into a home and not have our conversation confined to the grades of the child, and how the child is progressing academically, but to have *them* teach *me* the things that they knew—the culture that they practiced; the people that they networked with for different things.
>
> The first family I visited—at first I was very nervous. And at first I thought there really isn't anything here that I can bring out into the curriculum, in terms of funds of knowledge. This mother had four children. They lived in a mobile home, and this mobile home was very clean. The mother was very— she really cared about the children's appearance, and how they went to school, and that kind of thing. And she didn't have time maybe to sit down and read with the kids like she wanted to. But having four children, the husband would come home very tired, and he would expect her to take care of him, too—just all of the tasks that she had to do.
>
> How could I say then at school "your mother didn't read with you today," because I could see when I got there all the tasks that she was responsible for doing, and did, in a very, very conscientious way. That if she didn't have time to sit down every night with her child and read, or whatever I could see why. There were just too many things that she had to do, and it wasn't because she didn't want to.

This teacher was profoundly affected by the experience of encountering parents with different ways of conceptualizing the world, and how they raise their children, and in the process realized that she brought her own prejudgments to these interactions.

Several teachers had similar experiences of being challenged to change their ways of thinking about their students after their home visits. This was another common theme in the teacher study groups. The same teacher continues, describing the differences between home and school contexts, differences that can be both cultural and linguistic:

You know, so many times in the schools you'll hear the teachers say "Oh, they never showed up for the conference, they don't care about their children's education." But then you go into the homes and you see the kinds of things that they're dealing with and it's not because they don't care. They just have other things that need to be done. And a lot of times they don't feel comfortable in the school setting. . . . And so they don't come, not because they're not interested in their children's education, but they don't want to be judged. They feel that the school is a foreign environment for them. The language spoken in the school is English and their home language is Spanish. You know, all these things enter into it. They don't have transportation. This first family, she drove, but they had one car so he had to take the car to work so she had no form of transportation. So if I were to have a conference with her at school, there's no way she could get there. And a lot of times when you try to make contact it appears that they're not interested. But there are so many other reasons why they can't make it. So that's basically what I'm talking about. We need to be much more compassionate, understanding. And this program helps to do that.

[The parents] felt much more comfortable with me then, once I made the contact and sat down with them and talked with them about their family histories and all this. Then they felt the *confianza* with me. They could tell me more. You know before they might be embarrassed—"I can't tell her that I don't have a car" or "I can't tell her that I just don't feel comfortable at the school." You know, they felt more at ease with me and they knew that I wouldn't be judging them wrongly. And that—the rapport was much much better.

This teacher's discussion of her previous lack of compassion, and of initial understanding of her students' families, underscores the importance of teachers gaining firsthand knowledge of their students. As Amanti (1995) pointed out, when teachers complete their university studies, many assume that they have learned as much about their future students as they need to, despite the fact that their studies likely exposed them to thirdhand knowledge of multicultural communities and the differences of class, race, and gender that they would encounter among their students. For Amanti, the benefit of teachers doing qualitative research in their students' communities is that they gain firsthand knowledge. As Floyd Tenery mentions (this volume), teachers can serve as mediator between the worlds of home and school. It is this process of gaining firsthand knowledge that leads teachers to question their ways of thinking about their students' families. The social process of teaching and learning in the classroom can only be improved by building rapport and relationships of *confianza,* mutual trust, based on increased understanding between teachers and students with their families.

The teachers I interviewed all speak of stretching themselves and letting go of preconceptions over time. In the process they have experimented with new identities as teachers, and as learners and researchers.

When teachers look to their students for curriculum ideas, this involves a shift in perspectives, and a shift in the role of a teacher from "imparter" to "learner and researcher":

> This project makes that shift, and gives teaching a more human side. It is easy to be objective and treat the children like small machines, not really taking into account their personalities and their backgrounds. When you only see a child in a classroom this is very easy to do. If your only contact with them is an academic one, it is very easy to make assumptions, and not take into account outside information when you are evaluating the child. So I have found that the project gave me a chance to get to know the children in another context.

For this teacher, seeing the child in another context opens up possibilities of new forms of understanding and communication. One teacher observed that personalizing the institutional relationships is a key to educational change:

> So, it just really taught me a lot. About understanding people and realizing how much worth there is in a home that can be dealt with at school. Even if we didn't find a curricular connection—just interviewing and having the home visits I think in and of themselves was so helpful to give that human contact. I'm sure many years ago when teachers were required to live in the communities where they taught, and stay at the school board member's house, that kind of thing, they were invited all the time to people's homes and there was a lot of social interaction. But now there's a real barrier there between the teacher and the family and so many times they don't make that connection. That's really important, for a child's whole education to have that contact.

Getting to know a student in a different light, in a different context, as a whole person, rather than just as a "little machine" opens up many possibilities for teachers, and also for parents. This personalization can be accomplished through exchange (i.e., of ideas, or items for use in class). This type of exchange between teachers and families begins to break down the traditional hierarchical relationships, in which students and families are subordinate to teachers, who in turn are too often considered subordinate to their administrators and the researchers they may work with.

THE IMPORTANCE OF EXCHANGE
IN BUILDING RAPPORT

> The parent came in too and shared his expertise with the students in the classroom and the home visits I made with him were—ended up being probably six visits with each family. But the home visits I made with this student were—

and you know they could have gone on all year if I had had enough time because I got very close to the family. And they asked me to dinner, and, you know, it was really amazing. The mom went on two fieldtrips with us and the dad, who was very resistant, decided to come in and share his expertise when he was a cook on a submarine, [and] also a mechanic. And he brought slides and the kids really liked it. . . . So he had a lot of different skills. And so he shared a lot of those.

Building rapport between home and school can be as simple as increasing communication. A Funds of Knowledge project teacher developed a method to take advantage of household knowledge by sending home newsletters, telling family members about class activities, and inviting them to come into school and demonstrate some of their skills. She found that by simply asking more questions of "her families" she fosters the home–school connection and finds new ideas for classroom projects that can encompass a range of topics across her curriculum:

So it came about from that grandma. Later on in the year I was doing a math project. We were really learning about tessellations, which are basically tiling, where it's mosaics, where patterns fit together to make a solid design. And we got into quilting, which is a tessellation also. And so I started asking the kids if they had any quilts . . . children started to bring in quilts that somebody in their family had made for them. And they were beautiful! We just got really involved with the designs and how they were made.

When I questioned this teacher about how she had learned about her families' expertise for all the projects she undertook, she replied: "I talked to the parents. [laughs] I guess that's one thing that I didn't do before! Now it seems so natural, you know."

This teacher found that she never lacks in ideas for class projects, or for assistance in the classroom, since she sees students as contributors to the curriculum. The theme of reciprocity and exchange is also a key to the success of the Funds of Knowledge project.[2] A participant above talked of the importance of "what the student could bring *to* the class. And the other focus was what *I* could give the family. Like, *me* developing curriculum for them to do at home." In the Funds of Knowledge project there are constant exchanges of ideas, talents, goods (including, for instance, articles in the study groups, and crafts in the households and classrooms), and communication in general. The fundamental basis for the change in perspective and practice is exchange, coupled with the openness created by approaching the educational context as a learner, through ethnography.

---

[2]For an anthropological description of the importance of exchange, see Mauss (1950/ 1990).

CONCLUSION

As the editors say in the Introduction, we all felt the impact of this project:
Teachers see themselves as learners, students and families take on the role of
teachers, and fellow teachers become learners and "sharers" with each other
and with university researchers, who are also learning from fellow members
of the team. Professional development takes on new meaning as teachers reflect on their practices in a new way, in conjunction with this inversion in perceptions of hierarchical institutional relationships. What teachers experienced through participating in the Funds of Knowledge project constitutes a
restructuring of common practices in educational institutions whose hierarchical roles of principals, teachers, students, aides, and parents are laden
with unspoken, assumed dimensions of power (in an anthropological sense).
Through this questioning of tacit power dimensions and practices (Bourdieu, 1982), these teachers engaged in ethnographic projects have affected
change in the social contexts of their schools.

REFLECTION QUESTIONS

1. How have the Funds of Knowledge project teachers' practices
   changed as a result of their experiences with this project?
2. How is ethnography defined?
3. What do you identify with in the teacher's narratives?
4. What do you learn from this chapter that challenges you to think
   about your own role as a teacher? As a researcher? Can hierarchical
   (power) relationships in schools be challenged and/or changed?

REFERENCES

Amanti, C. (1995). Teachers doing research: Beyond the classroom walls. *Practicing Anthropol-
ogy, 17,* 7–9.
Bourdieu, P. (1982). *Ce que parler veut dire* (Language and symbolic power). Paris: Fayard.
Levinson, B., & Holland, D. (1996). *The cultural production of the educated person: An introduction.*
New York: SUNY–Albany Press.
Mauss, M. (1990). *The gift: The form and reason for exchange in archaic societies.* New York:
Routledge. (Original work published 1950)

Part III

TRANSLOCATIONS: NEW CONTEXTS, NEW DIRECTIONS

The chapters in this part provide a window into permutations that are possible by building on local knowledge. These four chapters are variations on the funds of knowledge theme. Each takes the concept and extends it in new and sometimes unanticipated ways in response to the dynamics of particular settings. The authors in this part "problematize" what we have considered the foundational premises of the work.

In chapter 12, Marcia Brenden presents an exciting variation of the approach, documenting how teachers in an actual field research project became social scientists, gathering usable data for a large funded project. This chapter takes the funds of knowledge approach to a new level. The author participated in a social impact assessment of the oil industry in southern Louisiana. Part of the process involved gathering information from two communities, and teachers were recruited as fieldworkers. In this approach, however, teacher-researchers gathered data that were to be part of a formal study and were systematic researchers of their own communities. Because the focus was on the oil industry, teacher-researchers quickly became aware of the impact that this entity has on their own lives. Many voiced the idea that they had been unaware that their personal experiences were part of larger patterns in the ebb and flow of oil revenues. They acquired a historical consciousness of the articulation of the household to market systems. The distancing and focusing of events in their own lives brought into sharp relief their embeddedness in globalization issues. They also came to fully appreciate how the structuring of work schedules deeply affects community and family life. These insights fostered a professionalization paradigm for the teacher-researchers as they presented their findings in public forums and received recognition for their work.

The next two chapters contain descriptions of work that took place in academic settings. In her chapter, Carmen Mercado describes how a funds of knowledge approach was used by teachers to conduct research on literacy practices within Puerto Rican households in New York City. She shows how the anthropological emphasis of the approach helped contextualize socially and culturally the life and literacy events found in the various households. She also emphasizes the heterogeneity of households they studied. As she writes, "We discovered, as well, that there is no typical Puerto Rican household and that differences across households are the result of broader and more complex social and structural forces on family life. These forces affect households, but households also mediate the effects of these forces, especially on the young and the vulnerable." Hence, a methodology that was field-tested in the Southwest can translate to the urban venue of New York, with accompanying modifications in response to the different realities and goals of the new setting.

Next, Patricia Buck and Paul Skilton Sylvester use local neighborhoods in Philadelphia as settings to help preservice teachers question their perceptions about inner-city urban communities and identify both the structural issues affecting community life and the resources available within those very same communities. They do this in the context of courses they teach that cover jointly the social foundations of education and social studies teaching methods. The authors describe the very challenging task of helping the students, middle- and upper-middle-class women venturing often for the first time into urban working-class communities of color, confront long-held perceptions and apprehensions about these neighborhoods, without ignoring the difficult issues of living found within these locations. Both instructors and students are constantly working out the following contradiction. On the one hand, their job is to present to the students an alternative perception of the neighborhoods based on a funds of knowledge approach. This is what the authors refer to as an *asset orientation*. On the other hand, it is important for both instructors and students to address the difficult structural issues found in these neighborhoods. The authors have explained it as follows: "Assuming that the ultimate goal is to position preservice teachers to view urban communities as reservoirs of strength, possibility, and talent, how can a teacher education program guide students in the articulation between their lived, possessed, and claimed privilege and the relative poverty and disadvantage within which urban community members must be equally embedded?" The authors invite teachers and teacher educators alike to think through with them the deeper significance of these issues, in particular the preservice teachers' apprehensions about entering these communities, in terms of the teachers' future ability to view their students' communities as sources of "ready-made, untapped educational resources."

In the final chapter, "Bridging Funds of Distributed Knowledge," Norma González, Rosi Andrade, Marta Civil, and Luis Moll examine critically how to both refine and problematize the approach that has been adopted throughout the book. The work in this chapter is based on the BRIDGE project, which focuses on understanding the mathematical potential of households as well as "mathematizing" household practices—that is, understanding the ways in which math is used in everyday tasks. The transformation of mathematical knowledge, however, was not unproblematic. Whereas other classroom knowledge domains (language arts, social studies, etc.) may draw in a rather straightforward fashion from households, mathematical knowledge may not be so easily incorporated. This chapter describes a theoretical refinement of the concept of funds of knowledge that helps conceptualize the distributed nature of a mathematical community. It also underscores that mathematics practices cannot be disembedded from social context and that creating a zone of mathematical practice depends on not only the store of funds of knowledge, but also the transformation of that knowledge into meaningful activity.

Chapter 12

Funds of Knowledge and Team Ethnography: Reciprocal Approaches

Marcia Brenden
New Mexico Highlands University

This chapter focuses on the funds of knowledge philosophy and methodology as a crucial mediating process that has assisted in creating joint research relationships between outside researchers and community members, in this case public school teachers, within the context of a specific team ethnographic project in southern Louisiana. After introducing the project, I clarify the following questions concerning the inclusion of public school teachers as team members in an ethnographic research project: What various roles did the differently situated teacher-researchers play in gathering and interpreting data and in constructing the meanings that become data for later investigations? As a result of participating in the project, what personal, professional, and social impacts did the teachers experience? What variations and extensions of the funds of knowledge methodology and philosophy were implemented during the course of the research?

THE PROJECT AND THE TEAM: GETTING STARTED

The focus of the ethnographic project was a 3-year Minerals Management Service (MMS) study titled "The Social and Economic Impacts of Outer Continental Shelf Activity on Families and Individuals." The research grant (Contract 1435-01-98-CT-30897) was awarded to a team within the Bureau of Applied Research in Anthropology (BARA) at the University of Arizona in July of 1998.

For this study, BARA researchers proposed a unique approach to the investigation of impacts of offshore employment on individuals and families in two southern Louisiana communities. We planned to conduct in-depth interviews with hundreds of individuals, predominantly offshore oil workers and their spouses, but also community leaders, school administrators, oil industry representatives, business leaders, and social service providers. We also planned to maintain a continual presence in both of the target communities so the research would be thorough and ongoing. But perhaps the most novel aspect of our research approach was to include a funds of knowledge component that brought public school teachers onto our research team as field assistants and crucial local contacts.

Before recruiting the teacher-researchers, the initial BARA team consisted of four anthropology professors, me (a doctoral candidate with a background in education and cultural anthropology), two research specialists trained in anthropology who lived in the subject communities for this 9-month study, and several graduate and undergraduate research assistants and data analysts. We first participated in an initial visit to the areas in order to make contacts, conduct preliminary research, and introduce town leaders to the scope and intent of the study. We then began regular month-long site visits over the next year to recruit, train, and work with the teacher-researchers, to conduct interviews and other fieldwork, and in general to talk to enough people to understand the multiple social and economic impacts of the off-shore oil industry on the area.

TEACHER RECRUITMENT: ADDING TO THE TEAM AND BUILDING A COMMUNITY OF LEARNERS

Having previously participated as a research assistant in several funds of knowledge university–public school collaborations, I was familiar with the usual methods of teacher recruitment. Team leaders would contact teachers or principals from a variety of local schools who were interested in the topic and arrange a presentation of the project. Interested teachers would attend a follow-up meeting and often suggest other colleagues from neighboring schools who might be interested in becoming teacher-researchers in their own classes.

Recruitment is never effortless. Teachers, as professionals, are regularly undersupported and overcommitted. In addition, participation in collaborative funds of knowledge projects demands a significant amount of a teacher's time to conduct household interviews, attend study group meetings, and analyze and write up the data. Consequently, the modest stipend that is offered to the teachers is a necessary but not always sufficient inducement to participate.

Our teacher recruitment approach differed in the two communities involved and varied somewhat from the norm established in previous funds of knowledge collaborations. In one school parish (district), we informed the superintendent, and his office directed us to the personnel director. This particular parish was wired with computers in every class. The personnel director posted an announcement on e-mail that introduced the social impacts study and noted the time and place of the follow-up meeting for interested teachers. The initial response was overwhelming. But after stressing the required time demands of the study, only three teachers came to the first team meeting. Through follow-up phone calls and visits to teachers, we ended up with a group of six teacher-researchers from that parish.

In the second community, recruitment followed a more traditional approach because the schools within that parish had very few computers and had not yet established e-mail as a mode of communication. Our initial administrative contact was through the school-to-work personnel. The superintendent had directed us there, presumably because the project primarily concerned issues related to work in the offshore oil and gas industry. The director of the school-to-work initiative sent a flyer to all the parish schools within the city limits explaining the project and inviting teachers to a meeting. Only three teachers, all from one school, attended. I started a school-by-school presentation that produced another eight interested teachers. We finally incorporated 14 teacher-researchers from the two communities that enabled us to schedule an all-day ethnographic training workshop.

The teachers and other members of the team were introduced to the methods and practices of the key ethnographic methods of research that would be used during the course of data collection. Though teachers may lack a certain familiarity with specific interviewing techniques, one rationale behind engaging them as social science researchers is that they are already primary mediators between parents and the school and between family-based knowledge and school-based knowledge. The workshop also introduced the teachers to several specific ethnographic techniques that were to become methods of household data collection in the social impacts study, specifically the mapping of family or kinship trees and the documentation of occupational timelines.

Though this kind of information is informally collected in the household visits in all funds of knowledge project designs, the specific training of how to construct and annotate a family tree and labor timeline was a new addition in this rendition of the research methodology. The importance of family tree documentation is to provide multiple types of information. This information includes the specific family members who are or have been involved in the oil industry across three generations, a pattern of family employment, rootedness within or outside the community, and leads to additional prospective oil field workers.

Families in southern Louisiana are extensive, with as many as 75 family members spanning three generations. Clearly the teachers found that constructing the family tree could be painstaking and occupied the major part of the first household visit. However, this process also created a comfortable place to begin discussing family history.

Likewise, the documentation of the interviewee's occupational timeline was an essential segment of the data collection in this project. Every job since the interviewee's high school years was noted on the top of the timeline with the reason(s) for leaving or changing the job noted below the line. Team members found some timelines to be exceedingly short and nondiversified and others to be extensive and quite varied. For example, if an employee had worked for Shell Oil all of his life and retired from that company, the only information noted across the years on his timeline was his change of location and advancement of position within the same company. However, a worker who was a contract laborer may have changed companies, positions, and work schedules numerous times a year. His occupational timeline was as much a marker of the restructuring of the oil industry and the resultant insecurity for employees as the previous Company Man's timeline was a marker of long-term security and expected occupational progression within the industry.

Both the occupational timelines and the family trees provided invaluable data concerning family decision-making processes in relation to changing economic conditions and periodic peaks and valleys in the oil industry.

COLLECTING AND SHARING DATA: THE TEACHERS AS FIELD ASSISTANTS

Identifying Families

The teachers were encouraged to choose three families to interview who were related to students in their classrooms, as was the customary practice in funds of knowledge research. However, because of the focus of this study, they were asked to choose families in which one parent was involved in the offshore oil industry. In both of the communities of study, it was not difficult to find adults who were in some way involved in "the oil patch." As one teacher remarked, "You have to work hard not to find oil workers around here." But not all of these parents cared to participate in the study.

The teacher-researchers approached the identification of families in various ways. One teacher sent a letter to all her students' families explaining the project and inviting parents who were interested to contact her. This approach was democratic since all families were invited and her students did not feel their parents were overlooked. It also introduced the study to her students and gave the teacher an opportunity to periodically discuss her involvement in the community research.

Other teachers contacted certain students' parents because they already knew a parent was employed in the oil industry and they felt that doing a series of home visits with this family would benefit the student. Still other teachers chose to interview neighbors, friends, or family members of the students.

The decision to interview families other than those of students was a significant deviation from funds of knowledge methodology. However, those teachers were still able to benefit from and add to the study because they developed new skills using ethnographic tools of inquiry and, more importantly, they extended their knowledge of the occupational lives and work patterns experienced by family members. Teachers who interviewed family members commented that the semistructured interviewing process operated as a mediating device that helped create the distance and objective stance needed to approach their relatives in a nonjudgmental manner. One teacher who interviewed her brother and sister-in-law spoke of the benefit of this distanced stance:

> The interview I enjoyed the most is my brother-in-law's. It gave me insight into them as a family. It made me more objective because I'm very opinionated. It's a fault that I have. It was the hardest thing to do to sit and listen and have them tell me the reasons why it works and it doesn't. And to realize there is nothing I can do to change it and that they aren't looking for my opinion. And that's the first thing I started off telling them. I'm not here to pass judgment. I'm here to interview you. But their stories were so different. Different from what they had told me all those years too.

This same teacher gained a new understanding of her brother-in-law's resourcefulness through her interviews with him. She also came to terms with the barriers that existed in her family between those who had a formal education and those who did not:

> And I never realized . . . I come from a family of educated people. College was expected. C [her brother-in-law] doesn't come from that type of family. And he's somewhat embarrassed about it. He didn't finish high school and obtain a degree, which I didn't even realize before. I assumed everybody did. I found that out in the interview. He gave me a different perspective. That guy is going to make it no matter what. I worry less about him than I do my brother—a mechanical engineer who if he got laid off from a job it wouldn't be as easy, in my opinion, for him to pick up and go on. C worked through the oil crunch and here we go again. He's one of the few at his work who is on his 40th day of going out. C never worries. He feels that if this oil company lays him off they'll hire him somewhere else. If not he can do carpentry work, he can do plumbing. He's never been without a job in all these years.

Who the teachers chose to interview depended on several factors, including their specific student population, their own history, and their relation to the community. The personal history of some of the teacher-researchers participating in the social impacts study positioned them subjectively close to understanding the life trajectories of the oil families they were interviewing. These teachers' families may have lived in the community for many generations and they themselves were the daughters or wives of oil field workers, so they were attuned to the effects of the particular stresses and struggles of rotational employment.

This form of flexible labor, where the work shift of 7 days on and 7 off, or 14 on and 14 off, or 21 on and 7 off, or in some cases, being constantly on-call, requires the intermittent absence of a husband or wife. This work situation has important repercussions for the organization of marriage and family life. Teachers who were a member of an oil family had an understanding of the dynamics of this life. They were also part of an intricate network of family and friends who had worked in the industry.

Yet these same teachers reported that even if they were familiar with the life and chose to interview friends or family members, they learned a considerable amount about how other families developed coping strategies, division of labor, accommodations to worker absence, and decision-making patterns.

A number of the other teacher-researchers had been recruited from the Midwest within the prior 5–10 years to teach in the local parish schools. These teachers were aware they were considered outsiders regardless of how long they had lived there. They chose families to interview from their own social and school networks, which contributed to a more heterogeneous sampling of households.

Although teachers had the choice in the Louisiana team ethnography project of interviewing student's families, relatives, or other community members, those who did visit the households of students benefited doubly from the experience. The simple but profound contact that was made outside the school boundaries helped teachers feel more like insiders and assisted them in becoming closer to their students and their students' families. This creation of more dynamic social relationships is a constant of the funds of knowledge research.

Conducting the Interviews

In the funds of knowledge research, the ethnographic interview is an in-depth conversation based on the building of trust and rapport. It usually starts with the labor history of the family and leads to a discovery of the family's historically accumulated resources, coping strategies, and social networks. Many of a family's resources are embedded in the social history of the work they have done, both formally and informally. These loosely structured conversations are guided by a discussion protocol that provides a framework for the interchange.

In the Louisiana social impacts study, the types of questions were similar in scope and content to other funds of knowledge projects except for the development of the occupational timeline and the formal rendering of the family tree. The guide led the interviewers into conversations that more specifically focused on the interviewee's work schedule, work responsibilities, and their family's accommodations and/or resistance to the demands of the work. These queries led to discussing the strategies the families used in raising and disciplining children, handling household division of labor, and coping with stress in relation to the frequent absences and pressures experienced by the parent employed in offshore oil work.

One other addition to the discussion guide particular to this study was the contact information sheet. This page was designed to provide a coherent listing of friends or relatives involved in the offshore oil business who were possibly open to being interviewed. The teacher-researchers used this tool to give other team members names gleaned from interviews they had conducted.

The household visits and interviews had an important impact on the teacher-researchers who participated in the study. Through the process of approaching the households as learners and ethnographers, the teachers took on the anthropological gaze and looked beyond surface social factors and their own assumptions about the family. Instead they noticed the family's resiliency and the funds of knowledge they used to cope and prosper in their everyday lives. Once the teachers entered the household with the purpose of learning about the family, their relationships with students and parents were altered. A new type of social relationship was developed.

One of the teachers new to her community spoke of the meaningful changes this altered stance gave her, and the barriers it helped her cross:

> The reason [for the household visit] has to be something besides school. Because even if I go into the home as a teacher to talk about teacher stuff, it's still a teacher/student, home/school kind of thing. But if we're talking about something that gives you common ground, that's really what I think is important. . . . All the at-risk programs in the world still keep that teacher/student and home/school barrier. Those lines are never crossed. You can go watch all the football and baseball games in the world and make yourself visible but you're still a teacher. But just to be seen in a different way is important. It's a fine line you have to walk because you can get too close. But I'd rather have the problems of too close than total conflict and confrontation all the time. I really wish in hindsight that I had interviewed more students' families. I think looking back I would target people who looked like a potential problem. Most kids who walk in with chips on their shoulders is because of some treatment

they have gotten from a teacher. So for them to see a teacher in a different way changes everything, everything.

This reciprocal view of the teacher in a different context was the flip side of the teacher seeing her students and their families differently. This re-visioning was crucial especially since the teacher did not share the student's sociocultural background. Learning to see and listen with new eyes and ears assisted the teachers in crossing barriers that have been normalized within the institutions of schools and operationalized in social and economic divisions throughout communities.

Study Groups: Debriefing and Building Trust

The experiences sparked by the household visits were collectively examined within regularly held teacher study groups. The study group meetings are an essential component of all funds of knowledge projects. They serve to support and guide the teachers in their family–community research by providing a safe, nonjudgmental forum to reflect and discuss the interviews.

Teachers were given the chance to share interviewing successes and difficulties and to collectively reflect on the interviewees' responses and perceptions. Sometimes discussions covered readings from other researchers who had looked at similar issues in various parts of the world.

Held every three to four weeks in each of the two communities, the study group sessions also helped the participating teachers to consider how they could develop pedagogical applications from these data for use in their classrooms. In addition, the two groups met jointly several times to discuss the similarities and differences in their neighboring locales and to touch on their preliminary findings.

These meetings often served to clear up confusions over methodological details, give and receive feedback on emerging analytical themes, and to ensure that the teacher-researchers stayed on schedule as much as possible. New questions and lines of inquiry emerged for all of us as we collectively reviewed our interview transcripts and fieldnotes and discussed the assigned readings. Erickson and Stull (1997) noted that sessions such as these help to keep team members in touch with both the theory and data while they are in the field.

In our project, the teacher-researchers, in essence, never left the field unless they moved away from their community. But the field, which was their community, had become for them an unusual–usual place during the course of the research. Through the focused distancing they experienced as social science researchers in their own towns, the teachers often felt as though they were seeing the way(s) things are for the first time. Just being from the community or being part of an oil family did not ensure that the teachers had a full understanding of the lives of the families involved. As one teacher remarked in relation to the study groups:

> I didn't know anything about the oil industry at all. When we sit in our groups, our study sessions, and I hear other teachers talking about it, it's very foreign to me although I'm from here. I lived in other places and then came back as an adult and have now lived here many years. Now I have a different understanding about the families who are involved in the oil industry and how they are run and how difficult it can be for them. When I grew up both my parents were there most of the time. But now I understand how difficult raising your children can be without one parent there very much. And then when that parent comes back, how different it can be with the changes that go on.

Another teacher who was the wife of an oil industry employee came to understand the way things were in her own family through the interviewing of similarly situated families in her community and through the exchanges with other teachers in the study group. This recovery of one's own history is similar to what Freire (1970) referred to as a recapturing of historical consciousness.

> [The study] helped me concentrate on the oil industry and its effect on the communities, the families and the children. Even though I was involved in it personally, I've been out of it and never thought of it affecting the children and the families. I realized how much it does affect the home life and the children, especially this being gone. Especially fathers of children. So I realize now how much it must have bothered my children. I didn't really look at this because you're in the middle of it and not standing back and looking in on it. Now I'm seeing more things—that periodic guest thing that came up—(and) I realize that this is the way it was for us. I've learned more about my own and others' relationships by doing this study.

This progressive distancing and focusing process, referred to by George Spindler as making the familiar strange, was repeated within the study groups by reading and discussing articles that reported on similar studies about offshore workers and their families in other locations. Several of the teachers whose experiences included being an oil wife or part of an oil family found that these readings sparked vigorous theories and questions concerning their own experiences. They noted the potentiality of offshore work to shape the functions of households and the social reproduction of household members and community institutions. One teacher whose father worked in the oil industry his whole life and died of a heart attack at an early age was very sensitive to the stress of oil field employment.

My main reason for [focusing on the stress of the work] is my father worked as a toolpusher in the oil field all his life and he had a heart attack at 47 years old. He was a very young man. He started having chest pains on the rig and he came in at the end of his hitch and two weeks later he had a heart attack. I knew it was associated with the rig because of the long hours that he worked. Sometimes he worked 18 hours straight because he didn't have any relief. My brothers have told me that he worked at a time when the oil field was really getting started. They were making money but their job was harder because they didn't have all the equipment they have now.

   The toolpushers had a hard job because they were responsible for everybody on every shift. It was a lot of stress. He was always worried about people and when he came in—he worked 7 and 7—it was either somebody got run off while he was gone or somebody quit so it was constantly stressful. He enjoyed his job. He loved his job. So until the day he died he wanted to go back to work. He died 14 years after his heart attack. He knew it was stressful but that's what he wanted to do. He'd been doing that since he was 17 years old. His parents were farmers but he loved the oil field.

This same teacher continued to reflect on her own family's experience and her mother's accommodations to her husband's work schedule and frequent absences:

They [oil field workers] make good money but can you afford to lose your loved ones because you want money? That's what it comes down to. They're gone for a lot of holidays. They're gone for all those special events in your life. They're gone when your kids have a problem. A lot of times they're gone. So is the woman at home strong enough to deal with all that on her own and make that family stick together? I can say my mama was. And I always wondered why my mother was always so tough. She's still alive today. She cuts her own grass and is very independent. I have four brothers and she still tells them what to do. But that's because she always did that 'cause my father worked offshore and she ruled that house. That was her job. And that has a lot to do with it all, being from an oil field family.

Personal reflection and collective analysis was the crux of the study group meetings. These sessions provided the ability to define a working relationship integrating research and practice. As Kingry-Westergaard and Kelly (1990, as cited in Bartunek, J. M. & Louis, 1996) wrote in *Insider/Outsider Team Research* (1996):

The assumed benefits of the collaborative style is that the discovery of information about the structures, roles, and norms expressed in context will enhance the authenticity, the validity, and therefore, the usefulness of the research. The collaborative relationship becomes a social structure by which the processes of discovery and understanding can take place. (p. 16)

Together we generated knowledge and theories about the families and institutions within the communities. We built trust by creating a shared agenda to discover and understand these community contexts. The teachers' roles as team members honored them as knowers and learners in their own classrooms and communities and within the study group. They were knowers and learners who were embedded in the contexts that structure their daily work and living situations.

THE PROJECT RESULTS: THE PROCESSES
AND PRODUCTS OF TEAM RESEARCH

The household visits and the study group sessions strengthened and deepened the participating teachers' appreciation of the cultural resources and circumstances of their own and their students' families' lives. Through this team ethnographic study, the teachers were introduced to a variety and plurality of family situations, traditions, and experiences. This greatly expanded and even transformed their teaching methods, their connection to their students' families, and their understanding of the many ways the oil industry affected their communities. As one teacher remarked:

> The oil industry touches a lot of lives. And it touches ours even though we're not personally involved in it. But my family is and I'm still interested in what happens to them. We're still an oil town. We're still an oil state. We get a lot of revenues from that. My pay comes from some of the oil revenue from the port. So it still affects me indirectly.

The research process had multiple effects on all the team members, on the creation and dissemination of the products generated by the team that did not begin at the mythical moment when data collection ended. Impacts were felt and shared from the moment the team began to take shape, to conduct interviews, to write up fieldnotes, and to explore preliminary findings. As the teachers delved into the interviewing process and began to reflect in their study groups on the personal impact of oil industry employment, many of them started to incorporate some of the ethnographic techniques they were practicing into their classroom curriculum. In some classrooms, the use of these epistemological tools helped students and teachers discuss difficult family matters and led to a deepening of relationships. One young teacher spoke of this relational shift:

> It was like we all had on white coats and gloves and nothing was personal [when doing the family trees]. One student has only seen her dad twice and

she wondered if she had to include him and I said not if you don't want to and that was it. We moved on. One of them said "My mother died. Should she go on there?" and I said "Yes, she's part of your family" because he sounded like he wanted to include her. But it was real. Nobody judged or commented on what they didn't have. The second time when they did it, they knew the format and just did it. They had confidence. They would ask a few questions but it was no personal thing. When I was working with C he asked what to put as last names because he had a real dad and an adopted dad. We added both and moved on. Because of the timelines and family trees that we have done now and before, this class has gotten to know each other well, doing all that personal stuff. But because of the research we [the teacher-researchers] have been doing and the questions we have been asking of the families we interview, I'll ask a question and if somebody wants to share it we share it. It led to the careers study and we went to a few places and came back and talked about the work.

In addition to showing their students how to construct the family trees and occupational timelines as extensions of history projects or career explorations, several teachers and 20 students from the two study communities in collaboration with university-based team members created an oilfield-related Web page. The students from one community interviewed and gathered photos of their family members who worked in the oil industry and then traveled to the second community to get assistance in creating the Web page. One of the teacher-researchers who coordinated the Web page spoke of her rationale for initiating this project as a way of involving her students in an extension of her own research on the impacts of the oil industry:

I was looking for something that would tie into careers and I like to do science-oriented careers. So the Web page became a medium where I can do both. The kids will come in and they will first of all have pictures they have collected of where their father works or their mother—whoever is in the oil industry. They will design that part of the Web page that describes what their father does. Then they'll interview a relative and do a page about job requirements and types of equipment they will have to use. Next they will tell us about themselves and create their own home page. We will also do a CD of it so in class I can put this in and show the kids what was done last year and then continue next year. That's the way we can continue to interview families in areas where we have gaps until we have covered the whole oil industry.

For these public school teachers, the first and perhaps most significant audience for the dissemination of the research process and preliminary findings was their own students. Another audience for the presentation of preliminary findings and experiences of collaborative team research was the annual meeting of the Society for Applied Anthropology (SFAA) in

Tucson, Arizona in the spring of 1999. Thirteen of the teacher-researchers attended the conference and participated in a panel presentation and discussion that centered on their experiences as coresearchers in the study. This professional collaboration publicly positioned the teachers as adept in the field and essential to the success of the team's ethnographic project. Several of the teachers mentioned that preparing for and attending the conference increased their sense of themselves as professionals and as social science researchers.

The teachers also gave local presentations to their school colleagues and principals and to community organizations such as the Chamber of Commerce, the Parent–Teacher Organization, the City Council, or the School Board. Through their participation in the study, they came to know their own communities in new ways that connected them to their community's history and actively positioned them as possible agents of change. As one teacher noted:

> I've been here for six years but I think that I didn't know anything about off-shore oil. So just knowing that makes me feel more rooted. It's not a tangible thing that has made me change but I just feel more at home now. I know more people now. I don't feel so much like the outsider.

Insider or outsider, public school researcher or university-based researcher, the basis of all the team members' strategies and data collection and interpretation was the joint construction of knowledge through observation, dialog, and reflective listening. The firsthand knowledge, insight, and reflective skills that teachers gained through their practice and their participation in community research was valuable to their practice as teachers and critical to the authenticity and validity of the team's research. Concerns about ethnographic voice, professional collaboration, coauthorship, and strategies for getting a useful, coherent, and readable report into the hands of community members and MMS directors is the present concern of the team. But one thing is certain. Our collective task of understanding and describing what is going on here, of documenting and interpreting the multiple social realities of the individuals and families in the two communities would have been more daunting and less grounded without the mediating presence of the teacher-researchers.

REFLECTION QUESTIONS

1. How does a teacher's perspective change as a result of participation in household or community research?

2. What challenges may teachers face when they cross the barriers between school and community to do ethnographic research?

3. How might you and fellow teachers design a funds of knowledge project that investigates sociocultural issues pertinent to your school and community?

4. What pitfalls and/or benefits might teachers encounter as participants in team research?

5. Who could you recruit to help you collect a similar study and why?

REFERENCES

Bartunek, J. M., & Louis, M. R. (1996). *Insider/outsider team research.* Thousand Oaks, CA: Sage.
Erickson, K. C., & Stull, D. D. (1997). *Doing team ethnography.* Thousand Oaks, CA: Sage.
Freire, P. (1970). *Pedagogy of the oppressed.* New York: Continuum.

Chapter 13

Preservice Teachers Enter Urban Communities: Coupling Funds of Knowledge Research and Critical Pedagogy in Teacher Education

Patricia Buck
Bates College

Paul Skilton Sylvester
University of Pennsylvania

> *From the standpoint of the child, the great waste in the school comes from his in-*
> *ability to utilize the experiences he gets outside the school in any complete and free*
> *way within the school itself; while, on the other hand, he is unable to apply in*
> *daily life what he is learning in school. That is the isolation of the school—its iso-*
> *lation from life. He the child gets into the schoolroom he has to put out of his*
> *mind a large part of his ideas, interests and activities that predominate in his*
> *home and neighborhood. So the school, being unable to utilize this everyday expe-*
> *rience, sets painfully to work, on another tack and by a variety of means, to*
> *arouse in the child an interest in school studies.*
> —Dewey (1902, p. 75)

Nearly a century ago Dewey noted the potential symbiosis between schooling and community. Dewey called on educators to be responsive to the strengths, struggles, and desires that bloom in the neighborhoods surrounding their schools. One of the purposes of schooling, suggested by Dewey and countless others, is to graduate citizens poised to engage in democratic, local governance. Since the Progressive Era, this larger educational aim has led many to adopt an experiential or hands-on approach that actively engages students in the construction of meaning around notions of work, community, democracy, and society. Progressive educational philosophy positions educators to make use of the communities surrounding schools as laboratories of learning within which lie multiple possibilities for greater understanding of self, place in society, and possibilities for social change. Such a philosophy situates neighborhoods as wellsprings of opportunity and calls attention to educators' responsibility to contribute to the growth and healing of community.

In this chapter we describe our efforts to guide preservice teachers at the University of Pennsylvania's Master's Program in Elementary Education through the process of conducting qualitative studies of the neighborhoods that surround their school placements during the summer before they begin as student teachers. Penn's program has an urban focus, and the majority of preservice teachers complete placements in low-income, majority minority neighborhood schools. Students' research in these communities is framed around identification of funds of knowledge. Our students locate potential funds embedded within their urban neighborhoods and use them in the construction of thematic and equity-oriented social studies curricula. The larger aim of this work is to focus preservice teachers' attention on those local resources available in the creation of challenging, nurturing, and respectful learning environments.

More specifically, in this chapter we explore the salience of preservice teachers' consciousness of self and the "other" in relation to their entrance into urban communities. This exploration occurs through reflection on ways we might help students better articulate between the power and privilege they enjoy as, for the most part, middle- and upper-middle-class White women, and the realities of poverty they witness while doing fieldwork. We also reflect on the need to shift students' inclination toward deficit-oriented research topics to ones that situate urban families and communities as resources of talent, knowledge, and possibility.

While maintaining focus on skills, assets, and strengths suggested in family-based funds of knowledge research, the context of our particular teacher education program necessitates a shift to community-based assets—the difference being that funds are assessed through community-based relationships rather than directly from the home. In some cases the significance of this distinction is small. Moll et al. (this volume) describe examples of family-based funds that include a relative's experientially learned knowledge about immigration as a potential resource to be tapped in the classroom. In another example they suggest that mechanical work completed by students and relatives together represent learning practices deepened by " 'thick' and 'multistranded' " relationships.

> The person from whom the child learns carpentry, for example, may also be the uncle with whom the child's family regularly celebrates birthdays or organizes barbecues, as well as the person with whom the child's father goes fishing on weekends. (p. 74)

In our neighborhood studies, preservice teachers might, similarly, identify a storeowner as a source of emotionally rich information about immigration or a local mechanic as an exemplar of hands-on learning and situated problem-solving.

Our appropriation of the concept of funds of knowledge is in part a practical choice. Whereas family-based research depends on the establishment of trust over long periods of time, our students must complete their study during an intensive summer term when elementary schools are not in session. Given these constraints, community resources are more immediately available. Although we are disappointed at the loss of opportunity to engage in a focused and systematic effort to bridge a common divide between urban classrooms and the parents of those students served within them, we posit that holistic investigation into community reveals infinite foci for curriculum development and fosters the creation of learning environments defined by community pride and realization of student agency. Within such classrooms the larger community's resources are constructed as belonging to and offering equal access to all students. Further, on a fundamental level, both family- and community-based research and curriculum development suggest opportunities for social change and the nurturing of student agency and complement progressive educational philosophy's attention to permeability between schools, families, and community. As such, we genuinely perceive them as mutually constructive. Finally, at the same time that we emphasize a community-based approach, we encourage students, as they look into their futures as reflective and adaptive practitioners, to view both family and community as reservoirs of pedagogical and curricular possibility.

THE INTEGRATED PROJECT

The depth and complexity of students' work is made possible through the integration of two courses: Social Studies Methods and School and Society, which students take simultaneously. The courses are integrated in the sense that students conduct neighborhood studies in our School and Society course and that research is used to inform the development of thematic social studies curricula for Social Studies Methods.

The integration of the two courses represents a significant shift in the program. Universities have long suffered from the strict subdivision of fields of knowledge. Among the unfortunate ways that knowledge is subdivided in universities, one that plagues many schools of education is the split between teacher education and the social foundations of education. Most teacher education programs have a social-foundations component, but too often these courses feel like the math class that English majors put off taking until their senior year.

The problem we had at the University of Pennsylvania 4 years ago was not as bad as it could have been—we were an urban-focused program, all of the professors teaching methods courses found ways to integrate issues of equity and justice, and the one course that was specifically focused on social foundation, School and Society, was reasonably well-liked by students. But although students found the social foundations course intellectually engaging, the faculty's perception was that it did not seem to transform the way they taught in their student teaching placements. At that time, School and Society was not taught by faculty within Teacher Education but by other faculty whose main constituency were doctoral students focused on the social foundations of education. At a time when we were reviewing the curriculum of the master's program in elementary education, we made changes in the way that School and Society is taught that have yielded promising results for integrating social foundations with teacher education in more meaningful ways. Through this curriculum review, the faculty restructured the program, dividing it into five multiweek terms, each with a particular focus, each with one main assignment that cuts across courses. During our master's students' first term, which runs from late July to late August, the focus is on "neighborhoods and schools" and the "integrative assignment." Students complete a study of the neighborhood that surrounds the school where they will student teach and, on the basis of that study, develop social studies curricula centered on a community-based fund of knowledge.

The neighborhood study assignment can be said to be "one assignment" only insofar as there is unity to its parts—(a) an initial "inventory" of the five-block area surrounding the school[1]; (b) follow-up interviews and observations; (c) triangulation of data using demographic and primary, historical sources; and (d) a rationale for a social studies curriculum that incorporates funds of knowledge that they came across in the neighborhood.

On the first day of class, students arrive having read John Dewey's "The School and Social Progress" in *The Child and the Curriculum and the School and Society* (1902a). We ask what John Dewey would suggest we find out about the neighborhood in which they will teach. To this list, students add their own ideas, and we email these questions to them that night as the questions for their initial "inventory." The following day, students meet an alumnus of our program who serves as a "neighborhood liaison" and takes them out to the neighborhood. Liaisons introduce students to a community member who has been hired to guide a five-block walking tour.[2] As one student told us the day after her tour:

> I was scared going there, but when we got out of the car this Puerto Rican woman named Diana gave us each a hug and then she walked us around. She

---

[1]Steinberg and Stephen's curriculum for high schoolers inspired this portion of the assignment (1999).

[2]Also inspired by Steinberg and Stephen (1999).

knew everyone in the neighborhood and introduced us to him or her. It's a poor area but there's an amazing amount of positive programs going on.

As her comments suggest, during the initial neighborhood tours the community guide introduces students to store owners, parents who have children at the school, local clergy, and youth workers. During this tour and follow-up visits over the course of the next week, students identify both funds of knowledge and possible themes or issues to pursue in subsequent parts of their study. These themes often end up serving as the foci for students' social studies curriculum rationale.

The readings, class activities, and elements of research that comprise students' neighborhood study projects convey a multilayered vision of school and community much like the intricate, vibrant, and proud murals that decorate the walls of many of the neighborhoods they visit. Drawing on knowledge gained through the research process, students paint their own interpretive vision of community strengths and potentials. The thematic curriculum that students develop represents the tangible creation of students' interpretive work. The less immediate but ideally more consequential product is to position preservice teachers to look toward families and communities as resources rather than constraints, a position that stands to affect not only curricula development but also interactional classroom dynamics, pedagogical approaches, and relations with family and other community members.

ASSESSING OUR WORK

While largely implicit, the concept of student engagement is at the heart of our work. We work with preservice teachers to find creative and informed ways to engage elementary students. Engagement requires that teachers connect with students on both an intellectual and emotional level. In order to do so, it makes sense that teachers pay attention to what is closest to students: their families and communities and to do so in ways that help to grow students' sense of themselves, their families, and communities as valuable, talented, and capable of joy. In order to engage in the life and work of the classroom, elementary students need to know that their teachers care about them, that, as Schultz (2003) writes, teachers listen and pay attention to who they are and what they care about:

> A focus on listening highlights the centrality of students as resources for the moment-to-moment decisions teachers make as they teach. . . . The phrase "listening to teach" implies that the knowledge of who the learner is, and the understandings that both the teacher and learner bring to a situation constitute the starting place for teaching. Listening encompasses written words as

well as those that are spoken, words that are whispered, those enacted in gesture, and those left unsaid. It is an active process that allows us both to maintain and cross boundaries. (p. 13)

It is through active listening and responsiveness that teachers earn students' respect and that students come to feel safe entrusting teachers to
guide their learning and development of self. The notion that teachers
need to earn students' respect and trust is also often an implicit understanding at the heart of what all educators do.

As teacher educators, we too need to stay attuned to our students' levels
of engagement, to note the places where they contest our guidance within
an overall commitment to reflect and adapt our practice. As professors, we
hold a type of power over our preservice teachers that means we rarely have
to grapple with the type of oppositionality and resistance that our students
may face once they enter the classroom. We can count on our students to
go through the motions, to complete their assignments—often quite well.
Yet, while our students are used to performing in the academic sphere, they
may not be accustomed to being moved by their work. As future teachers,
however, it is important that they not only finish assignments. We need
them to genuinely and passionately care about and value their students,
families, and communities' funds of knowledge: their strengths, assets, and
possibilities.

Given the charge to responsively listen and earn respect, we have to find
ways to assess our own work, to gauge whether we genuinely reach our students. As part of this assessment process, we submit to the general conversation around theorizing practices a number of questions and our own partial
readings that have arisen through the process of guiding students' community-based research and curriculum development. In offering these questions and our own interpretation of the events and issues surrounding
them, we invite teachers and scholars to help us think about what it means
to introduce preservice teachers to new and often unfamiliar community
spaces. How might we grapple with issues that arise in the employment of a
qualitative, funds of knowledge approach to curriculum development
within a teacher education program? What are our responsibilities as educators guiding students through the research process? What are the barriers to such a project? Where are potential areas of improvement? What
stands to be gained from a deep and rewarding but admittedly challenging
undertaking? Finally, we ask a more pointed question, the investigation of
which sends us along each of these lines of inquiry: What are preservice
teachers' intellectual and emotional experiences of conducting community-based research and curriculum development?

Students' responses to conducting neighborhood studies are overwhelmingly positive. They appreciate the opportunity to get to know their
neighborhood, to meet some of the community members who will be key

players in their lives over the coming year. They recognize the inherent value in learning about their future students' everyday lives and "stomping grounds." They also express a desire to learn about underappreciated elements of strength and resilience found in often desperately poor sections of the city.[3] Yet, even as they are eager to learn, many maintain a consciousness of self in relation to an unfamiliar other, a sense of self as vulnerable.

Out of the premise that engagement is about connecting with students on both an intellectual and an emotional level, we want to explore this dynamic of vulnerability as an emotional hot spot in our program. As our students begin their research, they often express profound discomfort at being asked to venture into the neighborhoods surrounding their placement schools. Their fear speaks to the responsibility we, as teacher educators, have to explicitly address—students' personal experiences around racialized, gendered, and classed productions of inequity.

In her 1989 article "White Privilege: Unpacking the Invisible Knapsack" Peggy McIntosh describes a process through which White, middle-class teachers might become attuned to the everyday privileges they enjoy on account of their race, gender, and class. In one example, she compares the taken-for-granted absence of humiliation White consumers enjoy as they shop, unhampered by suspicious storeowners and security guards. In this comparative example McIntosh calls forth readers' empathy for the everyday struggles and humiliations of people of color and makes clear that middle-class Whites walk a relatively unfettered road. The assumption underlying the visual image of White shoppers' carefree circulation through stores is that they do so within the safe confines of mainstream neighborhoods. Our experience of working with middle- to upper-middle-class White preservice teachers as they enter, often for the first time, into low-income communities of color suggests a question: Would the emergent issues McIntosh (1989) describes be different if White shoppers were to browse

---

[3]Some teams of students also study neighborhoods of suburban schools, but we chose in this paper to focus on the experience of those studying urban schools. Although all our students have at least one placement in an urban public school, students may choose to either a single year-long placement in an urban public school or two semester-long placements, one in an urban public school and another in a suburban or independent school. Although some students have suggested that, as an urban-focused program, our students should only study urban neighborhoods, we as instructors have resisted this for the following reasons: Social science research is overwhelmingly a literature of elite and European American researchers studying the lives of poor and non-European-Americans as subjects. The result is a tendency to see these latter groups as the sole bearers of culture and difference, reinforcing the perception of Whiteness and middle class status as normalcy and all others as "the other"—an analogous phenomenon to the "ethnic" section in supermarkets. Secondly, studying the city without studying the suburb obscures the connections between the two—the fact that all's well in an elite suburb is not separate from the challenges faced by those in the city but rather part of the same ecology that has grown out of balance.

among businesses within poor, majority minority neighborhoods? Would they still enjoy the same unexamined feeling of safety garnered as coveted consumers? Would the significance of their race remain submerged within their consciousness?

Students in our program are required to venture out into urban neighborhoods, to browse through corner stores, walk along the sidewalks, and map out residences, parks, and businesses. They are paired with a community member whose race, class, and history of personal experiences are most often markedly different from their own. They are expected to develop a relationship with the community liaison and to converse with others they meet along the way. They spend hours observing happenings in the neighborhood and witness the everyday life of children. While not expecting students to feel like insiders, we hope to foster a shift from self-consciousness, vulnerability, and suspicion to respect, confidence, and humility. To varying degrees, this is often achieved. In the first few weeks of the year, students begin to build connections that serve them throughout the year. They enter into relationships with teachers, community leaders, and parents and gain entrée into the daily workings and politics of the neighborhood. They identify buildings that relay the history of the neighborhood, city, and nation and the organizations that advocate for the community. As a promising sign of well-placed loyalty, they often become protective of community members in ways that raise ethical issues for them about their role as researcher.

Yet, as each new cohort orients to the program and their projects, students invariably express anxiety over personal safety as an immediate and dominant interest. This apprehension is often explicitly packaged as a gendered and racialized issue. We have had parents call to express concern that their "very attractive" White daughters won't be safe in "minority" neighborhoods.

Each year, we anticipate students' concerns and invite a police officer to lead a discussion on street safety strategies. We also pair or group students in research teams and arrange for a community member to provide a tour of the neighborhood and contact information of other "safe" community members who are willing to speak with students. Even so, students and occasionally their families experience apprehension that is often heightened by critical events in their journeys through placement neighborhoods.

One afternoon in Patti's section, a student relayed a story in response to a question about how neighborhood tours of the previous day had gone. The student explained that she and a few of her classmates had walked past a cluster of young Black men hanging out outside a subsidized housing complex. The tour leader explained that the two-story, single-family units represented a shift in federal policy away from high-rise units or "projects." The shift, the tour guide reported, was meant to deconcentrate poverty and to provide families with the experience of low-cost home ownership. As she explained this progressive move in social policy, the men reportedly leered and hurled crude sexual and racial comments at a couple of preservice teachers who hung back from the guide and main cluster of classmates. The tour leader turned to the offenders and "called them out" on their behavior saying, "These young ladies are going to be teachers in our school. You show them the respect they deserve!"

The men responded, "Oh, sorry, sorry, Martha. [Then, turning to the students] Welcome. We didn't mean no disrespect. We need teachers. You'll all be good teachers for us. Don't worry, you'll be safe here. We'll look out for you."

Embedded within preservice teachers' concern for personal safety is an understanding of that which is contained within urban communities. And here we use the language of constraint quite deliberately and ironically, as it is the perceived unlawful, unregulatable elements that dominate both our larger sociocultural attention and preservice teachers' particular images of contemporary, urban communities of color. In class the woman told this story with a tone that suggested a questioning of us as educators. She implicitly challenged us to answer these questions: What do you make of this? What do you want us to make of this? Are we expected to see such men as community assets? How does this fit into the analytic equation you have provided for us?

Thus far, ours has been a practical approach to assure the security and peace of mind of our students—street safety strategies and connections with "safe" community members—but this event and others like it leave us with questions about how we might better interrogate the (dis)connection between their anxiety and our desire for the same communities that many preservice teachers fear to be seen as funds of knowledge. And so, we offer some ideas about how we might improve our practice at the same time that we ask educators and scholars to help us think about how to do this work better.

What becomes apparent to us is that students' concern over personal safety carries more weight than we have thus far appreciated. It is about more than protecting the physical safety of "just anybody" going "just anywhere." It carries with it a sense of disruption of taken-for-granted privilege and power: the privilege of distance from harm and the power of families to ensure that distance is maintained. As a reflection of larger, class- and race-based structures of privilege and power, we posit that preservice teachers and their parents' worries about physical safety reflect a significant problematic in the larger effort to organize teacher education around an asset-oriented approach to urban schools and communities. After all, teachers who long to avoid the streets and residents of their school neighborhood are unlikely to capitalize on the knowledge possessed within that community. And so, we ask: Assuming that the ultimate goal is to position preservice teachers to view urban communities and their residents as reservoirs of strength, possibility, and talent, how can teacher education programs guide students in the articulation between their lived, possessed, and claimed privilege and the relative poverty and disadvantage within which urban community members are equally embedded?

As a program that draws on multicultural, feminist, and critical pedagogical theory, we already operate out of a framework that makes such an articulation possible. In the past, the Social Studies Methods course has been centered on the personalized exploration of multiculturalism from particular identity positions. In this way, students and their instructors are ready to make the obvious connection between our predominantly White female students' emotional experience of vulnerability within majority minority and low-income communities. Perhaps what we could do better is craft a more genuinely constructivist learning experience. What would it mean for students to look at the very feelings of discomfort they experience and ask what it tells them about inequities of power and privilege? Are their experiences of fear somehow different from those who live their daily lives in such communities? Should they be responded to differently? What might preservice teachers' pedagogy gain from a personal exploration of their positionality and that of community members in relation to race, prejudice, and opportunity? Further, could preservice teachers' personal exploration be deepened through appreciation of their place and that of their families and those of urban community members within the social history of race- and class-based segregation and discrimination?

The School and Society course also has a number of mechanisms already in place that could lend themselves to students' examination of personal fears and privileges. Early in the semester, we hire doctoral students from Penn's history department to act as docents on a walking tour of Philadelphia. They point out ways in which the physical make-up of varied neighborhoods reflect remnants of differing economic and social epochs in history. Varied physical structures and urban landscapes are shown to parallel shifting structures of inequity across time. Students are introduced to the walking city of colonial Philadelphia and to the later "sprawl" affected by streetcar suburbanization. The accelerating impact of advances in transportation wind the tour through early suburbs of the wealthy Main Line outskirts of the city, and a final stop in the downtown business district punctuates the current hypersegregation of the current "dual city."

Following the tour, we ask students to research the history of their particular neighborhood and to place it within the larger socioeconomic history of Philadelphia. They also do hypothetical family history projects in which they role-play the economic, religious, family, and residential lives of hypothetical urban families across time.

Taking into consideration the foundation laid in each course, perhaps, we could integrate the two curricular approaches in order to grapple with students' discomfort. We could ask them to journal about their initial emotional reaction to entering their placement community and later to formalize their thinking in an essay about the historical and social context out of which these emotions surface.

Again, building constructively on their actual experiences, we could read material, such as Elijah Anderson's *Place on the Corner* (1981) and *Streetwise* (1992), that provides ethnographic accounts of Black men's experiences in school and the labor force, accounts that theorize oppressed men's use of sexual prowess and power to compensate for a lack of social, political, or economic power. In other words we need to provide students with the tools to make sense of such critical events as the one that occurred on the neighborhood tour, events that run the risk of reinscribing fears and stereotypes. We could also model the interdisciplinarity we encourage preservice teachers to employ and get at the same set of thematics by assigning Toni Morrison's fictive exploration of African American male violence against African American women in *Sula* (2002). Finally, we could ask students to consider where, in a deeply unequal society, responsibility lies for underemployment, drug use, and sexual violence. Taken together, critical readings, neighborhood research, and focused class activities provide a framework for students to see the shared responsibility for such "bad behavior" as a production of our larger culture and society.

In short, taking a funds of knowledge approach does not mean that preservice teachers must go through the research process with blinders on to the negative and threatening aspects that may exist in many poor urban communities. We need to value preservice teachers' gendered, classed, and racialized experiences. If we don't provide these intellectual tools, the funds of knowledge philosophy runs the risk of being overwhelmed by students' emotional experience of the neighborhood and dismissed as naive. Our teacher education programs may inadvertently index preservice teachers' consciousness of self to a socioculturally produced fantasy/nightmare of morally pure and physically vulnerable White women set down among lascivious men of color raised within and re-creating a culture of poverty.

Unless we listen and respond to preservice teachers' concerns around racially and sexually charged safety issues, they may not trust that we guide their learning responsibly and carefully, and so they may not fully engage in reflection on the assets embedded in their placement communities. Students enrolled in our program could go through the motions to complete the work assigned to them only to later walk into their own classrooms without having had the experience of genuine emotional and intellectual engagement as student-teachers. This worst-case scenario, of course, wouldn't bode well for the potential of community-based research to accomplish its goal to position new teachers to view urban students, families, and communities as assets.

In order to be responsive educators, we continue to think about how we can help student teachers articulate between their fears, desire to be good teachers, and a positioning of urban communities as funds of knowledge.

PRESERVICE TEACHERS CHOOSING
A RESEARCH TOPIC

Part of realizing the promise of neighborhood studies to reposition families and communities as assets is found in the "teachable moments" that present themselves as we guide students through the research process. The work we do doesn't stop at helping our students make sense of the anxiety they might feel at entering communities. Developing an asset orientation is an ongoing process that carries through the actual process of conducting research.

The significance of preservice teachers' social identity, perspectives, and background also emerges as salient in their selection of research topics. That, as Vygotsky maintains, our thought processes are a product of our cultural history is as true for young, White, upper-middle-class Americans as it is for the "other" population groups to which we are accustomed to seeing Vygotskian theory applied. Many of the majority White, middle- to upper-middle-class women enroll in the program soon after graduating from college and without exposure to or experience in grappling with issues associated with urban life or schooling. At the same time, preservice teachers are familiar with and vulnerable to a dominant discourse that explains academic underachievement among low-income students of color as the product of the culture of poverty, a logic often presented under the cloak of "common sense." Although the program maintains an explicitly urban focus that students are aware of before accepting admittance, given the pervasiveness of deficit orientations to urban schooling, faculty recognize the need to provide students with the tools to constructively come to terms with what it means to complete a practicum in an urban school.

That students operate out of a "culture of poverty" logic is often revealed in their initial approach to data collection and analysis. We instruct students to choose an emergent theme from the data to look at in more depth. Rather than select a theme or topic that reflects community members' *emic*, or insider perspective, students often choose to look at those topics that strike them as relevant on a personal level. Despite our explicit coaching to look for assets in the community, students' topics often hint at the assumption of failure, of a communal falling apart, of a dissolution of the ideal—that ideal being the suburban, intact two-parent family living in spacious homes that presume privacy and a centering on the individual versus the community. Students choose topics that will allow them to investigate failure—statistics about academic underachievement and its articulation with family structure, read: family destruction. Others have wanted to look at drug use, teen pregnancy, and criminal behavior.

Preservice teachers are often driven by a desire to make sense of those elements of the community that scare them and turn toward familiar academic logics to do so: to sort and organize, to correlate negatives with negatives, to draw a line between cause and effect. They pose research questions such as: What are family structures like in the neighborhood, and how do they correlate with academic performance? Is teen pregnancy common in the community, and is it related to low birth weight and malnutrition?

In conversations with us, preservice teachers explain that they hope such research projects lead to curricula around the importance of staying in school or of good nutrition. The danger of familiar analytic tools is that, without developing an appreciation of the richness, resilience, and ingenuity harbored in poor families and whole communities, students think themselves into becoming impassioned pedagogues, or worse: saviors of innocent children cruelly exposed to debauchery and underprepared for mainstream, moral society. On the other hand, we as instructors who insist on an asset orientation, risk being misunderstood as naive liberals pretending that the social problems that often go with joblessness do not exist. How do we help students understand the very real social problems of many urban communities while still helping them to see the funds of knowledge that also exist?

Our dilemmas mirror a set of similar issues faced by urban social scientists since the 1960s. The sociologist William Julius Wilson did the social sciences great service in 1987 by naming "the elephant in the living room" of urban research: that since 1965, when Daniel Patrick Moynihan was labeled a racist for drawing attention to the problems in urban ghettos, social scientists had avoided discussing the pathologies of inner-city communities. While acknowledging the inherent racism of the earlier studies' posit that "cultural disadvantage" as the cause of urban problems, Wilson (1990) put forth a more comprehensive theory that stresses the structural changes in the economy. Wilson noted that northern manufacturing jobs disappeared just as Blacks arrived from the south hungry for work. This in-migration happened simultaneous to the instatement of fair housing legislation that allowed middle-class Blacks to move out of central cities, coinciding social forces that concentrated the poorest of the poor, which Wilson termed "the underclass," in urban communities. Within this broader frame, choices of individuals could be seen for what they were—choices drawn from a limited set of options, some better than others, made in response to broad socioeconomic challenges. Like Wilson, we want our students to see members of the neighborhoods they study as affected by larger social processes—not pawns of larger social forces, but also not individuals acting free of socio-economic constraints.

The work of a student named Lucy presents a good example of the challenges we face. Lucy was part of a group studying an African American neighborhood fraught with drugs and drug-related violence. When interviewed, members of that neighborhood shared a uniformly bleak outlook. When she looked into social programs designed for urban redevelopment, she found that all of them fell outside its boundaries. Ultimately, Lucy decided that this was one community that was devoid of assets and said so in her analysis of data.

What's a professor to do? How do you instruct students to see assets when markers of decay understandably obstruct even community residents' vision? In this case, it was I (Paul Skilton Sylvester) who had Lucy in my section. How could I argue with the admittedly bleak outlook that her informants seemed to have of this area? What sense did it make to have students do original research but not accept the findings?

When I got together with Lucy, I told her that I could not accept her paper as it was. The rubric for grading the papers was explicit in its expectation that students would identify funds of knowledge within the community. I also said that having taught at a school that was located in this neighborhood I knew that the hopelessness that she described was not inaccurate. It was just not the whole story. I suggested that—like in wartime—the strengths of a group are not separate from the challenges they face, but rather are often found in the courage or creativity shown in response.

Then I asked Lucy what she had majored in as an undergraduate. I shared with her my observation that she was an excellent student, but was stronger in some areas than others. She often had incisive comments to make in class—incisive like a knife. She had strong analytic skills that allowed her to cut into the weakness of a text or an argument. But I had also noticed—I told her—that she did not seem as adept at finding the positive elements of an argument (or a neighborhood, I thought to myself), that could be built on.

She saw my point. She had been an art major—she was (and is) a photographer. And rather than being defensive, she pointed out that art students spend a great deal of time doing—and submitting their own work to—"crits," critique sessions in which the faculty, students, and their peers tear apart each other's work.

As we finished this conference, I laid down the gauntlet for Lucy—she could try to go through our program relying on her admittedly excellent analytic "ripping down" skills, or she could take up the challenge of strengthening her skills in a different part of her brain: synthetic, "building up," ways of seeing. At least for my class, she would not pass if she did not try to do so.

Lucy rose to the challenge and then some. Here's a passage from her second try at the assignment—a paper that she presented on a panel with us at the Ethnography and Education Forum held at the University of Pennsylvania:

Walking into Young's Candies on Girard Avenue I felt like Charlie Bucket walking into Bill's Candy Store in "Charlie and the Chocolate Factory." The wood counters and cabinets with glass panes, the old-fashioned candy scale, and the rows and rows of mouth-watering traditional German confections made me feel like I was walking into the Brewerytown of 100 years past. The elderly man behind the counter seemed to be just as much the "Candy Man" of Brewerytown as Bill was in Charlie's town. . . . Mr. Young is the third generation of the Young family to run Young's Candies since his grandfather opened the store in 1897. When Mr. Young heard that I was going to be teaching at the Robert Feltman School, he walked to a set of shelves behind the counter and pulled down his 7th grade class picture from Feltman, taken in 1941. Mr. Young told me that he keeps the picture around because some of his classmates still come into the store. It intrigued me that people like Mr. Young and his classmates chose to stay in Brewerytown despite the economic and physical decline the neighborhood has undergone in the last half of a century. But after talking to Mr. Young for a few more minutes, I got the feeling that when he looked out the front window of his store, he did not see the same littered streets, abandoned factories, and boarded up homes that I saw. It seemed that Mr. Young looked out his window and saw the neighborhood as it existed in his youth.

Mr. Young told me of times on hot summer nights when he and his friends would walk down to the banks of the Schuylkill River where other neighborhood residents had already gathered. There the residents of Brewerytown would find respite from the heat by sticking their feet in the cool water of the river. On other nights, Harry Young and his father would keep the candy store open until midnight. When a show ended at the Fairmount Movie Theater, local residents would come to Young's Candies to enjoy homemade ice cream and the company of friends.

"OK, engaging opening," I thought to myself as I read Lucy's revised paper. But seeing the positive in a neighborhood's past is different than seeing it in the present, I thought. How could the artifacts of this charming candy store proprietor be used as funds of knowledge without fostering defeatism among the students with the bad luck to be born into the age of deindustrialization? Later in the paper Lucy answered this question as she told about the evolution of her own thinking from a deficit-oriented perspective to an assets-oriented one:

In my initial research on the neighborhood, I struggled to find positive community resources and organizations as I knew them to exist in the area where I grew up. This search only led me to find more and more articles that focused on the deficits of the neighborhood instead of its strengths. The more negative information I came across, the more important I felt it was for the students of the Robert Feltman School to realize that the current condition of the neighborhood is not their fault and is not a reflection upon them as members of society. Incorporating the history of Brewerytown and the economic and political factors that influenced the industrial booms and declines of the past century into the classroom curriculum is one way I believe students can gain an understanding of the current situation. More importantly, I believe that interacting with devoted neighborhood residents like Harry Young, and others that see the beauty and potential of the area will help students realize the potential within themselves. In this case, the classroom has the ability to serve as a breeding ground to help students develop into informed citizens who realize their potential to initiate and carry out change.

As my approach to Lucy's research process illustrates, we, as educators, have to guide preservice teachers through experiential meaning-making by directing them toward evidence that reservoirs of human strength and talent, as ready-made, untapped educational resources, do exist in urban communities. The perspective we take is a Deweyian one (1938), insofar as we believe that we, as teachers who have gone further and seen more in this area, we have a responsibility not to just stand back and let students come wholly to their own solutions. After all, a lifetime of experience with stereotyped, deficit-oriented views of urban inequality framing urban problems as the result of individual weakness or pathology scaffolds their "own" solutions. As Lucy's example shows, we explicitly ask students to find funds of knowledge in their communities through the experiences we design for them, the written assignments we ask them to complete in regard to these field experiences, and our ongoing dialog with them. Through the research process students develop genuinely grounded theory about their placement neighborhoods, which they have creatively employed to inform the development of age-appropriate, historically rich and contextualized curricula (Corbin & Straus, 1998). Table 13.1 displays students' research topics and corresponding curricular themes.

One student pair, placed within a neighborhood in which 55% of the residents were Puerto Rican, chose as their thematic focus residents' efforts to build community. These students, Eliza and Sage, found that residents identified a set of community-building practices including neighborhood beautification, information sharing about acquiring U.S. citizenship, support of local business owners who carried Puerto Rican foods and other products, parental control and involvement in school, and maintenance of connections with family in Puerto Rico. In an analysis of the collection of interviews and observations out of which their findings emerged, Sage wrote:

> Community activists work daily to promote whole neighborhood cleanups and park cleanups in order to make their community beautiful. . . . They feel

TABLE 13.1
Student Research Foci and Corresponding
Thematic Curricular Topics

Research Topic	Thematic Curricular Topic
Demographics and community building, Philadelphia neighborhood	Exploration of demographics and community building in students' specific neighborhood
Relations/historical conflict between African Americans and South Asians in West Philadelphia (e.g., origins and manifestations of the conflict)	Interdisciplinary neighborhood study
Economic, demographic, and social context of school neighborhood	Interdisciplinary neighborhood study
History of social work in Philadelphia and Pennsylvania	Interdisciplinary neighborhood study
Community activism	Community identity and activism through neighborhood study
Neighborhood involvement in the civil rights movement	Civil rights and community leadership
Urban revitalization in school neighborhood	Neighborhood revitalization
Community-building practices	Transportation (trains) and its role in economic, cultural, and sociodemographic change
Immigration/assimilation in North Philadelphia	Cultural diversity in the United States

that a sense of community is something they had back in Puerto Rico, and needs to be established here in the U.S. . . . The sense of community is building and members care very much about the neighborhood in which they live.

As our assignments indicate, students explore their placement neighborhood within the context of larger urban history. Eliza and Sage drew pertinent connections between national immigration patterns and economic shifts and their impact on the Fredricksburg community:

As Puerto Ricans immigrated in clusters around the time of the Second World War, the country was going through a period of adjustment. As the country transitioned from the Industrial Age to the Information Age, a lot of factory work in the area was lost. . . . The tragedy that faced the Puerto Rican population was the fact that people immigrated to the U.S. largely due to the industrialized jobs they thought were available.

Development of a thematic curriculum unit is the culminating component of both summer courses. Putting this curriculum together allows students to put progressive theory into practice while maintaining responsiveness to local contextual factors. The development of the curriculum is a quintessentially Deweyian task in that it asks preservice teachers to complete a hands-on project and to explore the social meaning of this assignment as they do so. As Dewey eloquently argued:

> If we look at this from the standpoint of preparation of the boys for sewing buttons and making patches, we get a narrow and utilitarian conception—a basis that hardly justifies giving prominence to this sort of work in the school. But if we look at it from another side, we find that this work gives the point of departure from which the child can trace and follow the progress of mankind in history, getting an insight into the material used and the mechanical principles involved. In connection with these occupations the historic development of man is recapitulated. (1902b, p. 20)

The curriculum units preservice teachers create share a similar premise. Eliza and Sage's curriculum compares the role transportation has played in the history of Fredricksburg and a suburban community on the outskirts of the city. The unit asked students to reflect on the impact trains have in building or challenging particular types of communities.

> Both of the school neighborhoods utilize public transportation in various ways that will be compared and contrasted throughout the duration of the program. We, as teachers, feel it is necessary and age appropriate to teach the students about the history of trains, the economic effects of trains, the environmental impact of trains, the socio-demographic context of train usage and the general geographic implications of trains.

Eliza and Sage's curriculum asks students to examine the relationship between employment opportunities, train use, and community well-being. They also looked at the environmental effects of the rail construction on communities and asked students to develop a historical timeline of train use and its impact on each neighborhood.

Eliza and Sage, as well as their classmates, created an exemplary curriculum informed by their research on community-based funds of knowledge and provided a structural analysis of underemployment and poverty issues as they affect their placement community. As Sage wrote:

> We will be teaching how trains have deeply impacted the United States and world economy throughout history. Many jobs have created through the train's development including hard labor and other employment opportunities. . . . While focusing on a subject matter that has some familiar resonance with the children, teachers can guide students into a deeper exploration of social, economic, and historical issues.

Such promising research and curriculum development encourages us that the organization of the program around neighborhood studies is fruitful. It interrupts deficit orientations and victim blaming even as it positions students to regard the community as a wellspring of curricular resources and reveals the power of community members' efforts to craft their neighborhoods into thriving, culturally rich environments. In this chapter, we introduce and reflect on questions and concerns as well as the promise of doing critical curriculum development. At the same time, we leave open lines of inquiry and invite readers to join us in discussion of what it means for teachers and preservice teachers to conduct research around funds of knowledge embedded in urban communities.

REFLECTION QUESTIONS

1. To what perceived problem in preservice teacher education are the authors responding in their work?
2. In what way do the authors hope to transform their preservice students?
3. How do the authors of this chapter model the type of educator they hope their students will become?
4. What are some of the differences between participants and context in the original Funds of Knowledge project and the work described in this chapter? How do these differences affect the impact of the work?

REFERENCES

Anderson, E. (1981). *Place on the corner.* Chicago: The University of Chicago.

Anderson, E. (1992). *STREETWISE: Race, class, and change in an urban community.* Chicago: The University of Chicago.

Castells, M. (1989). *The informational city: Information technology, economic restructuring, and the urban-regional process.* Oxford, UK: Blackwell.

Castells, M. (1996). *The rise of the network society.* Oxford, UK: Blackwell.

Corbin, J., & Strauss, A. (1998). *Basics of qualitative research techniques and procedures for developing grounded theory.* Thousand Oaks, CA: Sage Publications.

Dewey, J. (1902a). *The child and the curriculum and the school and society.* Chicago: Phoenix Books.

Dewey, J. (1902b). *The school & society.* Chicago: University of Chicago Press.

Dewey, J. (1938). *Experience & education.* New York: Collier/Macmillan.

McIntosh, P. (1989). White privilege: Unpacking the invisible knapsack. *Peace and Freedom, 49,* 10–12.

Morrison, T. (2002). *Sula.* New York: Penguin.

Moynihan, D. P. (1965). *The negro family: The case for national action.* Washington, DC: Office of Policy Planning and Research, U.S. Department of Labor.

Schultz, K. (in press). *Listening to teach: Responding to the demands of teaching in a pluralistic democracy.* [Need publisher]

Steinberg, A., & Stephen, D. (1999). *City works: Exploring your community.* New York: New Press.

Wilson, W. J. (1990). The truly disadvantaged: The inner city, the underclass, and public policy. Chicago: The University of Chicago.

Chapter 14

Reflections on the Study of Households in New York City and Long Island: A Different Route, a Common Destination

Carmen I. Mercado
Hunter College of CUNY

> *Going through the experience and listening in class . . . made me feel something was missing or I was doing something wrong. Everyone was finding and reporting rich experiences and funds of knowledge while I seemed not to be looking at what was probably there. ¡No podía ver lo que estaba ahi! (I could not see what was there!)*

Ethnographic research that situates the school experiences of language minority children within the context of culture, community, and society provides a rich and complex portrayal of variations in the range of social contexts and circumstances that influence academic performance (August & Hakuta, 1997). As Greene (1994) explained, there has been intensified concern on the part of educational researchers for the social and economic contexts that affect what is learned and taught.

Luis Moll and Norma González (González et al., 1995; Moll, Amanti, Neff, & González, 1992) have engaged teachers from Arizona as social scientists to identify intellectual, social, and emotional resources developed by modest income families, predominantly of Mexican ancestry, to help them survive with dignity and respect. These scholars believe that teachers need to be knowledgeable about the social lives of children because there are important resources for learning or funds of knowledge in students' homes and communities.

During a 4-year period (1996–1999), I collaborated with over 100 bilingual and nonbilingual teachers in New York City and on Long Island (Mercado & Moll, 1997) to conduct similar work. Of the 80 households that comprise the New York Study, 43 (54%) were Latino, a mix of households of recent immigrants and long-term Americans of Puerto Rican ancestry. Fortuitously, the selection of households, which was left to the teacher research teams, reflected city and state demographics.

Initial analysis revealed the wide range of funds of knowledge of local households acquired through life experiences and accessible through family and friends, income-producing activities, and connections with institutions such as schools and churches. We discovered, as well, that there is no typical Puerto Rican household and that differences across households are the result of broader and more complex social and structural forces on family life. These forces affect households, but households also mediate the effects of these forces, especially on the young and the vulnerable.

Presently, data from 14 Puerto Rican households have been reexamined using theoretical perspectives that locate and explain the language and literacy practices embedded in the funds of knowledge of local households (see also Mercado, in press). This new analysis seeks to (a) make transparent the hidden uses of literacy of Puerto Rican households in one local community in New York City, (b) reveal the values and beliefs that explain the uses of literacy in these households, and (c) explain how social and structural forces create social needs and influence local literacy practices.

HISTORICAL AND DEMOGRAPHIC BACKGROUND

With 1.1 million school-age children and youth, New York City is the nation's largest and most diverse urban school district. Although New York City has a long history of ethnic and linguistic diversity, the city has experienced dramatic changes over the past decade in the growth and diversification of its Latino population, which now constitutes 25% of the total population and 38% of the school-age population. A full one-third of the city's school-age population has been comprised of Latinos for the past 30 years, primarily Puerto Rican, but the influx of immigrants from the Caribbean and Central America, overwhelmingly from Santo Domingo (15.9%) and Mexico (9.1%), has transformed New York into the largest transnational Latino city in the United States. Presently, the school population is predominantly Latino and African American, comprising 78% of the school population.

In contrast, Los Angeles, one of the largest cities of Spanish speakers in the world, is predominantly (77.1%) of Mexican origin and Central American (2.3% Salvadorian), with minor representation of Latinos from the Caribbean (1.3% Puerto Rican and 0.0% Dominican). As recently as 1970, Los Angeles was predominantly White. However, as New York and Los Angeles have become less White, both also report high levels of negative racial stereotyping and discrimination on the part of Whites and Asians toward

Blacks and Latinos (Mollenkopf, 1999). Differences in space and place, beyond "ethnic" diversity, affect languages and cultures in contact. "In Los Angeles different people do not rub up against one another as they do in New York. It is a city without a center, a very segregated city" (National Public Radio, 2002). Moreover, New York has historically been the center of creative activity for Puerto Ricans as they have come in contact with mainstream and nonmainstream groups. Cultural fusions evident in music and the arts of the early Puerto Rican community, which began flourishing in the 1930s, continue to evolve as each new generation creates cultural transformations and new expressive media and cultural practices—for instance, hip-hop, neorican literature, and murals. Encoded in these cultural transformations is a history and social criticism of the Puerto Rican experience in New York, past and present.

Despite problems associated with ethnic classifications, they are used in this study to call attention to the different historical trajectories associated with membership in different social groups. Clearly, boundaries between social groups are far more fluid and dynamic than this classification schema allows, evident in the interpenetrating realities and synergistic relationships of social groups living in close physical proximity.

Fifty percent of the Puerto Rican households we studied resided in El Barrio or East Harlem, until recently one of the largest Puerto Rican communities in the United States. (El Barrio stretches north from 96th Street to 125th Street, and east from Fifth Avenue to the East River.) Harlem (due west of East Harlem) has had the largest concentration of African Americans in the nation since the great Post-WWII northern migration. New York Puerto Ricans have had continuous and intensive contact with African Americans more so than with other Latino groups.

In contrast to those residing in other states, the Puerto Rican community in New York City, first concentrated in Williamsburg, Brooklyn, then in El Barrio, and presently in the Bronx, has the highest poverty rate, lowest household incomes, and the lowest labor force participation of nonimmigrant Latino groups (Mollenkopf, 1999). The median income for a family of four is under $20,000 in a city where the median family income for a family of four is reported to be $50,000. Puerto Ricans were declared U.S. citizens by an act of Congress in 1917, yet educators know little about the historical forces that have shaped the experiences of Puerto Ricans in New York City in particular, and in the United States in general. These include (a) a 100-year colonial relationship between Puerto Rico and the United States, which brought U.S. citizenship to an island that is not a state; (b) the imposition of English in public schools in Puerto Rico even though Spanish has been and remains the language of wider communication; (c) the abrupt economic changes induced by U.S.-controlled government policy on the island in the 1940s, resulting in the "forced" migration of massive numbers of Puerto Ricans to New York, in particular; (d) the displacement of Puerto Rican workers in New York City as the economy shifted from manufacturing to service and information in the 1960s; and (e) the segregation of Puerto Ricans and African Americans, and recent immigrants, in large urban centers after the mass exodus of the White middle class to the suburbs in the 1950s (Bonilla, 1985; Portes & Rumbaut, 1996; Walsh, 1991).

This historical perspective has been relatively invisible in textbooks both in the United States and in Puerto Rico (Morales Carrión, 1989; Walsh, 1991) and has resulted in distortions and misrepresentations when it comes to understanding and explaining the lower social, economic, and educational status of the Puerto Rican community. Mainstream social science research on the Puerto Rican community, which is extensive, has lent scientific credence to the view that this is a population that is "dysfunctional." Because the media is a powerful educator in shaping public perceptions and opinions, the negative image of Puerto Ricans endures, even among teachers of Puerto Rican ancestry (Mercado & Moll, 1997). Recent scholarship documents that students of Puerto Rican ancestry have been subjected to differential treatment in U.S. schools, primarily because of their particular use of English (Urciuoli, 1996; Zentella, 1997), which lessens the opportunities of children and youth for advancement through education (Bigler, 1997; Nieto, 1995; Walsh, 1991).

Negative teacher and media perceptions, combined with economic and political marginalization, affect Puerto Rican families and influence students' perceptions of themselves, their families, and their communities (Nieto, 1995; Walsh, 1991). Relatively little is known about how sociohistorical and economic factors influence cultural practices of local Puerto Rican communities, especially the transmission and transformation of language and literacy practices through home-community socialization. Zentella's (1997) study of language socialization among New York Puerto Ricans is unique, illuminating what happens when languages and cultures of unequal status and power meet in the "contact zone" (Pratt, 1999). Although this is not a new phenomenon—it has been traced to the Spanish conquest of the Americas in the western hemisphere—it continues today through globalization, the media, immigration, and commerce.

LITERATURE REVIEW

This investigation seeks to understand literacy locally and historically, both in terms of the histories of individuals and in terms of the places and social relationships in which they find themselves (Barton & Hamilton, 1998). Several related theoretical perspectives from distinct intellectual traditions are relevant to and inform the present analysis. Social theories of literacy (e.g., the new literacy studies) shed new understandings of what literacy means, what it looks like, and how it develops within particular groups and communities. Accordingly, literacy is a social practice, located in the interaction between people (Barton & Hamilton, 1998; Gee, 1990); however, the practices of social groups include but go beyond literacy. Thus, what we know is mediated through social relations—who we live with, deal with, learn from, and talk to (Urciuoli, 1996). Literacy practices are almost always fully integrated into and constitute part of the very texture of wider practices that involve talk, interaction, values, and beliefs. Conceptions of literacy as a social practice forge connections between the activities of reading and writing and social structures in which they are embedded and which they help to shape (Barton & Hamilton, 1998).

Because language and literacy are not acquired without culture (Ochs, 1988), literacy is a cultural product embedded in an ideology that cannot be isolated and treated as neutral or merely technical (Street, 1984). In conceptions of literacy as a social–cultural practice, socialization processes, not just educational processes, play a significant role in the construction of the meaning and uses of literacy (Street, 1984). According to Ochs (1988), socialization is a process by which one becomes a competent member of a society through the transmission of social skills and knowledge. Language socialization research examines how socialization processes produce competences to use language as less experienced members of a community participate in verbal interactions with older and/or more experienced members. As Duranti and Ochs (1997) emphasized, "language is the most important semiotic tool for representing, transmitting, and creating social order and cultural world views" (p. 1). Consequently, language-mediated activities are key to the transmission of this knowledge, and the sociocultural contexts in which interactions occur become part of the pragmatic and social meanings that are acquired by members of a given community as they assume various communication and social roles (Ochs, 1988). However, these culturally organized activities are complex, overlapping, and intertwined. Further, socialization is a bidirectional process; novice and competent members of a community reciprocally stimulate new understandings and skills in each other. This explains constancy and change over time in the character of cultural practices, including socialization—an important insight to have in examining socialization within the context of transnational, bilingual, and multidialectal communities in the United States.

Thus, literacy acquisition and literacy activities display some variation across diverse communities, with attendant consequences for the development of specific cognitive skills (Ochs, 1988). This research shows that socialization is a lifespan experience that begins in the home and continues throughout the life of an individual. As a component of language development, literacy is dynamic and changes to reflect the influence of family, friendship, social networks, and social institutions such as schools as well as social, emotional, economic, and communicative needs of individuals, as these needs change over time. Some scholars emphasize that the importance of literacy cannot be understood in isolation or in terms of self-enhancement skills; rather, its significance lies in its relation to the transmission of morals, discipline, and social values (Ochs, 1988).

In their study of a working-class community in Great Britain, Barton and Hamilton (1998) made transparent the diversity of literacies that are rooted in everyday experiences and serve for people to make sense of their lives. Because of their lower social value, local literacies (in contrast to official, institutional, or colonial literacies such as essay writing) often go unrecognized in dominant discourses about literacies. Barton and Hamilton (1998) identified six domains of day-to-day life in which literacy is central: (a) organizing life (e.g., literacy associated with paying bills, keeping calendars, and appointment books), (b) personal communication (e.g., writing cards and letters to loved ones), (c) private leisure (e.g., reading books and magazines, writing poetry to relax), (d) documenting life (e.g., maintaining records of one's life—birth certificates, school reports, old address books, party souvenirs), (e) sense-making (e.g., literacy related to researching topics of interest or need, such as health, legal, employment, parenting), and (f) social participation (e.g., literacy associated with participation in groups and social clubs).

Not surprisingly, in light of Ochs' theory of language socialization, local literacies are hybrid practices that draw on a range of practices from different domains and are influenced by the media, official literacies, and the household's social networks. The notion of "local literacies" is analogous to what Ochs and Duranti described as "syncretic literacies," an analytic tool to account for the ways that the same language or code may be used for distinct cultural practices and the ways in which different cultural practices can be merged within the same literacy activity in linguistically heterogeneous communities. Further, findings from language socialization research have also revealed that literacy practices are never neutral; rather, they are political acts and are invariably tied to larger sociohistorical processes that have a bearing on ongoing social relations (Garrett & Baquedano-López, 2002). Because communication is a function of human relations, and the conditions shaping human relations are never equal, all forms of communication, including literacy, are politicized (Urciuoli, 1996).

A multidisciplinary team of scholars affiliated with El Centro de Estudios Puertorriqueños, which has as its primary mission research on the Puerto Rican communities in the United States, have studied language use in El Barrio since the late 1970s. Zentella (1990; 1997) and Pedraza (1987), sociolinguists affiliated with El Centro, interpret the bilingual and multidialectal code-switching among members of this community to be an expression of their different identities and social roles (e.g., gender). Pedraza explained that a person's migratory history is the most critical factor influencing language behavior. Zentella (1997) agreed and argued for the need to understand the conditions that give rise to language variation—meaning, how it is influenced and shaped by the larger political, socioeconomic, and cultural forces (the social context), including the specific dialects in contact. Zentella's (1997) two-prong longitudinal study of language learning and use, first among 20 households and subsequently 5 households that branched out from these, found that "dense and multiplex" social networks (many kinship networks) in which households are embedded played a role in the socialization of younger members of the community. Moreover, changes in the language and literacy practices of the community are attributed to changes in the social networks with which younger members are affiliated. To date, little empirical attention has been given to documenting the contextual uses of and need for literacy in U.S. Puerto Rican communities. Del Valle's (2002) study of Puerto Rican households in Chicago is a rare exception, but it examines uses of literacy in households with youth of high school age. As elementary school educators, we studied households with young children, as I describe next.

USES AND SIGNIFICANCE OF LITERACY
IN PUERTO RICAN HOUSEHOLDS: METHODS

Teacher-researchers conducted 2–3 home interviews or focused conversations of no less than one hour each at different points in time. These conversations were guided by in-depth, open-ended questionnaires, but teacher-researchers were selective in the questions they asked.

It is significant and unusual that a little more than half of the 103 teacher-researchers were Spanish–English bilinguals with an average of 4 years classroom experience in elementary schools in low-income communities. In addition, many teachers were first- and second-generation Puerto Ricans, and some had lived in the communities where households we studied resided. I, too, am first-generation Puerto Rican, raised and educated in New York City and a product of its public school system. Shared *cultural* understandings usually facilitated rapport and communication with the families we visited, although it did not always facilitate how we interpreted what we saw and learned in and from the homes. The fact that researchers were teachers also affected the information we accessed and, therefore, data creation and knowledge construction processes, as will be made clear.

Through interviews often conducted in Spanish or a combination of English and Spanish, teacher-researchers elicited information intended to locate the households' funds of knowledge within the family's migratory history, the household composition, the income-producing and recreational activities, child-rearing practices and beliefs, and their oral and written literacy practices in Spanish and English. Consequently, home interviews were frequently transformed into intergenerational literacy events ("talk over text") that yielded information on the uses of literacy in particular households while also giving glimpses into actual home language socialization practices as children participated directly in the interviews or as they interacted with caregivers from a distance, as the following example illustrates.

> The interviews were conducted in a very friendly manner. In all three interviews there were children and their friends present, conversing with us, too. This part of the interview was crucial because we set out to find out the funds of knowledge [and it was] right there at that moment, and also because there was mutual language involvement. What each of us said was important because it was spontaneous. *A cada rato teníamos interrupciones.* (There were many interruptions.) *Ita estaba al tanto de todo.* (Ita was aware of everything that was going on.) *Mantenía todo en control mientras los hijos pedían ayuda mientras hablábamos.* (She kept everything under control as her children asked for help while we were talking.) *La televisión siempre estuvo prendida aunque los niños no le ponían atención.* (The TV was on while we were talking but the children didn't pay attention to it.) *Preferían hablar y dibujar, mientras Hercules ponía una pared.* (They preferred to talk and to draw while Hercules [her 17-year old son] installed a wall.) (Final Report, 1996)

The way language is used during the interviews reveals the extent to which a relationship of *confianza* is shared by the teacher-researcher and the primary caregiver; *confianza* allows for the easy exchange of information and the expectation that this information will be used to help students or the teachers in some way (Mercado & Moll, 1997). The use of language reflects the influence of culture in other ways. The following interchanges are examples of playfulness with language that we documented in a number of homes; in the Alegría household (hence the pseudonym, "Happy") it was especially striking.

> Teacher-Researcher: *¿Ayudan los niños a cuidar los animales?* (Do children help with the care of animals?)
> IA: *Sí.* (Yes.)
> Teacher-Researcher: *¿Cómo?* (How?)
> IA: *¡Poniendo gritos en el cielo!* (Screaming!) [audio tape #2]

> I asked her, how many languages does she speak? She said, "Spanish, English and . . . *jeringonza* (pig latin)." We began a conversation in *jeringonza*. We laughed. I remember the times I spoke *jeringonza* with my grandmother,

mom, aunts, cousins and friends in Puerto Rico. . . . To my astonishment, her children speak it, too. Her youngest daughter got into the conversation. It was fun!

Note that much of the humor here lies in the prosody and gestures, and the unexpectedness of the response.

As Ochs (1988) described, our home interviews were culturally organized events that were complex, with overlapping and intertwined occurrences—examples of syncretic literacies—although there were differences across households in terms of how these events were organized. In addition, of primary concern throughout was the well-being of families and not the execution of a precise set of research strategies. We shared the understanding that in this community, representatives from social service agencies visited families frequently for purposes of detecting improprieties in the reporting of economic or social needs. In the next section, findings on the literacy practices in Puerto Rican households are presented.

EVERYDAY LITERACIES IN LOCAL PUERTO RICAN HOUSEHOLDS

As I have reported previously (Mercado & Moll, 1997), the content of knowledge and the range of activities in Puerto Rican households are both rich and variable (see Appendix). Barton and Hamilton's (1998) framework served as a useful guide in identifying and distinguishing "literacy practices" according to domains of use. For Barton and Hamilton, the term "literacy practices" refers to people's awareness of literacy, how they talk about and make sense of literacy, and the values, attitudes, feelings, and social relationships that are associated with it. However, unlike literacy events (defined as "any action sequence involving one or more persons in which the production and/or comprehension of print plays a role," Anderson, Teale, & Estrada, 1980, as cited in Heath, 1983) that are observable interactions involving print, or "talk over text" (Wells, 1990), literacy practices are inferred from patterns in the uses of literacy over time. In sum, "literacy practices are the general cultural ways of utilizing written language which people draw on in their lives" (Barton & Hamilton, 1998, p. 6).

A summary of the practices gleaned from the study of Puerto Rican households' funds of knowledge are presented and organized according to the classification schema generated from Barton and Hamilton's study of local literacies in a working-class community. However, our data allow us to comment on uses of reading and writing for sense making, social participation, private leisure, and documenting life.

Sense Making

Literacy mediates our interaction with the world, and many of the literacy practices we documented relate to making sense of lived experience. The everyday literacies we documented addressed a range of needs, including understanding (a) health and nutrition, (b) legal issues affecting household members, (c) the upbringing of children, (d) one's identity and the identities of those who are new to our community, and (e) the need for spiritual comfort and guidance. Drug addiction, alcoholism, asthma, diabetes, high blood pressure, and poor nutrition are serious health issues affecting the Latino community. Research to learn about health concerns that affect family and friends usually begins with literature that is available in the hospital or clinic waiting room that is relevant to the lives of families, but extends outward and involves conversations with experts (those with lived experience and those with scientific knowledge on the subject) and interaction with other symbolic media, for example, the informational videos that Ms. Navarro viewed to learn how to help her brother deal with a drug addiction problem.

The overriding concern in this community is keeping children and youth safe from the dangers of the street. Teaching children at home so that they will do well (and stay) in school is motivated in part by this concern, as it is by a profound belief in the value of education for improving the conditions of our lives. For example, Mrs. C most enjoys reading issues that affect parenting, such as articles on peer pressure to help her child, how to spot illnesses, and what are some treatments for some common health problems.

Legal concerns ranged from legal violations to the incarceration of a family member. They also included knowing the education law so as to challenge school policies and practices that affect children's educational opportunities. *Yo vengo hablándole a Muñeca y dejándole saber cuáles son sus derechos como madre, porque en ella he notado los deseos de pelear y saber defenderse de muchas cosas injustas que ella ha visto.* (I have been speaking to Muñeca for some time now about what are her rights as a mother, because I notice that she has the will to fight and defend herself against the many injustices that she has seen.)

In all instances, literacy as a sense-making practice is an ongoing quest to understand, through multiple symbolic media or multiple literacies, information that enables us to act on the world, as Freire and Macedo (1987) described. This need to know was primarily motivated by a need to assist or comfort loved ones, another way in which literacy is tied to relationships. Consequently, these local literacy practices result in a great deal of expertise that becomes a communal resource to be shared with others, as Barton and Hamilton found. However, although local literacies generate funds of knowledge, funds of knowledge are not exclusively literacy-based. What is important for teachers to understand is that local literacies are not likely to be visible through typical questions about the uses of literacy, such as "What kinds of things do you read?"

Social Participation

Household members participated in a number of different social groups—for example, church affiliated groups such as the elderly ladies organization, the tenants' patrol, the local parent association, and volunteers at local schools. Participation in these social groups required a range of literacies ("talk over text"). Jaclyn Navarro filled out police reports as part of her duties as a tenants patrol person. And, as a parent volunteer, her duties included: filling out admissions and registration forms for parents, translating documents from English to Spanish, and on some occasions, acting as an assistant teacher in some bilingual classrooms. However, as Farr (in Del Valle, 2002) has pointed out, different activities make different literacy demands so that the actual practices individuals engage in are quite variable.

Private Leisure

Getting lost in other people's lives, creating new family members or imaginary friends, rewriting one's life, or getting even with life may motivate reading about the lives of music, film, and TV personalities (*la farándula*) or reading a novella or love story, in English as well as Spanish. Characters from *telenovelas* (soap operas) also became part of the extended family and their exploits the topic of family conversations, much as the characters in best sellers are discussed in some circles. *Alondra* and *La Dueña* were among the *telenovelas* identified, as were *Primer Impacto*, tabloid journalism on the air, and *Las Noticias*.

This intergenerational practice may provide temporary distractions from life's stresses, as entering fictive accounts may also enable viewers to rewrite their lives, or get even with life given the many soap operas that depict the class wars in which the rich receive just punishment for wicked deeds.

Telenovelas also provide exposure to language and cultural practices in Spanish that influence community uses of language and literacy, in some cases from the print that appears on the TV screen and in others, from the performance of written texts such as *telenovelas*.

Household members also read newspapers and magazines in English and Spanish, although print materials are often (not always) read in transit—at a friend's home, on the subway, or at clinic.

Mrs. Castillo is an avid reader. She reads magazines, newspapers, comic books, and the Bible. She buys magazines in English and in Spanish at least twice a month. She buys magazines such as *Buen Hogar*, Vogue, *TV Novelas*, etc. She also reads newspapers such as *El Diario-La Prensa*, *El Vocero*, The *Daily News*.

Collecting and recirculating previously read newspapers and magazines, as Ita Alegría did, may be more common in Latin America where print materials, when they are available, are costly. News and entertainment are, after all, easily accessible on the TV screen, for "free" or a modest cost. "Doña Carmen enjoys reading religious books, but she will read the Daily News if someone buys it for her. She won't spend money on a newspaper."

Even in the U.S., children's books are more expensive than adult reading materials, and there are few local public libraries in communities such as East Harlem.

As others have found, in these households "literacy is restricted through class advantage and inaccessibility of reading and writing materials" (Del Valle, 2002).

Documenting Life

Maintaining records of one's life was evident in all the households we visited, especially through photos, party souvenirs and mementos: "We saw various souvenirs of the Navarro children's accomplishments, as well as graduation favors."

In documenting the collective experiences of her community and her cultural heritage, Ita Alegría added a new dimension to the meaning of documentation. Ita is a collector of antiques, photographs, paintings, magazines, people, language and culture. She has created a museum, a library, a community resource to her family and friends. She is a historian and storyteller.

Two areas of life where reading and writing are central, according to Barton and Hamilton (1998), are organizing life and communication. However, our study of households yielded limited data on these uses of literacy even though paying bills and keeping calendars and appointment books were forms of literacy present in all households.

What was distinctive about the Puerto Rican households that we study is not only the emphasis on literacy to make sense of life, but that in all domains of use, we documented, English and Spanish (and any variants of the two) were seamlessly interwoven into the day-to-day activities of each household. Similarly, print and speech in two languages were intertwined in complex ways in the literacy practices themselves. In these homes, however, reading and writing were not treated as skills that were isolated from interactive activities, but as abilities that enabled community members to understand themselves and their families and to relate to others, as Zentella (1997) also found in her study.

What was also striking about the Puerto Rican households we studied was the range of literacies associated with school—either children or adults—that were present in these households. Although institutional literacies (Anderson & Stokes, 1984; Barton & Hamilton, 1998) are an important means of socializing the young to literacies associated with success in school, they are different from the literacies required to meet the daily needs of families. The influence of school-related or "institutional" literacy, more readily visible to teachers and what is valued in our society, was especially strong in the Navarro home. In the words of one teacher-researcher: "The greatest asset Jaclyn possessed was her disposition to act as a teacher at home." . . . At the end of the first visit, all of the younger children came out of their bedrooms with their notebooks and homework, and showed off that they knew the alphabet or could spell. They showed pride in what they had learned and were obviously happy to have teachers in their home.

As I have described previously (Mercado & Moll, 1997), the long history of bilingual education in El Barrio has resulted in an increased number of administrative and instructional staff that are bilingual within the districts' schools. Consequently, in these schools, language does not inhibit contact with institutional agents who have "insider" information about the educational system and who are willing to share their funds of knowledge with the community, in and out of school. Viewed in this broader context, it is not surprising that institutional literacies were as dominant as they were in the homes we visited, even though there were differences across households. This is made clear in the two sketches that are presented in the next section.

LITERACY IN TWO PUERTO RICAN HOMES

Sketches of two households presented in the next section provide a glimpse into the lives of two Puerto Rican families and illustrate how social and historical forces affect families and family members. Of specific interest is how these forces shape the meaning and uses of literacy to meet household needs, and households use literacy to mediate children's interactions with the world. These two households were selected because they were, in time and space, representative of one type of Puerto Rican household in El Barrio. Subsequently, I discovered that the children who motivated the study attended the same dual-language program in East Harlem, important in terms of understanding specific influences of institutional literacies on home literacy and socialization. They were also learners who were identified as having literacy-related problems in school, as determined by scores on the statewide test. Every effort has been made to preserve the actual words of participants, which I have patterned into a narrative to give a sense of the uses of literacy in these households and the meanings primary care-givers attributed to literacy, including any evidence for how it affected children's socialization. Translations were unavoidable in order to weave together a cohesive and fluent narrative from conversations held with the research team, especially the learner's teacher, at different points in time. In the actual interviews English and Spanish were seamlessly interwoven in all discussions as "languages are not always clearly bounded from each other," as Urciuoli (1996) pointed out. Thus, it was not simply a matter of translating discourse from one language to another. Although the mixing of two or more linguistic codes is a common practice in multilingual, multidialectal communities, it was more pronounced in some homes than in others.

Literacy in the Navarro Household

Jaclyn Navarro (a pseudonym) lives with seven of her 10 children (three females, ages 16, 10, 9; and four males, ages 6, 5, 4, and 2) in a six-room apartment in government subsidized housing in East Harlem, the family's home for the past year. The 13- and 11-year old daughters live with their maternal grandmother in the Bronx, and a 14-year old son lives with his father in Puerto Rico. The building complex where the family resides is on the dividing point for some of the highest priced real estate in New York and some of the poorest in the city. Sensitive to race and language, Jaclyn comments that the only thing bad about living there is the racism. On their first home visit, teacher-researchers overheard a member of the tenant's volunteer comment that, "When you talk to those people, you have to talk Spanish. You go nenenenene (said mockingly with accompanying hand gestures)," after one of the teacher-researchers spoke Spanish to Ms. Navarro on the intercom.

Ms. Navarro is 34 years old and was born in Puerto Rico. She has lived intermittently in Puerto Rico and New York City and has attended schools in both, as have the four oldest children: "I came when I was five but my mother kept on going back and forth. I told my mother, 'taking me back and forth I'll never finish high school.' I ran away with my daughter's father when I was 14 so that I wouldn't have to return to Puerto Rico because of all those trips." She became bilingual but she never finished high school. At the time the interviews were conducted (October–November 1995), Jaclyn had been living in New York since 1991. There are disruption and fragmentation of routines and relationships and expectations that result from frequent moves and the "back-and-forth" that is so common among the migrant Puerto Rican community. Even so, these moves also foster cultural adaptability, including bilingualism.

Jaclyn chose to continue sending her children to the bilingual education program they had been attending, now 30 blocks away from home, not because they needed to learn English but because she values both languages. "If the kids are not bilingual, the transition between New York and Puerto Rico will affect them because NY is only English and PR is only Spanish. I teach them the two languages because you never know (*Yo les enseño los dos idiomas porque*—you never know). The Navarro children are as proficient as their mother in both languages.

Taking care of her children is Jaclyn Navarro's primary concern and occupation. However, she has worked for pay since she was 14 in a cafeteria, pizzeria, bar, discount store, as secretary to a building manager, and in Puerto Rico's patron saint pageants. At the time of this study, a government subsidy was the household's primary income, but in the past Ms Navarro has sold Mary Kay, Tupperware, and Stanley to supplement this income. She also volunteered on the buildings' tenant patrol and now works as a parent volunteer because Charles' kindergarten teacher could not handle him and asked Jaclyn for help. She said, "I do it for my children not for anything else." Although she has garnered a reputation for dealing with "out of control" children, secretarial experience and administrative skills took her to the office where she has worked copying and running the mimeograph machines as well as the computer. She also has planned decorations for the bulletin boards, obtained supplies for teachers, and even covered a classroom when a teacher had to go to the office. Her biliteracy enables her to interview parents who apply for the school, helping them fill the many applications this requires. Jaclyn aspires to be a teacher assistant. "I don't want to be trained; I watch, observe, and I capture things. I would love to go into a classroom to learn."

The same day she arrived from Puerto Rico, her stepfather bought a book on basic English. "He gave us lessons." Her teachers were amazed at how quickly she learned English. Now Jaclyn teaches her children at home, in both languages. She feels that 6-year-old Charles needs more help in reading and other studies. In school, he is quite playful—a comedian who loves to take the limelight and prefers to speak in Spanish although he understands when spoken to in English.

Jaclyn emphasizes that she reads the Bible at night to her children and then asks them to interpret what she read. In speaking, she sometimes interjects Biblical verses in Spanish ("*La Biblia dice . . .*"). Jaclyn reviews her children's homework with them and helps them make necessary corrections. She also reinforces facts and concepts on a chalkboard. Big Open Court phonics cards cover the walls of the boys' room, and she borrows school materials for home use. The oldest daughter also "teaches" the younger ones. In addition, the family media center has a TV, a Nintendo, a VCR, and a library of children's videos: Disney films and educational videos such as "Barney" and "Sesame Street." Jaclyn enjoys playing games with her children, but also giving advice (*consejos*), telling jokes, and telling stories. The family does "lots of things in the house, not outside." Jaclyn stated repeatedly: "*La calle es peligrosa*" ("There are dangers in the street!"). Through her participation in school, Jaclyn has acquired institutional uses of literacy she now uses to help others, especially her children, but her uses of literacy to shape the moral character of her children are cultural—tied to religious beliefs and practices.

LITERACY IN THE ALEGRÍA HOUSEHOLD

Ita (a pseudonym) lives with three of her five children (a 17-year-old son and two daughters, a 13 year old and a 9 year old) on the fourth floor of a tenement near the overpass to the Metro North, the suburban train to the wealthy suburbs north. Her 21-year-old son is in a detention center, and her 20-year-old daughter, who is a student in the police academy, lives with her boyfriend. The railroad apartment is small, old, and in bad condition, and everything appears to be scaled down in size. The researcher compares Ita Alegría's world to Macondo, the mythical town from *One Hundred Years of Solitude*, to highlight the impoverished living conditions of El Barrio. "Why bother to fix this apartment," Ita explains. "If there's a fire everything is lost. Besides, I have a nice house in Florida." On weekends, Ita and her husband, also live in a motor home with their 9-year-old daughter.

Ita was born in Puerto Rico in 1955 and came to New York in 1962 when she was seven years old. She attended the first 6 months of first grade in Puerto Rico but was forced to repeat the first grade in New York. Although she was married at 13 and had her first child at the age of 14, Ita was able to complete her high school diploma. Her first husband left her, and in 1986 she married her Cuban-born second husband. He is a licensed electrician, construction worker, and building superintendent. As the superintendent's wife, Ita has learned to paint walls; install windows, locks, and electricity; and repair electronic equipment. Her curiosity provoked her neighbor to teach her how to run a printing press he has in his apartment.

"I am bilingual like my children; I speak in English and I speak *español*," she says playfully. She says in Spanish that she loves to speak English. "I learned English because when I was seven, all I knew how to say was "*pollito* chicken *y gallina* hen *y lápiz* pencil *y pluma* pen" (a popular school song used to teach English in Puerto Rico and in New York City). "I called the principal 'stupid' because a kid lied to (mislead) me. This motivated me to learn English. My husband speaks terrible English. If I am very angry, I speak English so that my neighbor doesn't understand. I love to tell stories in English. Speaking English relaxes me because if someone is going to insult me it sounds harsher in Spanish. I also speak English because my neighbor likes to gossip. I teach my children how to speak pig Latin" (*Jeringonza* as a secret code). "My children speak English but I speak to them in Spanish; they answer me in English even when I speak to them in Spanish." The two girls displayed their biliteracy for us reading from their mother's magazines during the home interviews.

"Every day I have to read something. I love to read the newspaper, magazines, everything. I love to read everything. I read the novels that come from Mexico. I read love stories that are a bunch of lies. I read gossip. If I am interested, I read even a Brazilian magazine. The newspaper (from the Dominican Republic) *El Nacional* was given to me because I was interested in something. I like to read because when I am in a conversation with someone I want to know what I am talking about. I subscribe to a newspaper called the *Américas*. I like to learn and to explore. If my kids ask me something and I don't know the topic, I look it up in a book." Ita also reads food labels. However, reading recipes is for people who do not know how to cook, which is why she doesn't believe in cookbooks. Ita admits to learning from conversations. She described a conversation she initiated with her children's doctor to learn more about the culture of Indians (from Asia).

"The children have many books, from storybooks to mechanic manuals, even about the private (intimate) life of a person." Ita has found some of these books and magazines; neighbors and local merchants she has befriended have given others to her. In turn, she shares them with others—with teachers in her daughter's school so that children may enjoy them and learn from them the way she has. However, few printed materials have been purchased in a store. "I don't go to the library because I like to talk a lot and I can't sit still. I tell my daughter, 'oh honey (*mami*), take care of your books because they are like good friends.' " Ita's children read at home in English and in Spanish because the material she provides draws attention, but not school. The humor and laughter in the Alegría home are contagious. Ita Alegría does everything with love and humor. Her children reflect what she reflects: a positive attitude toward the world and toward others. Most importantly, language and literacy practices in the Alegría home serve to sustain and strengthen relationships between children and parents and connections to valued members of the community, for example, school personnel, merchants, and those new to the community.

DISCUSSION AND CONCLUSIONS

As the quote at the beginning of this chapter tells us, the greatest challenge in studying local literacies is seeing what's there. It is instructive that even bilingual teachers need to look closely to find the funds of knowledge and literacy practices accessible to Latino households in general, and Puerto Rican households in particular. The deficit lens is pervasive, even among those who identified themselves with local households. Similarly, introducing alternative ideologies that value the social practices and local knowledge of nondominant groups remains a challenge. Nontraditional life styles and traditional and nontraditional forms of literacy are described by some as resourcefulness and adaptability, and by others as dysfunctional. Studying local literacies requires that we substitute less familiar lenses for more powerful ones that color and define what constitutes social and cultural capital in our society. As Del Valle (2002) pointed out, what we value is decoding extended prose passages or the production of expository writing. However, even with the disposition to do so, it takes time to make shifts in thinking that are the products of long-term socialization.

However, failure to strategically harness these resources represents missed opportunities to increase the life chances of students at a time when high school graduation requirements have increased, when a college diploma is an essential credential for economic survival, and when the economic value of Spanish is growing in the United States. This is important because the limited household incomes that characterize these families is the economic reality that is the core of the health, social, and educational problems of this community and that requires attention through social policy. It is also this economic reality that motivated the literacy practices we documented. Even so, teaching is a moral and ethical responsibility, and educators are responsible for contributing in positive ways to the quality of life of children and families.

"What teachers know and can do is one of the most important influences on what students learn" (Darling-Hammond, 1998, p. 6). Students from low-income communities are often more dependent on schools than their more privileged counterparts to develop mainstream social and cultural capital needed to be successful in school. Teachers need to be prepared to address the the impact of changing U.S. demographics and to better understand the achievement gap among indigenous minorities such as American Indians, African Americans, Mexican Americans, and Puerto Ricans.

Cochran-Smith (1995) argued that teachers must come to know the schools and communities in which they teach because

> teaching occurs within a particular historical and social moment and is embedded within nested layers of context, including the social and academic structures of the classroom; the history and norms of teaching and learning at the school; and the attitudes, values and beliefs, and language uses of the community and its web of historical, political, and social relationships to the school. (p. 504)

Educators need historical information about the intellectual and literacy traditions of U.S. Puerto Rican communities. Primary and secondary sources housed in the library and archives of the Center for Puerto Rican Studies at Hunter College (www.centropr.org) are an important resource for educators. However, curriculum construction and pedagogy must be variable if it is to be locally appropriate and culturally sensitive.

The funds of knowledge approach is one variant of culturally responsive teaching that builds on the resources of the home to improve student engagement and participation, which have been linked to learning and achievement. It is an approach that begins with the study of households rather than the study of pedagogy. Practices derived from this systematic, intentional inquiry (research-based practices) are applied and reexamined in terms of their influence on student participation. The validation of community knowledge resulting from these visits transforms the relationship between and among students, families, and teachers. Positioning teachers as research collaborators who come together to think and to construct knowledge with others where they are funds of knowledge for each other, this approach also inspires teacher commitment and supports educational excellence.

The approach is also especially powerful for teacher development, particularly in large urban centers where even teachers with experience are challenged to address the constantly changing diversity of their student population and the many issues associated with poverty that affect schooling. In addition, direct participation in research can be an important influence on teachers' knowledge and, therefore, on the expectations they hold for students. It is also a powerful pedagogical approach that teachers may use to construct knowledge about students' homes and communities through collaborative inquiry with their own classes (Mercado, 2003).

I conclude with a quote from one of our participating teachers:

As teachers, it is our perpetual mission to make educational decisions based on what children bring to the classroom. We are often told alternately by administrators to use children's cultures and home life in our teaching or to ignore what children have at home because we can't have an effect on that. I have discovered that it is not in our hands, children's cultures and home lives come to school every day in the form of 5 through 12 year olds. To actually go to the home is to make the choice to embrace and learn from the home and then be able to teach the child. (Vivian Garcilazo, teacher-researcher, 2001)

REFLECTION QUESTIONS

1. To what does the term "invisibility" refer in this chapter?
2. What does the author mean when she writes that complex social and structural forces affect family life, but that households mediate the effects of these forces?

3. Under what circumstances is the question "What kinds of things do you read" problematic?

4. What tools does this article present to teachers to enable them to make visible literacy a fund of knowledge in modest income families?

APPENDIX

TABLE 14.A1
A Sample of Funds of Knowledge in Puerto Rican
Households in New York City

Material & Scientific Knowledge
  Education/pedagogy
  Health education/nutrition
  Electricity
  Domestic pets/animals
  Latin America
  Music & dance
  Computer technology
  Business
  Negotiation skills
  Economics
Business
  Entrepreneurship
  Business management: Pizzeria, Bodega
  Sales: Avon, Amway, Tupperware
  Food: Piraguas
  Babysitting
  Jewelry
  Crafts
  Tailoring
  Needlework
  Fundraising
Education
  Teacher: Music, Dental Hygiene, Technology
  Assistant Teacher
  School volunteer
  Clerical assistant
  Adult Education: GED, ESL, College
  Didactic teaching at home
Household Management
  Child care
  Comparative shopping
  Budget & finances
  Appliance repair
  Cooking & sewing

(Continued)

TABLE 14.A1
(Continued)

Communications
  Bilingualism
  Translation & interpretation
  Letter writing
  Journalism
Home/Building Maintenance & Repairs
  Wiring, Plastering, Painting, Wallpapering, Plumbing, Insulation
  Window Installation
Health Care & Medicine
  Nutrition
  Dietary planning as preventive medicine for treatment of ailments such as Diabetes
Recreation & Hobbies
  Computer games
  Trips
  Quilting
  Needlepoint
  Sewing dolls' clothes
  Framemaking
  Painting
  Toy & figurine collections
Activism
  Advocacy work in community
  Challenging school policies & practices
Performing Arts
  Classical, jazz, Latin
  Cello, piano, trumpet
  Solo & ensemble
  Salsa singer
  Composing & arranging
  Ballet
Institutional
  Board of education
  District/school structure
Policies & Practices
  PA organization
  Students/parents rights
  Hospitals
  Religion & Rituals
  Baptisms, Communions, Weddings
  Bible studies
  Moral knowledge & ethics
  Charity work with elderly & disabled
Folklore
  Oral traditions: Verbal play, jokes, storytelling, sayings, proverbs
  Celebrating traditions
  Music: Songs, dances, games
  Religious beliefs & practices
  Traditional foods

REFERENCES

Anderson, A. B., & Stokes, S. J. (1984). Social and institutional influences on the development and practice of literacy. In H. Goelman, A. Oberg, & F. Smith (Eds.), *Awakening to literacy* (pp. 24–37). Exeter, NH: Heinemann.

August, D., & Hakuta, K. (Eds.). (1997). *Improving schooling for language minority children.* Washington, DC: The National Academy Press.

Barton, D., & Hamilton, M. (1998). *Local literacies: Reading and writing in one community.* London: Routledge.

Bigler, E. (1997). Dangerous discourses: Language politics and classroom practices in upstate New York. *CENTRO, 9,* 8–25.

Bonilla, F. (1985). Ethnic orbits. *Contemporary Marxism.* San Francisco: Synthesis Publications.

Cochran-Smith, M. (1995). Uncertain allies: Understanding the boundaries of racism in teacher education. *Harvard Educational Review, 65,* 541–570.

Darling-Hammond, L. (1998). Teachers and teaching: Testing policy hypotheses from a national commission report. *Educational Researcher, 27,* 5–15.

Del Valle, T. (2002). *Written literacy features of three Puerto Rican family networks in Chicago: An ethnographic study.* Lewiston, NY: Edward Mellen.

Duranti, A. (1988). Literacy instruction in a Samoan village. In E. Ochs (Ed.), *Culture and language development* (pp. 189–209). New York: Cambridge University Press.

Duranti, A., & Ochs, E. (1996). *Syncretic literacy: Multiculturalism in Samoan American families.* Research Report No. 16, Center for Research on Cultural Diversity and Second Language Learning, University of California, Santa Cruz. Retrieved December 13, 2002, from http://www.ncela.gwu.edu/miscpubs/ncrcdsll/rr16/

Garrett, P. B., & Baquedano-Lopez, P. (2002). Language socialization: Reproduction and continuity, transformation and change. *Annual Review of Anthropology, 31,* 339–361.

Gee, J. (1990). *Social linguistics and literacies.* Bristol, PA: Falmer.

González, N., Moll, L. C., Floyd-Tenery, M., Rivera, A., Rendón, P., Gonzales, R., & Amanti, C. (1995). Funds of knowledge for teaching in Latino households. *Urban Education, 29,* 443–470.

Greene, M. (1994). Epistemology and educational research: The influence in recent approaches to knowledge. In L. Darling-Hammond (Ed.), *Review of research in education* (pp. 423–464). Washington, DC: AERA.

Heath, S. B. (1983). *Ways with words.* Cambridge, UK: Cambridge University Press.

Mercado, C. I. (in press). Seeing what's there: Language and literacy funds of knowledge in New York Puerto Rican homes. In A. C. Zentella (Ed.), *Language socialization in Latina/o communities.* New York: Teachers College Press.

Mercado, C. I. (2003). Biliteracy development among Latino youth in New York City. In N. H. Hornberger (Ed.), *Continua of biliteracy* (pp. 166–186). Tonawonda, NY: Multilingual Matters.

Mercado, C. I., & Moll, L. C. (1997). The study of funds of knowledge: Collaborative research in Latino homes. *CENTRO, 9,* 26–42.

Moll, L. C., Amanti, C., Neff, D., & González, N. (1992). Funds of knowledge for teaching: Using qualitative research to connect homes and communities. *Theory and Practice, 31,* 132–141.

Mollenkopf, J. H. (1999). Urban political conflicts and alliances. In C. Hirschman, P. Kasinitz, & J. DeWind (Eds.), *The handbook of international migration: The American experience* (pp. 412–422). New York: Russell Sage Foundation.

Morales Carrion, A. (1989). *Puerto Rico. A political and cultural history.* New York: Norton.

Nieto, S. (1995). A history of the education of Puerto Rican students in US schools: "Losers," "outsiders," or "leaders?" In J. A. Banks & C. A. M. Banks (Eds.), *Handbook for research on multicultural education* (pp. 388–411). New York: Macmillan.

Ochs, E. (1988). *Culture and language development.* New York: Cambridge University Press.

Pedraza, P. (1987). *An ethnographic analysis of language use in the Puerto Rican community of East Harlem.* New York: Centro de Estudios Puertorriquenos, Hunter College, City University of New York.

Portes, A., & Rumbaut, R. G. (1996). *Immigrant America* (2nd ed.). Berkeley, CA: University of California Press.

Pratt, M. L. (1999). *Arts of the contact zone.* Retrieved February 1, 2003, from http://web.new.efl.edu/~stripp/2504/pratt.html

Street, B. (1984). *Literacy in theory and practice.* New York: Cambridge University Press.

Urciuoli, B. (1996). *Exposing prejudice. Puerto Rican experiences of language, race, and class.* Boulder, CO: Westview.

Walsh, C. E. (1991). *Pedagogy and the struggle for voice: Issues of language, power, and schooling for Puerto Ricans.* New York: Bergin & Garvey.

Wells, G. (1990). Creating the conditions to encourage literate thinking. *Educational Leadership, 47,* 13–17.

Zentella, A. C. (1997). *Growing up bilingual. Puerto Rican children in New York.* Malden, MA: Blackwell.

Chapter 15

Funds of Distributed Knowledge*

Norma González
Rosi Andrade
Marta Civil
Luis Moll
University of Arizona

As we tried to make connections between household knowledge and community knowledge, we came to realize that we had focused much of our efforts in literacy, language, and social studies. One area that had not been adequately investigated was in looking at community mathematical practices.

The differences and apparent lack of connection between in-school and outside-school mathematics have been well documented in a number of studies (Abreu, 1995; Bishop & Abreu, 1991; Carraher, Carraher, & Schliemann, 1985; Lave, 1988; Saxe, 1991; Schoenfeld, 1991) that indicate that both adults and students are competent in performing mathematical tasks that they view as relevant. The practically error-free arithmetic in everyday situations provides a dramatic contrast with low performance in school-like circumstances. While we had affirmed that a funds of knowledge perspective could affect content areas such as language arts and social studies, the areas of mathematics and science were more problematic. It was to this end that the BRIDGE project was conceptualized. Could a funds of knowledge methodology, through ethnographic understanding of a community, reveal mathematical funds of knowledge that could affect classroom practice?

First, we had to understand the nature of classroom practice in mathematics. What is behind the leap to irrelevance once mathematics is moved into the classroom? The recent calls for changes in mathematics education (Na-

*Portions of this chapter appeared originally in González, N., Andrade, R., Civil, M., & Moll, L. (2001), Bridging funds of distributed knowledge: Creating zones of practices in mathematics, *Journal of Education for Students Placed at Risk, 6*(1), 115–132.

tional Council of Teachers of Mathematics, 1989; National Research Council, 1989) capitalize on the need to teach mathematics to all children, to help them make connections with their everyday world, to engage them in doing mathematics and in constructing meanings, and to move away from the teacher and textbook as the authority on what counts as mathematical activity.

However, because the discourse in mathematics has presented a Eurocentric and androcentric perspective on the development of knowledge and civilization, the domain of mathematics has been embedded in these frames of reference. Frankenstein and Powell (1994) presented cogent evidence of the "distorted and hidden history of mathematical knowledge" (p. 88) which has obscured the contributions to mathematical knowledge of those outside the rational, Western, male elite discourse (see McBride, 1989). Mathematical knowledge has resonated with unequal power relations. The images, texts, and discourse of mathematicians have not included perspectives on the situated nature of knowledge, nor on the language of power that often drives the pursuit of knowledge.

What does this mean in reference to diverse students learning mathematics? The impact of these discourses is poignantly stated by Adrienne Rich in "Invisibility in Academe": "When someone with the authority of a teacher, say, describes the world and you are not in it, there is a moment of psychic disequilibrium, as if you looked into a mirror and saw nothing" (quoted in Rosaldo, 1989, p. ix). At a macro, taken-as-shared mathematical level, these students do not exist as mathematicians. As Fasheh (1991) noted in his personal narrative outlining the role that mathematics plays in constructing symbolic power, "Hegemony is not only characterized by what it includes, but also by what it excludes; by what it renders marginal, deems inferior and makes invisible" (p. 59). Minority and linguistically diverse students in general have not been construed as visible players within mathematical discourses either in or out of schools.

One of the aims of the BRIDGE project, then, was to interrogate "What counts as mathematics?" How can we find mathematics within households that are economically marginal? How can we help parents and communities see themselves as mathematicians, "doing" mathematics in their everyday lives?

Our avenue to accomplishing these aims was to adopt our previous methodology, but to focus only on mathematics. The household interviews were revised to highlight labor histories that could be rich in mathematical potential.

WHAT DID WE FIND?

We began with the assumption that uncovering mathematical funds of knowledge would not be very different from discovering knowledge bases in other domains such as literacy or language use. Initially, it seemed that this was the case. As teacher-researchers entered the households armed with a lens to focus on mathematics within households, the mathematics of cooking, construction, and sewing, as well as the logical processes of schedule setting and time management were all in evidence. After this initial affirmation of mathematical processes, though, our study group was faced with a discomfiting reality. Although teacher-researchers found the aforementioned reservoirs of knowledge in households, the underlying mathematical principles were not always evident to household members. For instance, construction workers could explain their methods for tile setting and framing a house, but on deeper questioning could not elucidate why these methods worked. Similarly, seamstresses could produce wonderfully complex designs and patterns, but often it was a matter of trial and error rather than a logical progression. More disconcerting was the dawning realization that our mathematics researchers found it difficult to find the mathematics in many of these activities. Says Marta Civil, a mathematics educator, "My lack of knowledge with the practice itself (sewing, for example) may make it harder to 'visualize' the mathematics, and my training in academic/school math may make it harder to see other forms of mathematics."

We want to emphasize that we were convinced that the "split" between school contexts of mathematics and community contexts of mathematics was not due to the socioeconomic status of the households. Instead, it seemed to be a matter of perspective. On the one hand, although the households we interviewed certainly deployed mathematical concepts, the academic transformation of those concepts was elusive. On the other hand, academically validated school knowledge of mathematics seemed to obscure nonacademic forms of mathematical practices.

This left us in a theoretical vacuum. We were in need of further theorizing on how funds of knowledge could be applicable within the domain of mathematics. We had found that unilineal transference of mathematical knowledge from household to classroom was problematic. Yet, we were aware that deep and rich mathematical processes were being tapped in the forms of constructions, buildings, landscapes, gardens, and clothing. In order to account for this distributed knowledge, we activated our own funds of knowledge and drew from the insights of L. S. Vygotsky and his theory of socially mediated knowledge.

THE SIGNIFICANCE OF VYGOTSKY

The essence of Vygotsky was significant for our dilemma: that human thinking develops through the mediation of others (see Moll, 2001). Put succinctly, people interact with their worlds, which are "humanized," through mediational means and practices. This mediation of actions through arti-facts and practices, especially the uses of languages in both their oral and written forms, plays a crucial role in the formation and development of hu-man intellectual capacities.

Vygotsky (1978, 1997) concentrated primarily on what he called "psycho-logical tools," the semiotic potential of systems of signs and symbols, most significantly language, in mediating thinking and the making of meaning (see also Wertsch, 1985). Nevertheless, however crucial these psychological tools may be to the mediation and development of thinking, the construc-tion of meaning is regulated (or mediated) by social relationships (see Lee & Smagorinsky, 2000). It is in connection to this social emphasis that Vygotsky proposed the well-known concept of the Zone of Proximal Devel-opment (ZOPD), the contrast between what a child can do independently, representing his or her actual level of development, and what a child can do with the assistance of others, which represents the proximal level of de-velopment (Vygotsky, 1978). Much has been written about this concept in recent years (cf. Moll, 1990; Wells, 1999), and we do not intend to spill any more ink on the subject. However, for present purposes, we do want to em-phasize the importance of a broader understanding of the ZOPD, under-stood not only in terms of "more capable" others assisting "less capable" ones, but in terms of how human beings "use social processes and cultural resources of all kinds" as Scribner (1990) wrote, in helping children con-struct their futures.

In this broader sense, the concept of the ZOPD was also used by Vygotsky to capture the relationship in schooling between what he called "everyday" and "scientific" concepts (Vygotsky, 1987, 1934/1994). The key difference between the two is that scientific or schooled concepts (e.g., mammals and socialism), as compared with everyday concepts (e.g., boats and cars), are systematic: That is, they form part of and are acquired though a system of formal instruction. It is not so much that one is acquired in school and the other out of school, but their systematicity, that explains how scientific con-cepts form part of an organized system of knowledge and can thus be more easily reflected on and manipulated deliberately; consequently, through schooling, these concepts become objects of study. Furthermore, Vygotsky (1987) pointed out the reciprocal relation between everyday and scientific concepts, and how they mediate each other. Everyday concepts provide the "conceptual fabric" for the development of schooled concepts, but are also transformed through their connection to the more systematic concepts; sci-entific concepts grow into the everyday, into the domain of personal experi-ence, acquiring meaning and significance, but bring with them conscious awareness and control, which he believed to be two essential characteristics of schooling. This latter insight was crucial to us as we contemplated the in-school and out-of-school contexts of mathematics.

But how could we relate Vygotsky's theories to the practices we were encountering in our research on mathematics in households? One of the most provocative ideas to come out of Vygotskian-based psychology is that of distributed cognition (Salomon, 1993), and this was our theoretical starting block. Stated briefly, thinking is usually considered to take place solely within the head of the individual, what some psychologists refer to as "solo" or "in-the-head" cognition. Schools accept this notion, testing students to determine their individual ability or intelligence, considered as an immutable, fixed attribute or trait. Educators are too prone to reach ready conclusions about a child's abilities based on the results of these tests. These conclusions are usually connected to the children's social class background, if we are to judge by the sort of rigid and prescribed schooling lower social class groups receive. In contrast, conceptions of human activity, including intellectual activity, as mediated and distributed, bring forth a radically different idea about thinking (Moll, 2001). The key point is that human beings and their social worlds are inseparable. They are embedded in each other; thus, human thinking is irreducible to individual properties or traits. Instead, it is always mediated, distributed among persons, artifacts, activities, and settings (cf. Pea, 1993). People think in conjunction with the artifacts and resources of their social worlds, and these artifacts and resources, in turn, are made available through the social relationships and settings within which human beings constitute their lives. Schools and households are two such settings. However, as Cole and Engestrom (1993) have observed, "Precisely how cognition is distributed must be worked out for different kinds of activity, with their different forms of mediation, division of labor, social rules and so on" (p. 42).

How social relationships, ideas, or activities become resources for thinking, then, must be studied in relation to the concrete and varied practices of human beings. It was this idea that led to our rethinking of how we had been investigating the mathematical practices in households. Next, we describe how participation in a zone of practice integrated social relationships and activities into a finished product.

THE MATHEMATICAL PRACTICE OF A FEMALE
TAILOR DESIGNING AND MAKING A DRESS PATTERN

As the BRIDGE project progressed, we realized that although we had rich information based on household interviews of mathematical activities, we did not have a sense of actual participation in these activities. In eliciting information from the households, we had not adopted a stance of coparticipants in mathematical practices. We had been more observers than participants. It was evident that putting the "participant" back into participant-observation was necessary. At this point, within the study group format, we decided to build on work that had been emerging from another arena.

A teacher-researcher, Hilda González, who had participated in the original work that had been undertaken on literacy practices in the home, had continued her work in this area while pursuing a doctoral degree. Her interest was not only in documenting the funds of knowledge in literacy that are found in households, but to do so in a way that was more participatory and reciprocal (González-Angiulo, 1998).

To this end, she formed a mother's literature circle as a way of creating intertextual experiences between the mothers' lives and the themes of widely read books. By bringing these themes to a discursive consciousness, the women made connections to issues of social criticism in their own lives and came to a historical consciousness of how they came to be where they are now. Conceptualized as a critique of the passive documentation of household funds of knowledge, the "*Señoras'* literature circle" was made up of mothers of children who attend a school within an "at risk" area. The mothers, mostly immigrant women, met and continue to meet once a week. The literature circle encompassed the domains of multiple literacies, and the mothers began to see themselves as producers as well as consumers of knowledge. Andrade, González Le Denmat, and Moll (2000) explained the process of connecting the participants' experience in the world to their reading of texts:

> Their responses to text were too varied, dynamic, even unpredictable, and it includes a range of modes of engagement that varied from preoccupation about decoding smoothly to extracting insights about the role of language and social relationships in life. The books [or activity] became another social environment or context within which to develop new knowledge and experiences, new social identities, if you will. (p. 281)

It was a small leap, then, to introduce mathematics into this forum. What was true of the literature study group became true of the mathematics study group: The discussions that took place were but a vehicle for the transformations that occur as a result of the sharing and cocreation of knowledge and experience. What each participant brings to this experience and consequently takes away is multiplex. The study group was a safe place where one could question, discuss, comment, critique, and analyze in a mutually educative process.

THE ACTIVITY

On this early morning, Sra. María, as she is respectfully addressed, has offered to give a lesson on sewing in a format similar to our study group. Sra. María is an immigrant woman in her 50s who works from her home, caring for her family, nieces, nephews, and grandchildren while also practicing her profession as tailor. Participating in the group of more than 20 women were Hilda González and mathematics researchers Rosi Andrade and Marta Civil. Sra. María begins by walking us through the taking of measurements and design of a three-part pattern for a dress (front and back of the upper part, and the skirt). Teacher Hilda González was volunteered as the female model for the group. Throughout the several hours that elapsed during the course of this lesson, the other women in the group shared their knowledge of sewing, exchanging tricks of the trade and asking one another how to do certain things (e.g., make shorts, or a flounced skirt, or how to make a rounded collar stay flat).

After the key measurements (back, bust, length of upper body, waist, hips, and length of upper skirt) had been taken, the first thing she drew was a rectangle, which eventually would become both the front and the back half of the upper portion of the dress. The concept of symmetry would be used in making the other half. Soon the blackboard had a picture like the one shown in Fig. 15.1. The tools of Sra. María's trade used in today's lesson included a square ruler and a measuring tape. With these, Sra. María demonstrated flexibility with mathematical knowledge rooted in past formal educational experiences, as she had learned her profession at a trade school in Mexico.

Marta Civil, the mathematics educator in our group, admits that seeing Sra. María as she developed this drawing and listening to her as she would say things such as, "waist is 70 cm, let's add 6 because we need 3 for each pleat, and then we divide by 4," was as "mesmerizing and mysterious to her as mathematics lectures are to so many people—seeing bits and pieces but not getting the whole picture." Yet, it did not seem as mysterious to the other women in the group because they were much more familiar with the practice. Further, the collective knowledge and experience of the group on the topic of sewing and clothing manufacture (as learned through the scrutiny practiced in purchasing various types and styles of clothing), allowed a dialog of sophisticated meanings to be constructed.

Throughout the lesson, the repeated "ahs" demonstrated that Sra. María's explanations facilitated understanding. But for Marta, the mathematics educator, her lack of familiarity with making patterns for sewing and her formal training in mathematics seemed to be clear obstacles in her understanding of the conversation. This episode reminded Marta of Fasheh's (1991) account of his relationship to mathematics versus his mother's relationship to mathematics in her sewing:

> It struck me that the math she was using was beyond my comprehension; moreover, while math for me was the subject matter I studied and taught, for her it was basic to the operation of her understanding. . . . Without the official

ideological support system, no one would have "needed" my math; . . . in contrast, my mother's math was so deeply embedded in the culture that it was invisible through eyes trained by formal education. . . . Mathematics was integrated into her world as it never was into mine. (p. 58)

This was a crucial insight. The validation and privileging of academic mathematics was completely dependent on an ideological support system that constructed the hegemony of a particular type of mathematics. On the other hand, the mathematics of Fasheh's mother "was so deeply embedded . . . that it was invisible through eyes trained by formal education." This kind of mathematics goes beyond facile constructs of social context and must take into account the deeply felt relationships of coparticipants, the social relationships involved in undertaking the practices, as well as the deep engagement of connection with a product, and not just a process.

Sra. María and the women in the group were interested in making a skirt. Their object was not to uncover mathematics in this process. Yet the participation of Marta transformed the social interaction into one in which the concepts could be systematized instead of intuited. Yet interestingly, the shift in contexts problematized the notion of who held the spontaneous everyday concepts and who held the scientific or schooled concepts. The systematicity of the mothers' knowledge was based on familiarity with the practices involved. As Marta questioned the how and the why of the calculations, the answers seemed to be obvious to the mothers, yet, Marta admits, were difficult for her to visualize.

Additionally, the actual practices required skills and knowledge in other areas: efficiency in cutting only once, conservation of resources in using less paper for the actual pattern, and problem solving. In one example, the construction of a quarter of a circle, we can see the systematicity of everyday mathematics based on practice. In order to make the pattern for the skirt, Sra. María took a large square of paper and, holding her measuring tape fixed at one corner of her square (the center), she marked a few points 25 cm from that center point. She then joined them to get a quarter of a circle (see Fig. 15.1).

Why 25 cm for the radius? She came up with 25 by taking 1/3 of the waist measurement (to which she previously had added a few extra cm for the pleats). Then, based on the person's height and the favored length of the skirt, she drew another quarter of a circle, using the same technique. Figure 15.2 demonstrates the next step.

She then cut out the smaller quarter of a circle that was to then become one half of the skirt, as shown in Fig. 15.3.

Constructing the circles (or quarter of a circle) as she did certainly shows the circle as the geometric locus of points equidistant from a given point. This is the formal definition of a circle. Yet we wonder how many children experience this in school mathematics (instead of simply using a compass

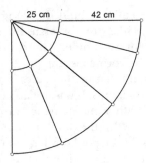

FIG. 15.1.   Drawing a quarter of a circle.

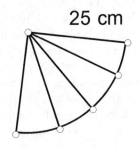

FIG. 15.2.   Toward a skirt 42 cm long.

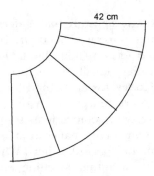

FIG. 15.3.   Half of the skirt.

to draw a circle). Even more, we wonder how many children are aware that this knowledge about circles may reside in their households. Would using a compass be considered more mathematical than using the tape measure (or a ruler) to mark a few points equidistant from a given point and then joining them? This concept of what we count as being mathematics is related to our values and beliefs about what mathematics represent. In particular, in this context we are reminded of the work of Harris (1987), in which she compared the mathematics behind the design of the heel of a sock, something that a woman is likely to do, versus the mathematics behind the design of a right-angle cylindrical pipe. Whereas the latter is considered a mathematical problem, the former is not.

In this example, we found that mathematics is not a possession residing within the head of the participants. It was not an immutable, fixed attribute or trait of one individual. Rather, mathematics was a practice, but we had to discover how to create a zone for the development of that practice. It is not enough to simply "possess" funds of knowledge in mathematical domains. These must be socially mediated into productive knowledge in order to be meaningful. We reiterate: The key point is that human beings and their social worlds are inseparable, they are embedded in each other; thus, human thinking is irreducible to individual properties or traits. Instead, it is always mediated, distributed among persons, artifacts, activities, and settings.

Within this example we find evidence of mathematics embedded in social knowledge. However, it must be mediated through the activity of the group, the artifact of the sewing patterns and tools, and distributed among the participants of the group, including those with more formal academic knowledge. This was the key that unlocked our previous disjunction in finding mathematical funds of knowledge in households. We had attempted to disembed this knowledge from its social meaning and access it through a linear process of dialog. We did not consider the shared and collective construction of mathematical knowledge that is often outside of the purview of individual households.

We began with a theoretical posture that underscored the uneven distribution of knowledge—that is to say, that culture could not account for the everyday lived experiences of every household. Our emphasis on practices of households, on what they actually do, helped us conceptualize mathematics in households. However, our method for doing this, through the narrative elicitation of overt and covert mathematical processes, decontextualized mathematics from its embeddedness in social activities. We had attempted to decouple doing mathematics from its zone of proximal development, that is, from interaction with others. When we viewed a community knowledge base within an authentic setting, with a group of mothers intent on accomplishing a specific goal, the socially mediated nature of mathematical meaning making came into focus.

DISCUSSION

In our theoretical refinement of a funds of knowledge methodology, we have come to acknowledge that we must go beyond a simplistic dichotomy between community (practical, out-of-school, intuitive, tacit), and academic (in-school, deliberate, explicit) mathematics. Our experience with the mothers' group demonstrates that the forms of meaning-making in which the mothers engaged can be characterized by the principles that undergird effective classroom instruction: authentic engagement in joint productive activity, connecting to prior knowledge, complexity and rigor, and the dialogical emergence of instruction.

Returning again to Vygotsky and his insights on everyday and scientific understanding, we reiterate that the difference is not that one is acquired in school and the other out of school. Instead, what is at issue is systematicity. Scientific (or mathematical) concepts form part of an organized system of knowledge. However, we also have demonstrated the systematicity of Sra. Maria's informal practices. As Vygotsky has postulated, we found a reciprocal relation between everyday and scientific concepts. While everyday concepts provide the building blocks for the development of schooled concepts, they can be transformed through a connection with the academic. Similarly, scientific concepts can be transformed into the everyday, into the domain of practice, acquiring meaning and significance but also enabling conscious reflection and meta-awareness.

Community funds of mathematical knowledge reside in distributed everyday and scientific knowledge that does not have to be reconstituted anew at every turn. Accessing this knowledge, however, is not an individual construction but is socially mediated through more knowledgeable others. However, we must remain aware of the dialectical relationship between the academic and the everyday, and the category of "more knowledgeable others" is a shifting construct.

What does this mean for educational practices? It means that we can create zones of practice, and we can invite children into a world with a concrete motivating activity in which the everyday and spontaneous comes into contact with the scientific and the schooled. The dichotomy of in-school and out-of-school mathematics can be elided into a dialectical practice within which students' engagement with both the activity and the social context are foregrounded. The mothers' study group created a practice zone for Marta, but Marta also created a mathematical zone for the mothers, and we came to an appreciation of how contexts are constituted by the contributions of the participants. Does this imply a mathematically sophisticated teacher? Yes, in some ways. Yet, although it might be more difficult to create these zones of mathematical practice, it is very much worth our while. Many teachers create such zones in domains such as literacy and language arts, yet a whole-mathematics classroom similar to a whole-language classroom often remains uncharted terrain.

What suggestions can we offer? First, we have to return to the initial assumptions of our approach and underscore that practices may not be uniformly distributed throughout a community. Thus a community of practice might encompass contested and contesting ways of sense-making. It is therefore important to look at the local contexts of practices and to acknowledge that uniform patterns might not be consensually agreed on or taken for granted. Indeed, subaltern discourses may construct particular forms of practice.

Second, we must be aware of the social relationships of participants in any given activity. This is evident as we think about "more capable others," because there are social issues of relative status surrounding the construction of knowledge. When we have carried out observations in classrooms, it is often the case that students are keenly aware of classroom social status, and negotiation of mathematical discourse is often less a function of coconstruction than it is one of jockeying for position within the social hierarchy. Students often accept as givens the answers supplied by the more popular students and the GATE (Gifted and Talented Education) students, and regularly disregard the answers contributed by those outside of the social loop. The existence of special programs for special children (whether "gifted" or "slow") puts students in cubbyholes and creates a set of expectations that influences the learning dynamics. The mere fact of students' placement in GATE makes students intelligent to the rest of their peers. This clearly affects the creation of an environment conducive to a mathematical discussion, as these children's statements are clearly more valued and legitimated by their classmates. In contrast, in the mothers' group, the women were equally validated as producers of legitimated knowledge by each other.

A third point concerns the kind of mathematics that mathematics educators assume students should be doing, especially as it relates to the perceived dichotomy between schooled and everyday mathematics. For example, Marta, with a formal academic background in mathematics, stated that:

> I enjoy mathematical explorations because of my values and beliefs about mathematics. To me, mathematics has a lot of playfulness in it. I do not enjoy doing meaningless computations, but I enjoy playing with numbers and looking for patterns. It is like a game and every time I find a new pattern, I still have the feeling of surprise and amazement at the structure behind it. Some patterns occur in seemingly very different situations, and that is for me, an aspect of the beauty of mathematics, the relationships between different areas. I have the feeling that many of the math educators who are working on developing "classroom cultures in which students do mathematics naturally," as Schoenfeld (1987, pp. 214–215) noted, share a similar set of beliefs about mathematics.

Constructivist approaches support a perception of mathematics as a creative art form, as a form of playfulness. Yet these are constructs of adult mathematicians, not of novice users. Instruction in mathematics continues to be defined in many cases as the development of novel methods to express and transmit mathematical representations that are self-evident to the expert. However, as Lemke (1990) cogently argued,

> The knowledge of mathematics consists of two parts: a practical knowledge of how to perform various manipulations of quantitative and logical relationships, and a theoretical knowledge of how those relationships fit together to form an overall system within which the manipulations make sense. It is only the first part that most people have any conceivable use for, but it is only the second part that enables you to understand why mathematical procedures work. . . . For nearly all students, abstract theoretical mathematics will remain a luxury, not a necessity, in their educations. While it should certainly be available to those students who want to study it, perhaps we should be honest with all students about the role of mathematics as a "tool" subject and the real reasons why they don't understand how it works. (pp. 164–165)

By "not being honest" with students about the adult mathematical experts' agenda in mathematics education, students do not view the playfulness of the second part of mathematics that Lemke referred to as a legitimate use of mathematics. Mathematics becomes subsumed under a veneer of positivistic assumptions that label knowledge as correct apprehensions of taken-as-shared mathematical principles, not open for contestation. We suggest that reform efforts in mathematics pay closer attention to the social worlds of children (cf. Andrade & Moll, 1993) in all of their multidimensionality in order to better formulate a child's-eye view of the forms and functions of mathematical discourses.

Finally, and perhaps most importantly, we learned from our experience that mathematics practices cannot be disembedded from social context and that creating a zone of mathematical practice depends not only on the store of funds of knowledge, but also on the transformation of that knowledge into meaningful activity. Like the mothers in the study group, students must be involved in practices in which they are not only consumers of knowledge, but producers of mathematical practices.

REFLECTION QUESTIONS

1. What do the authors mean by funds of distributed knowledge?
2. How did they come to problematize their approach?
3. What are zones of mathematical practice?
4. How can we transform funds of knowledge into classroom use?

REFERENCES

Abreu, G. de. (1995). Understanding how children experience the relationship between home and school mathematics. *Mind, Culture, and Activity, 2,* 119–142.

Andrade, R. A. C., & Moll, L. (1993). The social worlds of children: An emic view. *Journal of the Society for Accelerative and Teaching, 18,* 81–125.

Andrade, R., González Le Denmat, H., & Moll, L. C. (2000). El Grupo de las señoras: Creating consciousness through literature. In S. Hollingsworth & M. Gallego (Eds.), *Challenging a single standard: Multiple perspectives on literacy* (pp. 271–284). New York: Teachers College Press.

Bishop, A., & Abreu, G. de. (1991). Children's use of outside-school knowledge to solve mathematics problems in-school. In F. Furinghetti (Ed.), *Proceedings of the Fifteenth International Conference for the Psychology of Mathematics Education* (Vol. 1, pp. 128–135). Assisi, Italy.

Carraher, T., Carraher, D., & Schliemann, A. (1985). Mathematics in the streets and in the schools. *British Journal of Developmental Psychology, 3,* 21–29.

Cole, M., & Engestrom, Y. (1993). A cultural-historical approach to distributed cognition. In G. Salomon (Ed.), *Distributed cognition* (pp. 1–46). Cambridge, UK: Cambridge University Press.

Fasheh, M. (1991). Mathematics in a social context: Math within education as praxis versus math within education as hegemony. In M. Harris (Ed.), *Schools, mathematics and work* (pp. 57–61). New York: Falmer.

Frankenstein, M., & Powell, A. (1994). Toward liberatory mathematics: Paulo Freire's epistemology and ethnomathematics. In P. L. McLaren & C. Lankshear (Eds.), *Politics of liberation: Paths from Freire* (pp. 74–99). New York: Routledge.

González-Angiulo, H. (1998). *Las Señoras: Moving from funds of knowledge to self discovery.* Unpublished doctoral dissertation, University of Arizona, Tucson, Arizona.

Harris, M. (1987). An example of traditional women's work as a mathematics resource. *For the Learning of Mathematics, 7,* 26–28.

Lave, J. (1988). *Cognition in practice: Mind mathematics and culture in everyday life.* New York: Cambridge University Press.

Lee, C. D., & Smagorinsky, P. (Eds.). (2000). *Vygotskian perspectives on literacy research: Constructing meaning through collaborative activity.* Cambridge, UK: Cambridge University Press.

Lemke, J. L. (1990). *Talking science: Language, learning and values.* Norwood, NJ: Ablex.

McBride, M. (1989). A Foucauldian analysis of mathematical discourse. *For the Learning of Mathematics, 9,* 40–46.

Moll, L. C. (Ed.). (1990). *Vygotsky and education.* Cambridge, UK: Cambridge University Press.

Moll, L. C. (2001). Through the mediation of others: Vygotskian research on teaching. In V. Richardson (Ed.), *Handbook of research on teaching* (4th ed., pp. 111–129). Washington, DC: American Educational Research Association.

National Council of Teachers of Mathematics (NCTM), Commission on Standards for School Mathematics. (1989). *Curriculum and evaluation standards for school mathematics.* Reston, VA: The Council.

National Research Council (NRC). (1989). *Everybody counts: A report to the nation on the future of mathematics education.* Washington, DC: National Academy Press.

Pea, R. (1993). Practices of distributed intelligence and designs for education. In G. Salomon (Ed.), *Distributed cognition* (pp. 47–87). Cambridge, UK: Cambridge University Press.

Rosaldo, R. (1989). *Culture and truth: The remaking of social analysis.* Boston: Beacon.

Salomon, G. (1993). *Distributed cognition.* Cambridge, UK: Cambridge University Press.

Saxe, G. (1991). *Culture and cognitive development: Studies in mathematical understanding.* Hillsdale, NJ: Lawrence Erlbaum Associates.

Schoenfeld, A. (1987). What's all the fuss about metacognition? In A. H. Schoenfeld (Ed.), *Cognitive science and mathematics education* (pp. 189–215). Hillsdale, NJ: Lawrence Erlbaum Associates.

Schoenfeld, A. (1991). On mathematics as sense-making: An informal attack on the unfortunate divorce of formal and informal mathematics. In J. F. Voss, S. N. Perkins, & J. Segal (Eds.), *Informal reasoning and instruction* (pp. 311–343). Hillsdale, NJ: Lawrence Erlbaum Associates.

Scribner, S. (1990). Reflections on a model. *The Quarterly Newsletter of the Laboratory of Comparative Human Cognition, 12,* 90–94.

Vygotsky, L. S. (1978). *Mind in society.* Cambridge, MA: Harvard University Press.

Vygotsky, L. S. (1987). Problems of general psychology. In R. Rieber & A. Carton (Eds.), *Collected works* (Vol 1). (N. Minick, Trans.). New York: Plenum.

Vygotsky, L. S. (1994). The development of academic concepts in school aged children. In R. Van der Veer & J. Valsiner (Eds.), *The Vygotsky reader* (pp. 355–370). Oxford, UK: Blackwell. (Original work published 1934)

Vygotsky, L. S. (1997). The history of the development of higher mental functions. In R. Rieber (Ed.), *Collected works* (Vol. 4) (M. J. Hall, Trans.). New York: Plenum.

Wells, G. (1999). *Dialogic inquiry: Toward a sociocultural practice and theory of education.* Cambridge, UK: Cambridge University Press.

Wertsch, J. (1985). *Vygotsky and the social formation of mind.* Cambridge, MA: Harvard University Press.

CONCLUDING COMMENTARY

Chapter 16

Reflections and Possibilities

Luis Moll
University of Arizona

This book has provided a thorough review of a funds of knowledge approach. This review included theoretical and methodological details, the perspective of teachers who have collaborated with us, and the development of iterations of the work in different settings. In this final chapter I want to use the benefit of hindsight to provide some reflections about the work presented in this volume. In addition, I want to situate the work within the present social context of schooling, especially in relation to the children, families, and teachers with whom we do our work.

In November of 2000 Arizonans approved through their votes as Californians had two years earlier, a proposition, that imposes severe restrictions on bilingual education in an effort to dismantle this form of instruction. In denying Latino families and children, for all intents and purposes, access to bilingual schooling, a form of schooling that the overwhelming majority of Latino parents support, the enormous coercion and control imposed on these families and children becomes clear and evident. As Sleeter (1999) has observed, the dominant assumption guiding such actions is that

> monolingual Anglo members of the general public are perfectly capable of deciding what kind of educational programming is best for non-Anglo language minority children . . . and are better able to make such decisions than are bilingual education teachers or the communities the children come from. (pp. xv–xvi)

The passage of such propositions into law, through direct popular vote, illustrates the neocolonial ideological conditions under which working-class Latino children are schooled (Moll & Ruiz, 2002). Within these conditions, an important educational option that Latino families generally desire for their children, bilingual education, is outlawed, declared (in essence) a criminal activity, while ignoring any serious consideration of its educational merits. As important, such decisions not only curtail the ability of teachers to build on the language and cultural experiences of students, their most important tools for thinking, but fracture the families' history of learning from the school. Prohibiting the use of Spanish for instructional purposes, also imposes a (de facto) pariah status on both the language and its users, including teachers, students, families, and community, and is a continuation of the historical subtractive conditions for learning that have come to characterize, whether in English or in Spanish, the schooling of working-class Latino children in the United States (see Moll & Ruiz, 2002; Spring, 1997; Valenzuela, 1999).

It is impossible to ignore, then, that schooling practices are related to issues of power and racism in U.S. society, especially as related to the working-class status of these families. The key issue, therefore, from my perspective, is who has the power to decide the nature of schooling for working-class children, whether the children are Latinos or otherwise. As usually constituted, working-class children receive a reduced and intellectually inferior curriculum compared with their wealthier peers, as part and parcel of the stratification of schooling (Spring, 2001). Although with considerable variability across the country, this social stratification is systemic, not occasional, so it is a constant in the education of working-class children, especially as their numbers and cultural diversity increases.

The banning of bilingual education is yet another aspect of the constraining policies faced by these children, as is the high-stakes testing that passes for school reform, and the reductionist, phonocentric reading programs that pass for good literacy teaching (see Smith, 1999). As Gee (1999) has put it in relation to the teaching of literacy, "To ignore these wider issues [of power and politics], while stressing such things as phonemic awareness built on controlled texts, is to ignore, not merely what we know about politics, but what we know about learning and literacy as well" (p. 360).

It is in the context of this recognition that schooling practices are always intricately related to broader issues of social class, ideology, and power, that we must situate our study and understanding of funds of knowledge. The work presented in this volume has been concerned, from the very beginning, with the reduction and stratification of schooling by social class (see Moll, 1992). Indeed, as we wrote in the Introduction to this volume, we claim success to the extent that our work helps teachers perceive or define working-class or poor households and communities as containing important funds of knowledge. In addition, through our collaboration with teachers we have established that these funds of knowledge represent bona fide resources for teaching and learning in classrooms.

As such, much of this book contains examples on how to use this concept, funds of knowledge, for defining and classifying phenomena that occur in households, as our main unit of study, but elsewhere as well, especially in classrooms. This concept helps make sense of and give meaning to cultural objects and social practices in a particular way and within the concrete circumstances of life in which we find them. It is important, though, not to reify the concept, to keep in mind that it is both theoretical and transitory, even though through their documentation funds of knowledge attain a sort of objective reality, or at least we treat them as such. Therefore, it is necessary to emphasize that the concept is not static, that it evolves through each new iteration, and that it must be renewed, that is, modified and adapted to local conditions as discussed by the chapters in Part III.

Hence, we have addressed issues of social class and schooling in at least two indirect ways. One way is by documenting funds of knowledge and, in the process of doing this work, forming (sometimes intimate) social relationships with working-class families (see Floyd Tenery, this volume). This is the process of inquiry that we have highlighted in this book. A second way is by questioning, through our practices, why schools may not privilege the funds of knowledge of the working-class families with whom we collaborate. This aspect of the work took the form of teachers making the funds of knowledge of the families they visited pedagogically viable within their classrooms, and by questioning how and why they teach the way they do. This classroom work proved quite challenging, as many researchers have discovered, but we present several examples of how teachers managed to create the necessary social space to attempt such changes, and with positive consequences, although not always in a sustainable fashion. I will return later to this issue of sustainability.

However, given the importance of social class to the schooling of children and the work of teachers, perhaps we should have treated social class as a primary theoretical or conceptual tool, exactly the way we were treating funds of knowledge. After all, we did not just casually introduce the teachers to this concept (funds of knowledge) and then walk into homes to discover what we could find. Instead, we prepared diligently to conduct the work by doing the required theoretical and methodological readings to establish the ethnographic nature of the concept. As part of this preparation, we highlighted the relation of funds of knowledge to the history of labor of the families and to the extant household economy (see Part I), with the understanding that both were related primarily to the working-class segment of the labor market. Ideally, we could have also developed a more sophisticated understanding of social class as it conditions household and classroom dynamics, the production of knowledge, and the relationships between these settings.

Along similar lines, Tozer (2000) pointed out the important theoretical difference, one that seems particularly relevant for our efforts, between treating the concept of class as "gradations" of socioeconomic status (SES) or as "oppositional" economic classes:

> The SES approach is easily compatible with a "cultural-deficit" understanding of low-income students. In this explanation, low-income children do poorly in school because their "cultural backgrounds" ill-prepare them to succeed, and the source of the problem lies therefore in the home, an environment deficient in the language and practices necessary to support school success. (p. 157)

Our approach was developed precisely to challenge such deficit interpretations, but the point is that we could have also developed an approach, based on the same collaborative principles with teachers, to the study of the mediating role of social class in the phenomena we were addressing. As Tozer (2000) stated:

> An oppositional economic class analysis . . . reminds us of a different way of understanding the experience of working-class children and youth in schools, one in which their cultural practices and language are subordinated to the dominant class that governs the schools. This is the second major problem, then, of looking at "cultural background" without taking class seriously: The knowledge, language, and practices of one class are dominant and valued; those of the other classes are subordinate and devalued. Instead of a cultural deficit explanation for persistent school failure of low SES children, we can see the possibility of a cultural subordination explanation that is grounded in relations of domination and subordination in the economic and political order of society. (p. 157)

This emphasis, then, compatible with our efforts, would highlight the interaction between class-based school cultures, as variable as those may be, and the class-conditioned cultures of the families and students, as variable as those may be as well. A goal, then, is for teachers to develop ways of teaching that mediate between "the schools' class-based norms and the students' values, knowledge, and practices" (Tozer, 2000, p. 158). That is, just as the teachers developed (appropriated) a theoretical language about funds of knowledge in the process of redefining their understandings of households and communities, and in taking action to make those funds of knowledge pedagogically viable, they (and we) could have also developed a language to talk about class relations as the major source of inequalities in education.

I want to make a similar point about the role of gender in a funds of knowledge analysis. For a long time it has been quite evident to us that women play the central role in the formation of the critical social ties and networks of households. It has also been evident that if we were to establish enduring or reciprocal relations between households and classrooms, the role of women, as the central participants in both settings, was the key. Be that as it may, although we often took note of the nature of a household's division of labor, we did not develop an analysis of gender as central to a funds of knowledge approach. It is not simply a matter, I don't think, of highlighting the role of women in household dynamics or in school life. It is instead a matter of developing a theoretical analysis of the role of gender or, perhaps better stated, of gender relations as a variable social system, in the constitution of household and classroom settings and their relationships. Here I borrow ideas from the gender scholarship in understanding immigration dynamics (see, e.g., Hondagneu-Sotelo, 2001). A recent finding, for instance, is that, within certain contexts, labor markets tend to favor women over men, thus women exceed the earnings and job stability of the men. It is feasible that diverse and changing employment locations and remuneration may then shape not only gender relations within households but also social relations outside households, both with important consequences for the formation of funds of knowledge. The point is that an emphasis on gender relations may provide a more diverse and nuanced understanding of funds of knowledge formation and deployment, as it is providing a more sophisticated understanding of immigrant dynamics, and of the potential for home-school relations in changing contexts of work. It is also likely to be a topic of considerable interest to teachers, most of whom are women, and for the possibilities of sustained activism in education.

We have also long been aware that a funds of knowledge analysis, depending as it does on interviews with adults and participant observations in households, may inform us about adults and their social worlds but not necessarily about their children. We have often assumed, and it may be untenable, that what we learn from adults may inform us about children. We have also known that adults engage children selectively around particular funds of knowledge but not others. So, for example, a father may involve his son in welding activities through a sort of apprentice relationship, or in laying tiles, or landscaping, but not necessarily in other details of business ventures related to those or other activities. In addition, we have documented how it is children, not necessarily adults, who initiate many of the activities that end up in the communication of funds of knowledge. But we also know that children create their own social worlds, with accompanying funds of knowledge, which may be independent from the adults' social life (Andrade, 1994). It is this last emphasis, in particular, that needs careful elaboration in future studies. This focus is particularly important with immigrant families, whose children, because they usually develop English language skills before the adults, must assume the role of mediators in the families' communication with other social institutions (Vásquez et al., 1994). This brokering may range in complexity, but some are very much adult-like, such as helping the family negotiate house mortgages or bank loans, activities that carry serious consequences for a family's well-being.

The extent of children's roles in dealing with secondary institutions is not only a function of their English fluency but of the mothers' years of schooling and familiarity with such institutions in this country. It is well established in educational research that mothers' schooling experiences may influence not only their children's success in school but how mothers relate to the school as a social institution. Lareau (1989), for example, documented how working-class mothers generally do not have the educational history or the access to social networks that afford them symmetrical relationships with school personnel, and thus they defer authority to the school (but see Lareau & Horvat, 1999). Middle-class mothers, in contrast, have both the educational history and social ties to interact with teachers and other school personnel in more advantageous ways. That is, middle-class mothers can more readily position themselves in relation to the school in ways that allow them to monitor their children's schooling experiences.

Immigrant mothers, on the other hand, especially those from the working class, may not know enough about how the school system functions in this country or about its particular middle-class norms, or know enough English to interact confidently and competently with teachers, so that they may keep their distance, with an understandable distrust and detachment, and thus be perceived by teachers as not caring about their children's education (Valdés, 1996). We found that a funds of knowledge approach, through its emphasis on teachers engaging households as learners and thus forming what we call relationships of *confianza* with parents, may help create new options for parents, especially mothers (but see Hensley, this volume), to shape their relationship to the school and the schooling process. That is, we found that once the relationship level of the communication between parents and teachers becomes more reciprocal, where the teachers start forming part, even if peripherally, of the household's social network, it creates new possibilities for teachers to engage households and for parents to engage the school in fundamentally new ways—hence our emphasis on repeated visits to households to facilitate the formation of such reciprocal relationships. The household visits, then, can alter parents' relationships with teachers and, by implication, the parents' positioning with the school as a social system. In a sense, these parents now have some inside help in dealing with the schools.

The nature of such parental participation or relationship to the school was of definite interest to us, as the teachers have addressed in this volume.

There is, nevertheless, plenty left to study as to how this work may shape the quality of the parental relationship with schools and the consequences for the children. Of particular interest would be research that helps parents understand what resources, what funds of knowledge, may be advantageous in dealing with schools. The emphasis would not only be on how parents can accommodate to the routines of schooling, as is usually the case, but on how they can get the school to accommodate their needs, conditions, and desires. One such understanding may be related to the notion that all social structures, including the institution of schools, are generated in practice, especially through the specialized discourses of its many participants. Stanton-Salazar (1997), for example, has proposed seven forms of "institutional funds of knowledge," including knowledge about network development, academic tasks, problem solving, and institutional discourses that are specific to the working of schools and crucial for "decoding the system" (pp. 11–17). What sorts of arrangements may assist working-class parents in acquiring such specific institutional funds of knowledge remains a critical question. We are convinced, however, that the sorts of connections our approach facilitates are particularly crucial in mediating access to such knowledge.

During our project visits to households, the tacit arrangement with families was that their collaboration would be reciprocated through our efforts to improve schooling practices based on what we learned in the study, not only for their children but for all children in their schools. Thus, our commitment to reciprocity was usually indirect, through the teachers' classroom work with the children. Of course, given the repeated visits, there were times when other forms of reciprocity were requested, such as assistance in locating employment, enrolling in a course at the university, translations of documents, or general advice. In some cases, the teachers became confidantes (usually the women), as mothers would consult them about a serious problem or issue, but this did not happen often (but see Floyd Tenery, this volume). Another possibility for manifesting reciprocity would be to structure it in a more deliberate or formal way. The work of Andrade and González Le Denmat is one such example (see Andrade, González Le Denmat, & Moll, 2000). Their study involved organizing a literature study group with Spanish-speaking women within a community where we initially conducted the funds of knowledge research. The participants were mothers of students in an elementary school, most poor and in their thirties, who spoke little or no English and were often subjugated by men in their lives, not to mention by their low position in the broader social order. As such, their domestic ties to the home framed their exposure to the world outside the home, which the study sought to mediate through the collective readings of books.

The reading of a book took anywhere from 2 to 8 weeks depending on the selection made from the Spanish-language literature and at a level that could be considered academic. These books, all challenging texts, presented many opportunities for reflection and discussion, which the women eagerly accepted, engaging in penetrating and often highly personal discussions. They not only read for meaning, but formulated new meanings from their readings that generalized to their lives, including their relations with men, as expected, but also their children's teachers and school.

These women, then, with the assistance of their teachers, have turned the study of literature into a critical examination of their own situations in their families, communities, and society at large. During the course of the work, a primary goal of this study group became to help the women discover their knowledge in ways that would facilitate a self-motivated transformation of their private lives that would subsequently be projected into the public sphere (see also Benmayor, Torruellas, & Juarbe, 1997). There are indications that these changes in "public identities" have occurred. In fact, some of the women helped organize a second group of mothers at a nearby middle-school community, in collaboration with the school's librarian and university researchers from Education and Women's Studies, forming a new, extended network. These women, therefore, have become resources and inspiration for others, as they confront the tension between constraints and possibilities in their lives.

This literature study group is analogous to the ones that form part of the basic design of the funds of knowledge approach, with similar consequences for identity formation and dealing with tensions between constraints and possibilities in teachers' lives and work. We consider these settings mediating structures, as these are settings deliberately designed to create the time and discursive space necessary to think about the work conducted in households and classrooms and its consequences. In our approach, the formation of these settings is absolutely essential for the productive collaboration of teachers and researchers, as we have emphasized in this book.

It also strikes me that learning within these study groups, especially as one crosses cultural, class, and experiential boundaries in visiting households, always involves certain shifts in identity. We have underscored in this book that project participants are always changed in some ways, not only theoretically and emotionally as a result of the social relationships forged with others, but in terms of their personal identities as teachers (see Mercado, this volume). That is, as teachers learn about others, and about what others have learned, they also learn about themselves; they produce insights about themselves in relation to the households they study and in relation to their work within classrooms and schools as particular, socially created settings.

The key process in this shift of identities is the internalization of perspectives. This internalization implies not a simple transfer of perspectives from one person to another but the development and appropriation of perspectives based on the teachers' active participation in all project matters, from giving intellectual direction to the study as coresearchers, to collecting and analyzing data, to conceptualizing consequences for practice. This internalization of perspectives is aided, or mediated, by the theoretical concepts and lexicon they acquire and use in conducting the work, by the household relations formed through the visits, by their discourse with peers to develop a shared understanding of the work, and by the production of novel artifacts (their data and narratives) that result from their own actions.

There is a strong element of self-determination, of agency, in this process, as teachers develop the dispositions to visit households, form social relationships with strangers, and develop new working relationships with colleagues. There is also the disposition to question and redirect (or not) how one teaches and for what purpose, and recognition of the social and political constraints on one's work, as these become issues in study group discussions. All these processes take time to develop, which is why long-term collaborations are most useful in this work. That is, a teacher's access to the resources of the study group, and by implication, to the cultural resources of the households, involves what Manyak (2000) called "evolving trajectories of participation." This term refers to how, over time, one comes to participate in a variety of ways within a particular community—in this instance, the study-group settings—gaining access to its resources. Manyak put it as follows: "Through engagement in increasingly central roles and responsibilities in practice, participants' access to community members, activities, discourses, and technologies expands and they experience new opportunities to develop knowledge, skills, and identities" (p. 6). This is precisely the "expanded" participation we attempt to facilitate in our approach. In direct contrast, a "confining" participation would limit access to learning resources and constrain possibilities for change.

A similar dynamic has come to characterize the classroom work of the teachers. Consistent with our perspective, the general emphasis has been to conceptualize classrooms as cultural settings. That is, the intent is to conceptualize classrooms in the same sense that we have come to conceptualize households, as built environments characterized by certain historically developed, socially mediated, cultural practices and funds of knowledge. The goal, then, is to facilitate new ways of perceiving and discussing students, not only as individuals but also as situated or embedded within a broader educational ecology that includes their households' funds of knowledge, and the realization that these funds of knowledge can be accessed strategically through the formation of social ties or networks. Thus, the formation of such social networks can form part of any classroom pedagogy.

In addition, we have emphasized how within classrooms students should be active in the production of knowledge, not solely recipients of knowledge from teachers and curricula. Notice that this emphasis is consistent with how we collaborated with teachers in the study groups, and their expansive participation as producers of knowledge. An important point to convey here is that it is not primarily the infusion of funds of knowledge into existing classroom lessons that is of primary interest to us; we worry about reinforcing the reductionist forms of schooling that comprise the status quo. A more critical goal from our perspective is how schooling may be reconceptualized to support new and broader possibilities than is now the case.

As such, from early in the study, we proposed an inquiry approach to instruction as a way of expanding the roles, activities, and resources available for learning in classrooms, to include those resources made available through the funds of knowledge research of teachers. The emphasis within such inquiry is the student as active learner, displaying competence, within the expanded possibilities for action made available by exceeding the limits of tightly prescribed lessons, so typical within the reductionist school programs that are in vogue in the current education scene. Within these inquiry arrangements the emphasis is on literacy for action, as situated by the nature of the activities as developed by both teachers and students.

There are several ways that such inquiry arrangements can take place, probably as many as there are teachers participating in a study, given their different histories, interests, students, and so on. I am partial to theme cycles, where students have a say on the topics of inquiry, and which may involve prolonged exploration of that theme or topic through various oral and literate means, including the careful or critical analyses of texts, and different forms of representation of the knowledge produced through the student-generated activities (e.g., Moll & Whitmore, 1996). These theme units present both teachers and students with multiple opportunities to transcend the classroom and tap the social life and funds of knowledge of the surrounding communities, including classroom visits in which parents (and others) contribute their living knowledge and experience to the academic task of the students.

To be sure, several authors have elaborated versions of inquiry-oriented models that are compatible with our approach, although they may not emphasize the use of funds of knowledge (see, e.g., Luke, 2000; Nystrand, 1997; Wells, 1999). These models also emphasize, as we do, learning and development as sociocultural processes, where outcomes are an open question, for these processes are not deterministic but interactively constructed, so that they come about through the quality of work of teachers and students. These models also view classroom change not as the simple implementation of an innovation, but as intimately related to the development of teachers' identities as professionals.

I want to close this section with some comments about the sustainability of the innovation and about the process of generalization of these experiences elsewhere. Central to both is the authentic participation and, once more, the professional development of teachers. This development includes internalization of the core theoretical principles of the funds of knowledge approach. Along with these principles are new methodologies that must be mastered, and forms of talk about children, families, households, and communities, but also about teaching and learning that must be exercised and appropriated. Especially important is to learn how to think about culture as dynamic and changing, never fixed or static, and full of agency and versatility in response to the many different circumstances of material life. This approach, then, places a high premium on respecting and understanding cultural diversity.

We have also stressed the need to situate the work in the context of collegial and reciprocal relationships with others. We are partial to the formation of study groups among teachers and researchers, a social organization intended to mediate between school and community, and between school and university, to create the space necessary to talk and think about our joint research. The key is to facilitate a new relationship between teachers and household funds of knowledge. We have also tried other designs, similar to the course-based arrangements reported by Mercado (this volume). In any case, these study groups are relatively easy to develop but not necessarily to maintain over a prolonged amount of time. Three factors, among others, may inhibit their sustainability. One is that schools are not organized to facilitate the learning and development of teachers. Most state-sanctioned reform efforts do not even take teachers into account, and when they do, it is in a very restrictive and prescribed way. The overwhelming national emphasis on high-stakes testing, a dubious strategy to improve schools, is also a major constraint on the flexibility of scheduling needed to involve teachers in professional or extracurricular intellectual activities such as participation in research. Nevertheless, although never easy, teachers and principals oriented to the goals of this work seem to find ways to create new structures or settings for collaboration, no matter if they are fragile, and need care and perseverance to maintain.

University professors are only in marginally better situations to embark on this type of work. Although we enjoy much greater flexibility of scheduling than school-based teachers, universities tend to recompense individual work, and tenure is granted for individual achievement, usually in the form of individual publications. Collaborative and applied projects are generally discouraged among nontenured professors because it places them at risk, and teaching novel courses will rarely count toward promotion. Embarking on collaborative studies with teachers may not carry much weight in academia, unless significant publications are an outcome of the enterprise.

There is also the nature of the relationship between teachers and researchers, a point we have emphasized throughout this work. The status may be with the university professors but so is the responsibility for creating symmetrical and additive relations for the collaboration. This work has no chance of succeeding or of being sustained if teachers are not treated with respect, as colleagues, in the best sense of the word, where they can contribute intellectually to the endeavor. The responsibility for financing the study has also been on the professors, although we have worked with schools that have responded in kind, by providing space and time for the work. In general, the teachers we have collaborated with certainly appreciate being remunerated for taking part in the work—we all do—but have rarely if ever made it a condition for their participation.

We could say, then, that sustainability of such an innovation is related to the strength of the social networks among teachers and between teachers and researchers that form part of the study. This social network is particularly important in involving others who share a vision and values for the importance of cultural resources, funds of knowledge included, in teaching and learning. Such networks are also crucial to be able to sustain the innovation in the face of adversity, as when the school and district are preoccupied with other matters such as increasing test scores at any cost. It is through these networks, not only through the teachers' individual efforts, that such an approach can become part of the social and cultural capital of school, where not only the families' but the teachers' funds of knowledge become resources for others, thus expanding the school's capacity for developing new social practices.

The issue of generalization has to do with the applicability and adaptation of the work to other settings. We have strong indications that our concepts and methods travel well, but with the necessary modifications to local contexts to provide the study with vitality, energy, and flexibility. The intent would not be to have others replicate the project, but to adapt or recontextualize it to new social conditions. Some aspects of this approach, however, must perdure, regardless of social location. One is the emphasis on household analysis as the primary unit of study—it all starts there. Another is the use of ethnographic methods for the study of social relationships and practices—it is the method that is more sensitive yet malleable to contextual variations. Next is the creation of the study group settings, which can be located in sites that range from schools and community settings to university classrooms. These settings facilitate thinking collectively and developing the collaborative and reciprocal relationships with teachers, which is indispensable if the research is to have any school-related validity. And, of course, there is the relationship with the families, the heart of this work, without whom nothing presented in this book is possible.

REFERENCES

Andrade, R., González Le Denmat, H., & Moll, L. C. (2000). El grupo de Las Señoras: Creating consciousness within a literature club. In M. Gallego & S. Hollingsworth (Eds.), *What counts as literacy: Challenging the school standard* (pp. 271–284). New York: Teachers College Press.

Benmayor, R., Torruellas, R. M., & Juarbe, A. L. (1997). Claiming cultural citizenship in East Harlem: "Si esto puede ayudar a la comunidad mia . . ." In W. Flores & R. Benmayor (Eds.), *Latino cultural citizenship: Claiming identity, space and rights* (pp. 152–209). Boston: Beacon.

Gee, J. (1999). Critical issues: Reading and the new literacy studies: Reframing the National Academy of Sciences Report on Reading. *Journal of Literacy Research, 31*, 355–374.

Hondagneu-Sotelo, P. (2001). Immigrant women and paid domestic work: Research, theory, and activism. In J. Blau (Ed.), *The Blackwell companion to sociology* (pp. 423–436). Oxford, UK: Blackwell.

Lareau, A. (1989). *Home advantage: Social class and parental intervention in elementary education.* Philadelphia: Falmer Press.

Lareau, A., & Horvat, E. M. (1999). Moments of social inclusion and exclusion: Race, class, and cultural capital in family–school relationships. *Sociology of Education, 72*, 37–53.

Luke, A. (2000). Critical literacy in Australia: A matter of context and standpoint. *Journal of Adolescent and Adult Literacy, 43*, 448–461.

Manyak, P. (2000, December). *Legitimate peripheral participation, classroom literacy and Latina/o children.* Paper presented at the National Reading Conference, Scottsdale, Arizona.

Moll, L. C. (1992). Bilingual classroom studies and community analysis: Some recent trends. *Educational Researcher, 21*(3), 20–24.

Moll, L. C., & Ruiz, R. (2002). The schooling of Latino students. In M. Suárez-Orozco & M. Páez (Eds.), *Latinos: Remaking America* (pp. 362–374). Berkeley, CA: University of California Press.

Moll, L. C., & Whitmore, K. (1993). Vygotsky in educational practice. In E. Forman, N. Minick, & C. A. Stone (Eds.), *Contexts for learning: Sociocultural dynamics in children's development* (pp. 19–42). New York: Oxford.

Nystrand, M. (1997). *Opening dialogue.* New York: Teachers College Press.

Sleeter, C. (1999). Foreword. In A. Valenzuela (Ed.), *Subtractive schooling* (pp. xv–xviii). Albany, NY: State University of New York Press.

Smith, F. (1999). Why systematic phonics and phonemic awareness instruction constitute an educational hazard. *Language Arts, 77*(2), 150–155.

Spring, J. (1997). *Deculturalization and the struggle for equality* (2nd ed.). New York: McGraw-Hill.

Spring, J. (2001). Equality of educational opportunity. In J. Strouse (Ed.), *Exploring sociocultural themes in education* (2nd ed., pp. 217–247). New York: McGraw-Hill.

Stanton-Salazar, R. (1997). A social capital framework for understanding the socialization of racial minority children and youths. *Harvard Educational Review, 67*, (1), 1–40.

Tozer, S. (2000). Class. In D. A. Gabbard (Ed.), *Knowledge and power in the global economy: Politics and the rhetoric of school reform* (pp. 149–159). Mahwah, NJ: Lawrence Erlbaum Associates.

Valdés, G. (1996). *Con respeto: Bridging the distance between culturally diverse families and schools.* New York: Teachers College Press.

Valenzuela, A. (1999). *Subtractive schooling.* Albany, NY: State University of New York Press.

Vásquez, O., Pease-Alvarez, L., & Shannon, S. (1994). *Pushing boundaries: Language and culture in a Mexicano community.* Cambridge, UK: Cambridge University Press.

Wells, G. (1999). *Dialogic inquiry.* Cambridge, UK: Cambridge University Press.

Author Index

Subject Index